CW00418594

Talking With
THE RED BARON

ALSO BY PETER KILDUFF

The Red Baron

That's My Bloody Plane

Germany's Last Knight of the Air

U.S. Carriers at War

A-4 Skyhawk

Germany's First Air Force 1914-1918

Richthofen – Beyond the Legend of the Red Baron

Over the Battlefronts

The Red Baron Combat Wing

The Illustrated Red Baron

Talking With
THE RED BARON

'Interviews'
with Manfred von Richthofen

PETER KILDUFF

BRASSEY'S

First published in 2003 by Brassey's

A member of **Chrysalis** Books plc

Brassey's
The Chrysalis Building, Bramley Road, London W10 6SP

North American orders:
Casemate Publishing, 2114 Darby Road, Havertown, PA 19083, USA

Peter Kilduff has asserted his moral right to be identified as the author of this work

Library of Congress Cataloging in Publication Data available

British Library Cataloguing in Publication Data
A catalogue record for this book is available from the British Library

ISBN 1 85753 381 X

Edited and designed by DAG Publications Ltd
Designed by David Gibbons. Cartography by Anthony A. Evans

Printed and bound in Great Britain

CONTENTS

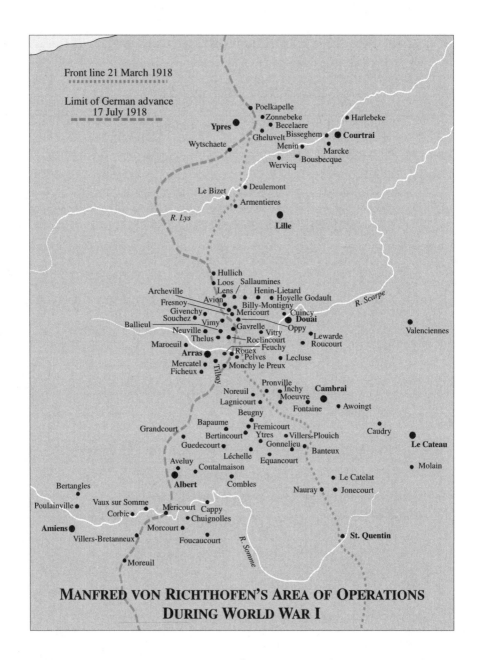

MANFRED VON RICHTHOFEN'S AREA OF OPERATIONS
DURING WORLD WAR I

INTRODUCTION

Manfred Freiherr von Richthofen was, without dispute, the most successful fighter pilot of the First World War. He received official credit for shooting down at least eighty enemy aeroplanes, the highest score of any fighter pilot of the 1914-1918 War. He may well have shot down other aircraft for which he did not receive credit. Historical records also confirm that he received more high decorations than any other German combatant in that war. Richthofen's bold use of red aircraft made him easily identifiable and, combined with his aristocratic stature as a Freiherr [baron], led to his being called 'the Red Baron.' That distinction added to his reputation in life and has served to perpetuate his memory in the more than eight decades since his death in combat at the age of twenty-five on 21 April 1918.

Many books have been devoted to Manfred Freiherr von Richthofen (including a translation of his memoirs and three other volumes about him written by this author) and he is mentioned in accounts by a number of his contemporaries; yet, questions about him and his activities continue to be raised into the present time.

This volume presents Richthofen's candid views as they could have been told to a journalist assigned to cover him as a wartime personality of growing prominence. The journalist's objective would have been to obtain Richthofen's comments, consistent with the openness found in some of the famous ace's uncensored comments in letters and other texts published posthumously after the war. The responses in this volume are adapted from Richthofen's own comments, drawing on existing and newly discovered factual material, which is edited and interpreted into dialogue that Richthofen could have used to talk about his experiences. In the interests of accuracy and completeness, other historical sources have been used to help shape events described. In the opening sequence, for example, Richthofen gave one account in the official combat report that he submitted for credit for his eighteenth victory, but related a different version in his autobiographical work *Der rote Kampfflieger (*The Red Air Fighter*)*. A post-war statement from one of the British survivors of that combat clarified the situation and enabled the author to select sentences from both of Richthofen's statements to depict the most likely scenario. Comparison of dates and events in various Richthofen texts with official records also shows discrepancies; generally, aligning some narratives with documented dates that do not match the events described. Also taken into account are text differences in the 1917 and 1933 editions of *Der rote Kampfflieger*, as well as the 1920 edition of Richthofen's memoirs, *Ein Heldenleben* (A Hero's Life). However, contemporary military documents and media reports, such as the *Kriegs-Echo* (War Echo) article of 30 March 1917 quoted in Chapter 4, and comments from people who knew or met Richthofen are entirely consistent with original sources.

Governments of the First World War belligerents bolstered popular support for the war effort by exploiting newspapers, magazines and cinemas. In Germany, articles, photo spreads and motion picture newsreels glorified the nation's heroes, holding up as worthy of emulation a variety of soldiers, sailors and airmen. In particular, the government recognised the propaganda value of combatants using new technology of the time – particularly submarine crewmen and aviators – and their successes were publicised heavily. Hence, it would have been normal for Richthofen to discuss his experiences with journalists and various dignitaries who visited him at the Front or whom he met while he was in Germany on leave. He would have been aware that any published results of his comments would have to be approved by censors who maintained the government's official attitudes towards the war.

First, however, basic facts about the man: Manfred Albrecht von Richthofen was born in the Lower Silesian town of Kleinberg near Schweidnitz (now Swidnica, Poland), on 2 May 1892, the second of four children of Albrecht Phillip Karl Julius and Kunigunde (*née* von Schickfus und Neudorff) von Richthofen. His siblings were: Elisabeth Therese Luise (called Ilse), born 8 August 1890; Lothar Siegfried, born 27 September 1894; and Karl Bolko, born 16 April 1903. Their father, a career Army officer with the Silesian mounted unit Leib-Kürrasier-Regiment Grosser Kurfürst Nr. 1, stationed in Breslau (now Wroclaw, Poland), had to retire because of an ear injury that occurred after he leaped into the Oder River to save a subordinate who had fallen off his horse. Despite his being descended from a family elevated to the nobility by Friedrich II of Prussia (better known as Frederick the Great) in 1741, the retired Major von Richthofen had no estates or other sources of wealth. The Richthofen family is divided into five Main Lines (Hertwigswaldau, Barzdorf, Michelsdorf, Ruppersdorf, and Heinersdorf, respectively) and Albrecht von Richthofen and his children were from the Second (or Barzdorf) Line, First (or Kohlhöhe) Bough and the Third (or

Gäbersdorf) Branch of the family lineage and, while he was able to retire to a pleasant villa in Schweidnitz, the Major had only his modest military pension to provide for his family; to ensure his sons' higher education, he had them qualify for admission to the Prussian Cadet System. Indeed, Manfred was named for his great-uncle and godfather, the cavalry General Manfred Freiherr von Richthofen – a pre-war aide de camp to Kaiser Wilhelm II and commander of Prussia's élite Garde du Corps before going on to command the 6th Division, IIIrd Armee-Korps during the First World War – a clear indication of the path the boy was expected to take in life.

The younger Manfred von Richthofen left the wooded beauty and stirring hunting jaunts of the Weistritz (Bystrzyca) Valley at the age of eleven when he entered the Cadet Institute at Wahlstatt (now Legnicke Pole, Poland) in August 1903. He was slightly built and smaller than other boys his age, which made him a target for the inevitable bullies in his group. Rough treatment by bigger boys, however, toughened Manfred's resolve and helped to form him as a scrapper of daring and courage, as would become evident in the sky-high hell over the Western Front. Manfred was a bright boy who, admittedly, did not apply himself to his studies, but who excelled in athletic activities, where he learned the value of teamwork.

In 1909, he graduated to the Main Cadet Institute at Gross-Lichterfelde, near Berlin. He enjoyed his time there more than at Wahlstatt, but did not become any more serious as a student. In fact, on leaving the Cadet Corps during the Easter season of 1911, Manfred qualified for officer's rank only after his second examination, which gave him status junior to his peers. In 1912, he was commissioned as a Leutnant (Second Lieutenant) in the Silesian-based mounted unit, Ulanen-Regiment Kaiser Alexander III. von Russland Nr. 1, and settled into what promised to be long-term garrison duty among the people of his own region.

The outbreak of war in August 1914 enabled him to refine his talents as an officer, a leader and a fearless fighter – especially in the age-old military tradition of individual combat. Richthofen soon became frustrated by ground warfare, in which mobile mounted troops could no longer dash across battlefields to reconnoitre the lines and engage the enemy directly. Looking skyward, he realised after nine months of protracted ground warfare that the fledgling air service had become, to use a now trite phrase, the 'cavalry of the clouds'. Aircraft were unhindered by the long lines of trenches, barbed wire, shell holes and other physical barriers that became emblematic of the bloody and fiercely destructive struggles in Europe during the war.

After writing a cheeky letter to his regimental commander, stating that he did not go to war 'to gather cheese and eggs', Richthofen was allowed to transfer to the air service in May 1915. He and twenty-nine other officers from various ground units were screened for suitability as candidates at Aviation Replacement Unit (Flieger-Ersatz-Abteilung 7 (FEA) 7) at Cologne. Richthofen was one of the few who passed all the tests and, on 10 June, he was sent to FEA 6 at Grossenhain to train as an aerial observer.

After eleven days of training, he was posted to the Eastern Front, where the Field Aviation Unit (Feldflieger-Abteilung 69) was being formed for operations with General August von Mackensen's 11th Armee in Poland and Galicia. The relative calm of the next two months allowed him to become accustomed to his airborne observation and photographic reconnaissance platform in the lumbering but steady old Albatros two-seaters deployed against the Imperial Russian Army. When not involved in visual or photographic reconnaissance, he had a flexible machine-gun to ward off aerial opponents. Opportunities to use the gun were scarce, however, and by mid-August 1915, he was ready for the more intensive combat on the Western Front. Once again, he got his wish and was assigned to the deceptively named Brieftauben-Abteiling Ostende (BAO) (Carrier Pigeon Section at Ostend), a unit which had nothing to do with birds and which deployed single- and two-engine reconnaissance and bomber aircraft over the battlefields in Flanders. While serving with the BAO, Richthofen persuaded a comrade to provide him with 'informal' pilot training in a Fokker Eindecker (monoplane), the aircraft type then being flown with stunning success by Oswald Boelcke, Max Immelmann and other early German fighter aces. Even a crash landing in a Fokker Eindecker did not deter Richthofen from his new found mission in the German Luftstreitkräfte (Air Force): to combine his hunting passion with flying in aircraft equipped with forward-firing machine-guns to become a modern air combat hero like Boelcke.

Indeed, following a brief meeting with Boelcke, he received formal fighter pilot training at FEA 2 in Döberitz, east of Berlin, and completed his final examination on Christmas Day 1915. The following August, he was refining his air combat skills at Kampfgeschwader 2 on the Russian Front, a successor to the BAO, when Boelcke visited the unit and personally selected him for the newly created single-engine fighter unit Jagdstaffel 2 in France. Within five months Boelcke was dead, following an in-air collision with Erwin Böhme, the other former Kagohl 2 pilot chosen along with Richthofen to create Jasta 2, and Manfred was in command of his own unit, Jasta 11. Like his mentor Boelcke, he also became a recipient of Prussia's Orden Pour le

Mérite – often called 'the Blue Max' – which gained the stature of the German Empire's highest award for valour.

Tracing Richthofen's fast rise to success, the following series of interviews could have taken place during the last fifteen months of his life. The author is grateful to the following German aviators who survived the First World War and, via correspondence and/or personal visits beginning some forty years ago, provided insights into the times and events in which Manfred Freiherr von Richthofen became such a notable part: former Leutnant der Reserve Oscar Bechtle; *Pour le Mérite* recipient Major der Reserve a.D. Carl Degelow: Generalingenieur der Luftwaffe a.D. Wolfram Eisenlohr: former Leutnant der Reserve Hellmuth Frank; Pour le Mérite recipient Major der Reserve a.D. Jürgen von Grone; Generalleutnant a.D. Erwin Jollasse; former Leutnant der Reserve Friedrich Kamfenkel; Pour le Mérite recipient Generaloberst a.D. Alfred Keller; former Leutnant der Reserve Johannes Knauer; former Leutnant der Reserve Oskar Kuppinger; Pour le Mérite recipient Generalleutnant a.D. Theo Osterkamp; Oberstleutnant der Reserve a.D. Hanns-Gerd Rabe; and Generalmajor a.D. Carl August von Schönebeck.

The author expresses sincere gratitude to succeeding generations of German friends linked in one way or another to flyers of the First World War, especially to: Fritzcarl Prestien, son of a Richthofen flying comrade; Donat Freiherr von Richthofen; Hartmann Freiherr von Richthofen, nephew of the illustrious flyer; Botschafter a.D. Prof.(h.c.) Dr. Hermann Freiherr von Richthofen, GCVO; Manfred Freiherr von Richthofen, nephew and namesake of the ace; and Wolf-Manfred Freiherr von Richthofen, son of Lothar and nephew of Rittmeister Manfred Freiherr von Richthofen. For helping an American learn more about the intricacies of German military and civilian customs and traditions, the author offers special thanks to the late Dipl.-Ing. Klaus B. Fischer and Alfred von Krusenstiern.

The author is grateful to the late Cole Palen, founder of The Old Rhinebeck Aerodrome, for providing the experience of being in the air, in the backseat of an open cockpit two-seat biplane during mock combat between replica and original First World War aircraft. Other resources, only slightly less adrenalin-producing and just as valued, were provided by Major Dr Harald Potempa, Director of the Luftwaffenmuseum der Bundeswehr in Berlin; Falk Hallensleben, Director of the Richthofen-Geschwader Museum in Wittmund;Iris Lorenz of the Bayerische Staatsbibliothek; and many helpful members of Bundesarchiv facilities in Berlin, Dresden, Freiburg and

Potsdam, as well as the Elihu Burritt Library at my alma mater, Central Connecticut State University. Special thanks for comments, observations, photographs and much other help go to: Charles H. Donald; the late Ed Ferko; Peter M. Grosz, Andrew Mazur, the late Neal W. O'Connor; Les Peters; Lothair Vanoverbeke; Aaron Weaver and George H. Williams.

Sincere thanks go to Roderick Dymott, Publisher of Brassey's, who encouraged me to undertake this work and has been most understanding of tribulations along the way. To my son Karl, whose degree of computer expertise goes far beyond mine, I express special gratitude for his help as my guide in the intricacies of twenty-first century technology. And, from my own generation, a grateful and loving acknowledgement to my wife Judy for her proofreading skill, pointed questions and being a compassionate sounding board during the development of this (for me) new type of writing project.

Many hours of research preceded and accompanied the writing of this book and a variety of sources, listed in the bibliography, provided factual materials that are presented here in the author's first semi-fictional work. This English-language book aspires to a place among thinly veiled fictional accounts that appeared after the First World War, including *Soldat in den Wolken* (Soldier in the Clouds) by Werner Chomton (1933); *Zwischen Wolken und Granaten* (Between Clouds and Grenades) by Johannes Fischer (1932); *'rangehn ist Alles!* (Getting Close is Everything!) by Thor Goote [pen-name of Werner von Langsdorff] (1938), and *Above the Bright Blue Sky* (1928) and other works by American writer Elliott White Springs. The rationale for producing a volume to honour these early air warriors is found in *They Fought for the Sky* by the late American journalist Quentin Reynolds (1957), one of the books that attracted the author to study First World War aviation history. Reynolds's introduction, titled 'Confessions of a Thief', characterises a writer's pursuit of such stories and expresses views with which I concur: 'Now that the book is finished I am disturbed by the thought that I didn't really write it – I merely typewrote it. I picked the brains of hundreds of men, dead and living, and this is the result . . . The material in this book was for the most part written by those who figure in it, and I, the predatory professional writer, have stolen their thoughts, their emotions and in some cases their very words. I make no apology – I think they bear repeating.'

PETER KILDUFF
New Britain, Connecticut, USA   May 2003

THE NEW SIEGFRIED

*I*nitially, *I was assigned to write an article about the fallen air heroes Max Immelmann and Oswald Boelcke, for use on 12 January 1917, the first anniversary of their receiving the Pour le Mérite. After learning that the Kaiser would present the same decoration to Germany's current highest-scoring fighter pilot on that day, my editor called his government contacts and arranged for me to travel to the Western Front for a series of interviews with the new falcon in the imperial aerie: Leutnant Manfred Freiherr von Richthofen. Who better qualified to help me tell my readers about this new form of warfare, taking place at more than a thousand metres above the ground?*

Despite the War Ministry's glowing reports, I know that these are bad times for the Air Force. Successful people seem to emerge and then are cut down. Immelmann and Boelcke died within four months of each other, and, two days after last Christmas, Leutnant Gustav Leffers, another Pour le Mérite hero, fell victim to a British 'Vickers' Fighting Experimental (F.E.) two-seater. Now, a new air combatant, whose successes are greater than Immelmann's and Leffers's, but not even half of Boelcke's total of aerial victories, is rising to prominence. The German people love heroes. Indeed, they <u>need</u> heroes. So it is that I, too old to fight in this war, have the good fortune of being assigned to write articles about the latest heroic figure. The new Siegfried. It is a choice assignment for me. I hope he lasts.

* * *

Wednesday, 24 January 1917: It is a long journey from Berlin to Douai, the old fortress city that has become a focal point of air warfare in our struggle to push the Tommies out of France. A staff officer accompanies me all the way from Valenciennes and peppers me with information about Germany's new air hero. By the time we reach La Brayelle airfield, on an old castle ground off the south-western edge of the old city fortress, I could write an article on the myths I have heard about this superhuman person. Worth noting, though, is that Manfred von Richthofen has been transferred from Jagdstaffel 2 at Pronville, where he was a Boelcke protégé, up here to Jagdstaffel 11, to lead, instruct and inspire a group of new air warriors.

I learn on arrival that Richthofen teaches by example, having shot down one aeroplane last evening and one at mid-day today. 'This previously luckless unit is seeing what a real warrior can do against the enemy,' notes my all-too-helpful companion. At the airfield, we leave the warmth of his car and hurry through the bitter cold wind to the Officers' Mess, where Richthofen is explaining to his men his latest air fight.

Richthofen is a splendid figure of a man, standing straight and proper in his smart Uhlan uniform. The young officer is compelling to look at: although of medium height, he has a slender, athletic build topped by a strong face with short-cropped blonde hair and piercing blue eyes that make him the very picture of a Germanic hero. Gleaming at the neck of his jacket is the deep blue Pour le Mérite medal; it is in the form of a Maltese Cross and the points of the badge seem to catch every facet of light in the small room. His audience of about a dozen people is silent, as he speaks with a low but firm voice.

Recognising my escort, Richthofen deduces that I must be the latest admiring guest. He looks in my direction and beams like a boy greeting a favourite uncle who has brought sweets. He motions for me to sit down with his men. He has very sharp instincts; quickly grasping the situation, he anticipates my first question by speaking directly to me:

'I was just telling my gentlemen here about today's work. It began when I saw a formation of enemy aeroplanes photographing our artillery emplacements. I signalled my wingman to follow me down towards the leading plane, a big "Vickers" two-seater. A formidable opponent. But this one was far ahead of the others and I caught him unawares. Closing in behind him, I sent a stream of bullets into him, forcing him down. Two other Englishmen attacked me … but I slipped away from them and went back after my target, firing several times more. The observer was wounded, I think. He did not return fire. I could see that the pilot wanted to get down to the ground because his plane was leaving a thin ribbon of smoke behind it … a sure sign he was burning. He managed to land and, before our troops arrived … the machine was on fire. I watched it burst into flames. Then I had to land, as one of my wings cracked at about three hundred metres. It was almost funny – my enemy had landed smoothly, while I came in right near him and turned over on to barbed wire near some trenches.'

I take advantage of a brief pause to ask: 'What did you do with your opponents? Did you take them prisoner? Were you able to talk to them?'

14

'At first, I was unable to do anything. Before I got out of my plane, troops from a nearby reserve emplacement were at the scene to take charge of the enemy crewmen. To answer your second question: they were the first Englishmen I had brought down alive. Of course, I wanted to talk to them. Using the English I had learned at school, I asked whether they had seen my machine in the air. "Oh yes," one of them said. "I know it quite well. We call it le petit rouge (the little red one)."'

'Doesn't it make you more of a target to be so well known by your enemies? Why is your aeroplane painted all red?'

'Yes, of course it makes me more visible. That is what I want. When I began to become successful flying with Boelcke, at first I was annoyed that the enemy could see me from far away. I tried using various colours – especially earth colours – to disguise my plane. If my opponent were directly above me, he might not see me for a few seconds until I moved. So that was impossible. Except for flying into a cloud, which has its own hazards, there is no place to hide in the sky. One cannot make one's plane invisible, but at least it can be made recognisable by our own airmen. One day I got the idea to have my crate painted in glaring red. Now, everyone knows who I am. '

'Are there any disadvantages to being so recognisable, as happened today?'

'Yes, in some ways. After our friendly exchange, one of the crewmen played what was, in my view, a typically British dirty trick. He asked me why I had been so careless in my landing. I did not tell him that my plane had been damaged; I said only that I could not do anything else. Then the scoundrel said that, in the last three hundred metres, he had tried to shoot at me, but his guns had jammed. Can you imagine that? I could have killed him, but, instead, I gave him the gift of his life … and he repaid me with an insulting personal attack! After that encounter, I don't care if I never talk to another one of those arrogant Lords.'

'Why do you call them "Lords?"'

'Because the Englishmen act as if they are Lords of the air. Well, you can see one of their lordly wrecks over there, west of Vimy.'

'What happened to the wrecked British aeroplane?'

'Nothing. Members of my Staffel managed to salvage two machine-guns, but the plane itself was not worth retrieving. It was completely burned up. My men left it in the field where it fell.'

At this point, Richthofen's subordinates determine that my questions are of little interest to them and they leave quietly. Thank goodness, they take the staff officer with them. I am, of course, glad for the opportunity to question Richthofen alone about the new form of combat, in the air, and events leading up to this prominent point in his career. I ask: 'How did you become Germany's latest most successful air fighter?' With a laugh, he responds:

'I shot down sixteen opponents and I am still alive. A year ago, when I was in flight training, a friend asked me what my goal as an airman would be. As a joke, I told him that it would be nice to become the leading fighter pilot. Neither of us believed it would ever come to that, but here we are a year later.'

'Since then you have shot down two more and now have eighteen victories to your credit. Were they all aeroplanes or have you also shot down observation balloons?'

'All have been planes, despite a rumour that a fighter pilot could not receive the Pour le Mérite until he had shot down at least one balloon. After my victory score reached a dozen, I received a note from higher up, asking whether I had attacked a balloon. I thought it was a joke and ignored it. Then came a telegram asking where the balloon was. That irritated me. Still thinking it was a joke, I replied by telegram: "The balloon remains up in the sky." Next, a staff officer, an old friend of mine, called and said: "So, Richthofen, you have shot down so many aeroplanes. We would like to award you the Pour le Mérite. But getting a balloon has just become a requirement. You should shoot one down so that everything is in order." I listened patiently to the harangue. When he finally finished, I told him that I had not given any thought to shooting down a balloon. I also told him: "For the moment, shooting down aeroplanes is more fun for me than your Pour le Mérite." With that, I hung up the telephone in disgust.'

'You still have not shot down a balloon and yet you have received the Pour le Mérite. If the so-called "balloon requirement" was not simply a prank, do you feel that your high number of victories over aeroplanes has proven you worthy of the honour?'

'Absolutely. Boelcke and Immelmann received it after their eighth victories. I had double that amount and wondered when I would receive mine. I was very excited about the prospect and when word came that I was to become the leader of Jagdstaffel 11, it was not the news I had been waiting for. I felt very close to my comrades in Jagdstaffel Boelcke and had no desire to leave them. The local army corps air commander told me privately that it was only a matter of time until I received the Pour le Mérite. But it was still a nice surprise when, during a brief farewell celebration in Pronville two days later, a telegram from Headquarters informed me that His Imperial Majesty had approved the high award for me.'

'Now that you have received the Pour le Mérite, as well as command of your own unit, what is your next objective?'

'I want to be as successful as Boelcke. I have him to thank for all that I have become. Now I want to teach my men to be successful in combat, just as he taught my comrades and me in Jasta 2.'

'Will you teach them special flying "tricks" so they can shoot down many aeroplanes?'

'No. I place little value on the skill of flying itself. Even now, I have difficulty flying the plane. I don't need aerobatic artists. I need daredevils. I don't care if a pilot can fly only in left-hand turns, as long as he goes after the enemy. Every air battle breaks up into individual combats. I can summarise the subject of air combat Tactics in one sentence: "I approach the enemy until I am about fifty metres behind him, take aim at him carefully, open fire and then he falls." That is what Boelcke told me the first time I asked him how he did it. Now I understand that his approach is the way to shoot down an enemy plane. You do not have to be a trick shooter; you simply have to have the courage to fly right up to your opponent and shoot him down. That method works every time.'

'Even for a new man?'

'For a beginner, it is just as important to know what he has to do to keep from being shot down. The greatest danger for a single-seater pilot is a surprise attack from behind. So many of our best and most experienced fighter pilots were surprised and shot down that way. The opponent looks for the most favourable moment to attack the rearmost aircraft of a flight. He dives on him from out of the sun and sends him down with a few shots. Without fail, everyone must be aware of what is behind him. A competent pilot is almost never surprised from the front. If a beginner is attacked from behind, however, he should not try to escape by simply slipping away. The best – and in my view the only correct – method is a sudden, very tight turn. Then, as quickly as possible, go on the offensive.'

'What do you do when you are attacked?'

'First, I try to not let the enemy get at my back. I turn towards the opponent and, by pulling up, I try to get up to his altitude and behind him. But I tell my men that if their opponents get lucky, they should never let up on the throttle; just continue to turn and then dive at full speed to gain momentum. '

'Wouldn't it be simpler to make a frontal attack, to charge right at him, as you would have done on horseback?'

'No. It may seem that you can attack a single-seater from the front. But you can't. I believe that shooting down an enemy from in front, even a single-seater, is rare. Our closing speed is so high that I would be at the right distance for such a combat for only a fraction of a second. The simplest thing is to surprise a single-seater from behind. Then the main point is to make tighter turns and stay above him.'

'Would it be any different if you attack a two-seater from the front?'

'No. I never make a frontal attack on a two-seater. That would be even more dangerous than trying to hit a single-seater from the front. First of all, I would be within the field of fire of the pilot's fixed gun … Then, I would pass by the observer's field of fire. Even if I squeeze below the two-seater and try to turn, while I am in the turn, I would offer the observer a good target.'

'Have you ever pursued an opponent who was clever – or lucky – enough to evade your bullets when you attacked from behind?'

'Yes, and there is a lesson in that circumstance. I tell my men not to stay with a single-seat opponent whom they could not to shoot down. There comes a time when the chase must end. The battle might last until it is far on the other side of the lines ... and then the German would be alone and perhaps face a greater number of opponents. It depends on the wind.'

'What does the wind have to do with it? Doesn't the power of your engine cut through the air and take you where you want to be?'

'No, it is not that simple. Wind direction and strength are critical at altitude. With a favourable wind, an air fight will end with your opponent on your side of the lines. Then he must decide whether he wants to land or risk flying straight ahead – as a perfect target – in order to make it back to his own lines. If he does the latter, I can sit behind him and easily shoot him down.'

'You proved that point last 23 November, when, even with a defective machine-gun, you shot down the top English fighter pilot, Major Hawker. How did you do it'?

'Quite simply, I followed Boelcke's instructions. Two comrades and I were on patrol at the Front and we spotted three small Vickers single-seaters that were out hunting, as we were. They were looking us over and, since I felt ready for combat, I let them come closer. I was below the Englishmen and waited for them to come down to me. Before long, one of them dived and tried to get behind me. I made a sharp left turn and fired a burst of shots, which stopped his attack. Then, both of us flew after each other in a circle like madmen, with our engines running full out at three thousand metres altitude. First to the right, then to the left, each of us intent on getting into the favoured position. Soon, I realised that I was not dealing with a novice. Clearly, he had no intention of breaking off the fight.'

'How did you finally defeat him?'

'By persistence. His little Vickers was very manoeuvrable, but my Albatros climbed better. Finally, I got above and behind him. By this time we were down to two thousand metres, and my opponent must have realised that it was high time to make himself scarce. The wind worked in my favour and we circled more and more until, finally, we were almost over Bapaume, about a kilometre behind German front lines.'

'*Were you close enough to see your opponent?*'

'Oh, yes and, at about a thousand metres, he waved to me quite cheerfully as if to say: "Well, well, how do you do?" The circles that we made around each other were so close … no more than eighty to a hundred metres apart. I could see him in his cockpit and observe every move he made. If he had not been wearing his flying helmet, I would have been able to see his expression.'

'*How did the fight finally end?*'

'Gradually, this round and round got to be too much for the brave sportsman. He had to decide whether to land on our side or try to fly back to his own lines. Of course, he attempted the latter – but only after trying to get away from me by looping and other tricks. Prior to that I had not fired a shot, but then I opened up on him. At about a hundred metres altitude, he tried to escape by flying zig-zag … making his plane more difficult to hit. This was the moment for me. I followed him down from fifty to thirty metres altitude, firing steadily. The Englishman had to fall. Then my guns jammed and I almost lost him! At about fifty metres within our lines he dropped to the ground. Shot through the head.'

'*How did you learn the identity of your opponent?*'

'Our men went back to the wreck. They determined that he was Major Lanoe Hawker, twenty-six years old and leader of a British squadron. Prisoners have said he was the British Boelcke, so I had his machine-gun pulled out of the ground and sent home as a souvenir.'

'*What happened to his body?*

'He was buried where he fell, with the wreckage of his plane standing as his monument. A fitting end for a warrior.'

'*How do you attack a two-seat reconnaissance aeroplane? As you have said, the pilot of a two-seater has a fixed, forward-firing gun, just as a fighter pilot has, and the observer has a flexible machine-gun that gives him a wide range of fire. Don't those qualities make them more formidable opponents?*'

'Of course. You attack a two-seater from behind at great speed, in the same direction he is flying. The best way to avoid an observer's field of fire is to stay calm … and put him out of action with the first shots.'

'As you did today?'

'Yes, I thought I hit the observer. Just to be careful, when the pilot went into a turn, I stayed behind him – not above him. A long fight with a two-seater is the most difficult. I open fire only when the pilot flies straight ahead or, better yet, when he starts to turn. But never from the side or when the two-seater is tilted to one side. That is the time to harass him with warning fire … sending streaks of phosphorous ammunition at him.'

'What do you do if an aggressive two-seater crew attacks you from the front?'

'I do not pull away. When he flies over and away from me, I make a sudden sharp turn below him … pull up and shoot him down. But if the observer has been careful and, while making the turn, I am still within his field of fire, I fly out of his range … turn away and make a new attack.

Individual combat against a single-seater is by far the easiest. If I am alone with an opponent and on this side of the lines, I can shoot him down unless I have a gun jam or an engine defect.'

'Jagdstaffel 11 is made up of new men, who are largely inexperienced in aerial combat. How will you mould them into an effective fighting force?'

'I will teach them as Boelcke taught me. I will make sure they understand certain key points that lead to success.'

'Can you tell me what they are?'

'Certainly. The man must have passed his flying qualification tests. Here at the Front, however, he must learn the terrain without a map … and the course to and from the Front by heart. He must have practised many long orientation flights at home, even during bad weather. When a pilot satisfies me in all of these points, he will make the very image of the man who can be trusted at the Front. When he meets these requirements at Jasta 11, he will fly the first few times fifty metres behind and to the left of me and pay attention to his flight leader.'

'*Anything else?*'

'Yes, a successful combat pilot must have iron discipline … which any good soldier needs to triumph in battle. For example, a fighter pilot must master his machine-gun. I believe in practice firing machine-guns on the ground until they are parallel to a target a hundred and fifty metres out. My men fire their machine-guns at the testing station, and they practise on targets from the air until they become very good at it. I insist on target practice in flight and at high altitude in tight turns and at full throttle.'

'*How do you avoid a stoppage or jam in the machine-gun?*'

'There is no such thing as a gun jam! Only an improperly maintained weapon! When it occurs, I blame only the pilot. The pilot, not the armourer or the mechanic, is responsible for having his machine-gun fire faultlessly. A well-firing machine-gun is better than a smooth-running engine. While loading the ammunition belts the pilot must measure every bullet with a special jig. He must be find time to do this – in bad weather during the day or good weather at night. But it must be done.'

'*But your gun jammed when you were chasing Major Hawker . . .* ' *I catch myself too late. His pleasant expression turns rock-hard. His piercing blue eyes seem to flare, as if they could shoot ice daggers at me. In an instant, I can see myself hauled away by military police and sent back to Berlin in disgrace. Then, just as quickly, his composure returns, with a hint of a forced smile, and he answers me in clear, deliberate tones:*

'Yes, that was my fault. And I learned a good lesson from it. That fight was the most difficult one I'd had up to that time. Since then, I have never gone into battle without checking my guns very carefully.'

'*Of course. Now, to turn to another subject, do you ever see any of your former comrades from Jasta 2?*'

'Oh yes, their airfield is about sixty kilometres south of here and we are trying to compete with them. There are some really aggressive fellows there. For the moment, they have the advantage of having shot down over a hundred enemy planes. It seems they are not to be outdone … but we will equal them.'

'Equal their score of over a hundred victories? How will your Staffel do that?'

'The best thing about being a fighter pilot is that the decisive factor of victory is simply personal courage. You could be a splendid stunt flyer and still not shoot down a single enemy plane. It is a matter of determination. Next, it depends on which opponent we face – the sneaky Frenchman or the plucky Englishman.'

'What is the difference?'

' Generally, the Frenchman lies in wait for his prey so he can surprise him in a trap. That is hard to do in the air … only a beginner will let himself be taken unawares. Ambush in the air does not work … you cannot hide and the invisible aeroplane has not yet been invented. Now and then the Gallic blood rages in the Frenchman and he launches an attack. But it is like soda water: for a moment there is a lot of spirit, but then it goes flat. He lacks tenacious endurance … he flinches, and then dives away.

The Englishman, on the other hand, shows some of his Germanic blood. I prefer to fight an Englishman because he displays pluck and daring.'

At that moment, an aide interrupts us and whispers something into Richthofen's ear. It is clear that he must leave. Indeed, I am just as glad that the first interview is over. He is such a compelling personality that he can communicate his pleasure or displeasure – and very forcefully, at that – with a gesture, and I feel very uncomfortable after our brief exchange about the machine-gun jam. I am unsure whether he will want to talk to me again. But he allays my fears with his parting comment:

'I will see you at dinner and then, I take it, you will be with us for a few days. We will have other opportunities to talk.'

2

THE MOST BEAUTIFUL TIME

Saturday, 3 February 1917: Leutnant Manfred von Richthofen went home on leave yesterday and, as other events demanded his attention, I had no further opportunity to speak with him at the airfield. I am told that when he brought down his eighteenth enemy aeroplane, on 24 January, a wing problem made landing his red Albatros precarious. And, the day before, Jasta Boelcke lost planes in similar accidents; among them, one flown by an old friend of Richtofen's, who was killed. A few days after that – on the usually festive Kaiser's birthday – all Albatros fighters were withdrawn from service. Richthofen and his people were busy arranging for the older, Halberstadt fighters to be sent as replacement aircraft. Richthofen dispelled any doubts about the Halberstadts' effectiveness two days ago when he flew one and achieved his nineteenth victory. Now he is off on a well-earned short rest and I am pleased to have been invited to accompany him back as far as Berlin. As expected, he is in good spirits during our ride in a very nice chauffeur-driven Mercedes touring car to the railway station at Douai. Germany's heroes travel in comfort, even on the train, where the privacy of a First Class compartment offers a marvellous opportunity for me to question him without interruption, save for the occasional steward who looks in on us to ensure that we have food and drink.

First, I ask him what had happened to the Albatros biplane fighters – they had performed so well after trouble had developed with the Fokker monoplanes and biplanes last year:

'I don't know yet. There seems to be some sort of structural problem. As I told you, when I was following Number Eighteen, at about three hundred metres, one of my lower wings broke. It was nothing short of a miracle that I reached the ground without mishap.'

'You said you had a problem, but I did not realise that you lost a wing.'

'I did not lose it, but it came loose and I was able to land before it tore away completely. Jasta Boelcke lost three planes and two pilots that way, including little Imelmann . . .'

'Any relation to Max Immelmann, Boelcke's great rival?'

'No. My friend Hans Imelmann – different spelling – had no connection to the Saxon airman, but was still a fine pilot. We flew together with Boelcke and were successful in some of the same fights. What a pity that he is gone.'

'Have you had to change your tactics to make allowances for the older Halberstadt aeroplanes that you now fly on missions to the front lines?'

'No. In fact, flying to the Front is not a fighter mission. We fly to the Front ... to the centre of our sector ... to watch enemy flight operations. When we fly away from the Front, we try to climb higher ... so that we can attack the enemy with the sun behind us. The fighter mission is a series of thrusts over the lines and back again. When we see no enemies over there, these thrusts over the lines are useless.'

'So you do not fly to the Front, in the manner of knights of old, looking to engage the enemy in individual combat?'

'Ach, knights of the air! What a myth! We just fly towards the English formations and the battle begins. It ends in a series of individual combats. I do not try to shoot down the entire enemy flight ... I seek out one opponent. Then it is a matter of You or Me. A knightly combat with equal weapons, each with a machine-gun and a plane and a bit of athletic skill – is really only a dream. I am more concerned with finding artillery-spotting aircraft ... they generally fly on the other side of the lines and at fairly low altitude. They help to rain down the heavy fire on our ground troops. If I cannot find one, then I watch five, six or even ten single-seat aircraft at a time. I observe their altitude and course changes, and try to determine whether they have high-flying escort aircraft. Then, I fly away from the Front a bit and come back to the enemy lines at higher altitude than my next target. As I distance myself from the Front, I keep them in view constantly. The best time to attack an artillery-spotter is when it flies from its own lines toward the Front. Then, allowing for the east to west wind factor, I drop down on him in a steep dive from out of the sun.'

'Is that what you did two days ago, to bring down your nineteenth victim?'

'Yes. One of my new men, Leutnant Carl Allmenröder, and I were at about eighteen hundred metres when I saw a two-seat artillery spotter. I managed to approach, apparently unnoticed, to within fifty metres of him. Then, about a plane's length away from him, I opened fire. The enemy plane went down in a wide uncontrolled right-hand curve, and Allmenröder and I followed it until it crashed in the barbed wire of our forward lines.'

'What happened to the crew and to the aeroplane?'

'According to reports, both crewmen were wounded and were taken prisoner by the infantry. It was impossible to remove the plane.'

'So there was no opportunity to take a souvenir from the wreckage, which I have been told you have been doing for some time?' He laughs heartily at that remark and says:

'Not this time. But I am a hunter by nature and hunters like trophies. They are proof of one's deeds. While I was still an observer with the Brieftauben-Abteilung Ostende, my pilot and I shot down a French plane, but could not prove it and therefore received no credit for it. Or for another plane that I shot down some months later.'

'That so-called carrier pigeon detachment at Ostend. I would like to hear about those flights, but, for the moment, please tell me about your first combat with this unit. There is no reference to it in the information I was given by the War Ministry.'

'The BAO was the cover name for the air combat unit based at Ostend to attack British sea and air units near the Belgian coast. I arrived there in August 1915 and stayed only a short time. Soon, fighting in the Champagne region flared up and we flew there with our big two-engined aeroplane. We soon realised that the big crate was a grand plane, but it would never make a fighter.'

'*Do you recall when your first aerial combat took place?*'

'I remember it distinctly. On the afternoon of 26 October, I flew with Oberleutnant von Osterroht, who, for this flight, had been assigned a somewhat smaller plane than the barge, as we called it. We encountered a French Farman two-seater about five kilometres behind his Front. Calmly, Osterroht approached him and for the first time I saw an opponent up close in the air. Osterroht flew so close to him that I could easily fire at him. The observer had not noticed us at all … and so he did not fire back until I had my first gun jam. After I had fired off my entire magazine of a hundred rounds, I could not believe my eyes, when all of a sudden the enemy went down in a peculiar spiral. I followed him with my eyes and tapped Osterroht on the head to watch it. The Farman fell into a big shell crater. We saw it, standing on its nose, with the tail up.'

'*Is he the same Oberleutnant Paul Henning von Osterroht who leads Jasta 12?*'

'Yes. He and I flew together many times.'

'*The combat you mention took place well over a year ago. How can you be so sure of the date after all this time?*'

'I marked the date, time and site on my map. Later, Osterroht and I submitted a combat report about the event. I can show you a copy of it. But at that time, planes shot down behind enemy lines did not count. Otherwise, I would have one more on my victory list today. I was very proud of my success, but the main point is that the enemy went down … not that anyone was credited with a victory.'

'*Tell me about the second plane you shot down. Were you still flying with the BAO?*'

'No. By this time I had become a pilot and was assigned to Kampfgeschwader 2 at Verdun, flying a smaller two-seater. My accomplishment is mentioned in the Army Daily Report of 26 April, although I am not named personally.'

'*Who shot down the enemy, you or your observer?*'

'I did. I had ordered that a machine-gun be mounted on the top wing of my Albatros two-seater … just as I had seen done on French Nieuport fighters.

Some people laughed at it because it looked very primitive, but I was very proud of this construction. Then I had an opportunity to use it practically.'

'What did you do?'

'I met a Nieuport that, apparently, was also being flown by a beginner, because he acted foolishly. I flew towards him and he pulled away. Evidently, his gun had jammed. I did not feel that I would be able to engage him further. What would happen if I were to fire at him? I flew after him and ... getting closer, fired the machine-gun for the first time, a short series of well-aimed shots. Then the Nieuport reared up and rolled over. At first my observer and I believed it was a trick the Frenchmen like to use. But this trick did not end. He went down lower and lower. Then my observer tapped my helmet and called out to me: "Congratulations! He is falling!" In fact, he came down in a forest south of Fort Douaumont and disappeared among the trees. It was clear to me that I had shot him down. But – on the other side! I flew home and reported nothing more than: "One aerial combat, one Nieuport shot down."'

'And, since that time, you have tried to collect your own proof of any victories?'

'Yes, on numerous occasions and especially for the eighth victory.'

'According to the records, that was on 9 November 1916. And wasn't that at a time when eight victories was the standard for earning the Pour le Mérite?'

'Yes. In Boelcke's time, eight victories was quite a respectable number. With the higher numbers of victories recorded these days, people must think that shooting down planes has become easier. Let me tell you that it has become only more difficult from month to month, from week to week. Of course, we find more opportunities to shoot down the enemy nowadays ... but the possibility of one of us being shot down has become even greater. The enemy's armament has improved and he has more planes. When Max Immelmann shot down his first plane, he had the good luck to find an opponent with no machine-gun. Now, the only place you will find such easy pickings is over a training field such as the Johannisthal aviation facility outside Berlin.'

'Yes, I understand. How did you come to score your eighth victory?'

28

'On that morning, I flew with my comrade-in-arms Hans Imelmann. He was just eighteen years old. We came to know each other at Jasta Boelcke and we got along together very well. Comradeship is the main thing. We pulled our planes closer together. I already had seven and Imelmann had five. That was quite a lot for the time.'

'So I understand, but how did the fight start?'

'We were over the Front just a short time when we saw a bomber formation. They came toward us boldly, in enormous numbers, just as they did during the Battle of the Somme. There must have been forty or fifty planes, although I could not tell the exact number. They were looking for a target not far from our airfield. Then, just before they reached their objective, I caught up with the straggler. My first shots knocked out the observer's machine-gun and most likely grazed the pilot. In any case, he decided to land, even with his bombs. I singed his hide some more, which increased the speed and he headed for the ground even faster. He crashed near our airfield at Lagnicourt.'

'What did Imelmann do while you were chasing your opponent?'

'He was involved with another Englishman and bagged him in the same area as mine. Quickly, we flew back home so as to be able to see the machines we shot down.'

'Were you able to land alongside the downed planes?'

'No, they were in a muddy field. We flew back to our airfield and went by car to the crash site. Then we had to run across the field to where the wrecks were. It was very hot, so I undid some of my clothes, even my shirt and collar. I had taken off my jacket and hat and left them in the car. I took a knotty walking stick with me to help get through the mud, which was up to my knees. I must have looked awful. Finally, I got to my victim. Of course, a lot of men from the area gathered around the wreck.'

'What happened to the crew?'

'There was only one and he was very badly wounded and taken away. A group of officers stood on the other side of the field. I walked over to them and asked one of them if he had seen the air fight and how it looked to him. I find it interesting to hear from people on the ground how the fight looks to them.'

'*What were they able to see?*'

'A Rittmeister told me that the other Englishmen had dropped their bombs, but that this plane still had its load. Then he asked my name and led me by the arm over to the other officers and introduced me to them. That was not a very pleasant experience for me ... I had messed up my clothes – and these gentlemen all looked fastidious. I was presented to their leader, but he did not look quite right to me. He wore a general's trousers and had a high award fastened at his neck. For someone in such a high position, he looked quite young. I saw. his epaulettes, but could not tell his rank. Yet, there was something exceptional about him and, in the course of the conversation, I felt compelled to straighten out my shirt and trousers and take on a more military bearing.'

'*Who was he?*'

'I did not know at the time. Eventually, the group of officers left and I returned to our airfield. That evening, however, I received a telephone call and learned that he was the Duke of Saxe-Coburg-Gotha. I was ordered to report to him ... it had been determined that the English had intended to bomb his headquarters. I was told that His Royal Highness felt that I had saved his life from those assassins. For that, I was awarded the Oval Silver Duke Carl Eduard Bravery Medal.'

'*Had you received decorations from other members of royalty prior to that occasion?*'

'No, this was the first. But after the eighth victory, I hoped to receive an award from His Imperial Majesty, the Kaiser. But, in this case, it was especially nice because His Royal Highness, the Duke had already helped to establish a flying school in Gotha. In fact, my old comrade Osterroht had been an instructor there before the war.'

'*Did Hans Imelmann also receive an award from the Duke?*'

'Yes, he did.'

Then Richthofen's mood shifts from bright to sullen. I cannot tell whether it reflects the loss of Imelmann or his disappointment in having to wait for the Pour le Mérite. I change the subject to break the awkward silence and ask: 'You were flying with Jasta Boelcke at this time. Tell me about Hauptmann Oswald Boelcke. How did you meet him?'

'Pure luck. It was in early October 1915 and I was on the train used to transport the BAO from Ostend to the Champagne Front. The battle was raging and the French airmen seemed to be everywhere. Due to the changing situation, we were assembled as a Kampfgeschwader. In any case, I was in the dining-car and at the next table sat a young, plain-looking Leutnant. There was no reason to take special notice of him, except for one fact: of all of us, he was the only one who, up to then, had shot down an enemy airman. Indeed, not only one, but four. He had even been mentioned by name in the Army Reports.'

'And you wanted to meet him?'

'Of course. I was impressed by him and by his exciting experiences. I had tried so hard and did not bag even one, in any case not one that was confirmed. I wanted very much to learn Boelcke's secret. So I asked him: "Tell me honestly, how do you really do it?" He had a good laugh at my bluntness. Then he answered: "Good Lord, it is quite simple. I fly right up to him, take good aim, open fire and then he just falls down."'

'Did you tell Boelcke that you had tried to shoot down enemy aeroplanes?'

'No, I just shook my head because I had also done that, but my opponent had not fallen down. The difference, of course, is that Boelcke was flying a Fokker and I was flying my big barge.'

'Did he give you any advice about changing that situation?'

'No. But I tried to get to know him better. Often we played cards and took walks together, and I asked him questions. And then I decided that I must learn to fly a Fokker and perhaps things would get better.'

'Could Boelcke have helped you by recommending that you receive training as a fighter pilot?'

'I don't know. I never asked for that. My only thoughts were on learning how to work the stick. Then, while Kagohl 2 was in the Champagne sector, a good friend taught me how to fly an old crate. I pursued flying passionately! I was an observer, but, after about twenty-five hours of instruction, I was ready for my first solo flight so that I could qualify to become a pilot.'

'When did you make your first solo flight and how did it go?'

'According to my logbook, it took place on 10 October 1915 and the result was terrible. I landed nose-first – with, of course, laughter from all sides. Two days later I went up in another plane. I flew the prescribed Figure Eight and made a number of landings. I was proud of myself when I got out of the plane – only to learn that I had failed again. Eventually, I passed and became a two-seater pilot. Then, in mid-November, I was ordered to the training facility at Döberitz.'

'To become a fighter pilot?'

'No, not yet. Osterroht and I had been assigned to learn to fly a "giant" aeroplane. This huge barge is quite impressive. It holds as many bombs as a Zeppelin and has a crew of five men: two pilots, an observer, a mechanic and a machine-gunner. I was interested in these giant planes from the beginning, but after flying one for a time, it became clear to me that only the smallest plane would enable me to become the combat pilot I wanted to be. The big barge was not quick and responsive enough for combat, and that is important for my work.'

'I understand that the giant aeroplanes were organised into specialised units and I gather you were not assigned to one of them. So, how did you become a fighter pilot?'

'More good luck, I suppose. I returned to Kagohl 2, then opposite Verdun, and flew a two-seater, which is what I used to shoot down a Nieuport in April 1916. From the beginning of my career as a pilot, I had only one ambition: to fly a single-seat fighter. I pestered my commanding officer until he gave me permission to fly a Fokker, the plane in which Boelcke and Immelmann had achieved their tremendous successes.'

'Did you shoot down enemy aeroplanes during your time with Kagohl 2?'

'No, I did not have my first air combat success until I served under Boelcke some months later. Kagohl 2 was sent to Russia, where many times all I did was haul one-hundred-and-fifty-kilogram bombs with an ordinary two-seat aeroplane. I also had two machine-guns, but was never able to try them out in Russia. It is too bad that I do not have a single Russian item in my collection of air combat souvenirs at home. The cockade would look very colourful on the wall . . . '

Richthofen becomes dreamy-eyed, no doubt thinking about less hectic times on the Eastern Front. I interrupt him by asking him about Boelcke. I knew that, after Max Immelmann's death, Boelcke had been ordered not to fly and had then been sent on a good-will visit to German allies on the Southern Front. I did not know, however, when he returned to duty or how he became connected to Richthofen. Instantly lucid, Richthofen responds:

'In mid-August 1916, Boelcke came to Kovel to see his brother, Wilhelm, a flight leader in Kagohl 2. One evening Boelcke appeared before a gathering of pilots and told us many interesting things about his trip to Turkey. He was on his way back to report to Supreme Headquarters. He talked about returning to the Somme Sector to continue his work and to set up an entire Jagdstaffel. For that reason he was selecting people from the Air Service who seemed suited to the new task.'

'And, of course you volunteered immediately.'

'No, I did not dare ask him to take me with him. Not on the basis that it was too boring in our Geschwader. But the thought of going back on the Western Front to fight tempted me. There is nothing more exquisite for a cavalry officer than going off on the hunt.'

'How did you end up in Boelcke's new Staffel?'

'Early the next morning, there was a knock at the door of my little hut. I opened it and there stood the great man wearing the Pour le Mérite. I really did not know what he wanted of me. It did not occur to me that he would invite me to become a pupil of his. I could have hugged him when he asked whether I wanted to go to the Somme.'

'How long did it take for you to be allowed to leave Kagohl 2?'

'Three days later I was on a train, travelling across Germany to my new field of endeavour. I was as happy as could be. At last, my fondest wish was fulfilled and now the most beautiful time of my life began for me.'

'I know that censorship is important in wartime, but am I correct in assuming that you are the Leutnant R. referred to by your mentor in his book Hauptmann Boelckes Feldberichte *(Captain Boelcke's Field Reports)? And the other pilot who was assigned to the new Jagdstaffel at the same time – Leutnant B. – is your friend Erwin Böhme?'*

'Yes, there is no point in trying to disguise these names ... as most people who read the book can determine who they are.'

'And Böhme had already a confirmed victory to his credit. One he shot down on the Russian Front in August?'

'That is true, but I caught up with him quickly. On 17 September, I achieved my first <u>confirmed</u> aerial victory.'

'Oh yes, that date is noted in Boelcke's book (a copy of which I pull out of my valise and open to the marked page). He writes: "Number twenty-three was a stubborn opponent. I had cut off the formation and busied myself with the second machine. The first one pulled away. The third was attacked by Leutnant R. and was soon being twisted and turned by Leutnant B. and Leutnant R., but, despite that, was able to get away over the Front . . ."Surely, the Englishman did not get away. How did you bring him down?'

'Exactly the way Boelcke told us to do it. Before we took off, Boelcke issued precise instructions which we took as gospel. When we arrived at the Front, still over our own lines, bursts of our anti-aircraft fire pointed out an enemy formation flying in the direction of Cambrai. Boelcke was, of course, the first to see it ... he always saw more than other people. Soon we also grasped the situation and each of us struggled to stay close behind Boelcke. It was clear to all of us that we had to pass our first test under the eyes of our revered leader.'

'And so, in cavalry parlance, he led the charge?'

'Carefully. We approached the formation slowly … it could no longer get away from us. We were between them and the Front. If they wanted to go back, they had to get by us. We counted eight enemy planes. There were only five of us. In a matter of seconds, the situation would explode. Boelcke was the first to get close to them … but he did not open fire. I was the second, with my comrades close behind me. The Englishman flying just ahead of me was in a big, darkly stained boat. I did not think about it long and took aim at him. He fired. I fired. I fired and missed. He did, too.'

'When you say your opponent was a big boat of an aeroplane, do you mean it was a two-seater, bigger than your Albatros?'

'Yes, but the pilot was no beginner. He seemed to sense that the moment I got behind him, his last hour was being chimed. At the time I was not convinced that he must fall; I was more concerned about whether he would fall. I was so close to him that I was afraid I would ram into him. Suddenly, his propeller stopped turning. He was hit! His engine was shot up and he had to land on our side. I noticed the machine making swaying movements. Something was not quite right with the pilot. Also the observer was no longer to be seen, his machine-gun pointed unattended up in the air. I must have hit him and he was lying on the floor of his fuselage. The plane came down near one of our airfields.'

'Did you follow it down?'

'I was so excited that I had to head for the airfield. But in my haste to land, I almost nosed-over, not far from him. I jumped out and ran along with a bunch of soldiers heading towards the wreckage. When I got there I found that my assumption was correct. The engine was shot up, the observer was already dead and the pilot died on the way to the field hospital.'

'Did you obtain a souvenir from your first official victory?'

'No, I had another thought in mind. I wanted to order a stone in remembrance of the foes who had fallen with honour and have it placed on their grave.'

'Hauptmann Boelcke must have been proud of you.'

'When I returned home, Boelcke was already having breakfast with my other comrades and wondered where I had been. Proudly, I reported to him: "One Englishman shot down." It turned out that I was not the only one. In addition to Boelcke, each one of us beginners had been a victor for the first time.'

'In his book, Boelcke wrote that a pilot receives a silver Cup of Honour for shooting down his first enemy aeroplane. Did you and your comrades receive yours at some suitably festive dinner?'

'Not right away. We had a party that evening, at which Boelcke presented Böhme with the Iron Cross First Class that he had earned in Russia, but that had arrived only that day. I came up with another way to commemorate my victory. That evening I wrote to a jeweller I know in Berlin and ordered a special memento: a small plain, silver cup with the inscription 1. Vickers 2. 17.9.16. It is for my first victory, which was a Vickers two-seater shot down on 17 September 1916.'

I want to ask Richthofen more questions about Boelcke and other victories, as well as the sad connection between Boelcke and Böhme. But the train's chief steward and two subordinates appear outside our compartment with a heated food tray that gives off the most wonderful aroma. It is time to eat. The long journey ahead of us will provide other opportunities to gather information.

* * *

Manfred von Richthofen is devoted to his tasks; our conversation ceases and we eat in silence. And what a feast! It is incredible that in wartime the train chef is able to prepare a marvellous big duck in orange sauce and farm-fresh vegetables for our lunch. The meal is accompanied by what the steward promises is a splendid white burgundy to make the repast more enjoyable. I know the wine will make me sleepy, but I hope it will make Richthofen less inhibited and that he may tell me some candid anecdotes for my articles. I offer to pour for him, but he declines. I have heard that he allows himself an occasional cigarette, but not that he is a teetotaller. 'Not a drop,' he says smiling, as he sips from his water glass. He is as well disciplined as an athlete; clearly, much of his success is due to his fine physical condition. Likewise, I pass on the wine and even one of the fine cigars on a silver plate. Richthofen appears to be quite satisfied with his lunch and ready for more questions. I ask about his second confirmed victory, a bomber brought down on the morning of 23 September 1916. He looks into his small logbook and then replies:

'Not much to say. I have it recorded as a single-seat Martinsyde, which I attacked over Bapaume. It took three hundred rounds to send him down. The pilot was fatally wounded and came down near Beugny. His machine-gun was knocked out by a bullet of mine to the breech block. I kept the gun as a souvenir. I also took a piece of fabric with the plane's number on it.'

'What about your third victory? What was that like?' Again, he peers into his logbook before responding:

'That was on 30 September. Just before noon, right over our own airfield. There were five of us against many more of them – all Vickers types. I singled out a machine and fired some two hundred rounds at it. Finally, it began to go down towards Cambrai, making big circles. Your heart beats a little faster when your opponent, whose face you have just seen, goes roaring down from three thousand metres.'

'Did you follow him down?'

'Not at first. The shooting had stopped and I could see the machine was out of control. We were rather far from our lines, so I left the stricken plane and went after a new opponent. Without success. Later I saw the first machine, on fire, being pursued by another Albatros. It crashed near Frémicourt. By the time I got to the site, little remained of the men or the machine. But I did retrieve a small insignia as a souvenir.'

'How are you able to learn the identities of the airmen you shoot down?'

'Sometimes the crewmen carry personal effects or other items that are examined for their intelligence value.'

'As they would make your claim for victory credit stronger, are you shown such materials?' He pulls a folded piece of paper from his logbook and, reading from it, he says:

'Not always in a direct way. I learned the name of the fourth pilot I shot down from an official Army report, which said: "The biplane single-seater, Lt Fenwick, shot down by Leutnant Freiherr von Richthofen near Equancourt belonged to the 21st Squadron and, indeed, according to the papers found in it, to a B.E. Flight. The aeroplane is apparently one of new construction."'

'You said that, after you had disposed of the crew of your third victory, another Albatros pilot fired at it and possibly set it on fire, but that you received credit for it. There seems to be some question, however, that, on 10 October, you shot down an enemy plane that should have been credited as your fifth victory. Boelcke was credited with his thirty-second on that date and in his book writes: "The day was also profitable for the Staffel. Leutnant R. shot down his fifth and Leutnant S." – Jürgen Sandel, perhaps? – "got one, so that all together we accounted for five." Yet, Sandel, if it was he, received no credit and, despite Boelcke's statement, your official score does not include a confirmed victory for that date. Why was that?'

'I do not recall Sandel as being successful. In any event, the Chief of Field Aviation has strict rules about victories. I am convinced that I shot down a big two-seater on 10 October, but the higher-ups are not. And that's the end of it.'

'What happened that day?'

'Boelcke led us against a flight of Vickers planes east of Arras and, as usual, I singled out a machine. I fired about three hundred rounds into it. Then it began to smoke and to glide steeper and steeper. I followed, firing almost the entire time. The enemy's propeller became slower and clouds of black smoke came from the engine. The observer had stopped firing and, just as I getting closer, I was attacked from behind and went into a tight turn to get rid of the second plane. Later, I learned that my Vickers had crashed and a crewman was dead. But a pilot from another unit received credit for shooting it down.'

'The Chief of Field Aviation's office states that you achieved your fifth victory six days later. Yet, for that date, Boelcke's book mentions only his thirty-fifth, that he flew with – Böhme, I assume – and that he witnessed the eighth victory of Leutnant Leffers, who was not even a member of Jasta 2. What do you recall of these events?'

'There is no doubt that Boelcke achieved a victory that day. And, of course, Leffers was a fighter pilot rising in success. He received the Pour le Mérite a few weeks later. It was not unusual for Jasta 2 and other German units to join up in their efforts. As for the enemy plane credited officially as my fifth, my logbook shows it was a B.E. single-seater that I attacked over Bertincourt. It took about three hundred and fifty rounds, but I brought it down, east of Léchelle.'

'Boelcke is mentioned often in our conversations, yet you have not told me much about him. Now, of course, he is a legend – but how was he to the people who saw him every day?'

'In the air, Boelcke was a mystery to us. It was incredible the way he could shoot down an enemy plane almost every time he went up. On the ground, though, Boelcke was quite an ordinary fellow. He did not let his fame go to his head. Everyone who came to know Boelcke imagined that he was his one true friend. I have met about forty of these one true friends, whose names Boelcke never knew, but who believed that they were especially close to him. It was a strange phenomenon that I have observed only in Boelcke. He had no personal enemies. He was equally friendly to everyone, no more to one, no less to another. Yet, he had a maturity about him that left no question that he was in charge. He was a born leader and his men would follow him anywhere.'

'Did you think it was ironic that Boelcke, the victor in more combats than any other German pilot, should be killed in a collision with one of his own pilots?'

'Ironic? No. Combat in the air is as unpredictable as it is on the ground. In fact, the Battle of the Somme was an extraordinary time for us. Boelcke called it an El Dorado for fighter pilots. Within two months, he increased his victories from twenty to forty. We beginners did not have the experience that our master had and were quite satisfied to get home without being scorched. But it was beautiful!'

'"Beautiful"? How so?'

'Every time we took off there was a fight. Often, great air battles of forty to sixty Englishmen against, unfortunately, not always so many Germans. They had quantity and we had quality. But the Englishmen are cheeky fellows, we must give them credit for that. They came back and forth at quite low altitude to visit Boelcke at his own airfield – with bombs. They challenged us to fight and we accepted. Rarely have I met an Englishman who refuses to fight. Unlike the Frenchman, who embarrasses himself by avoiding encounters with his opponents.

'We had beautiful times at our Jagdstaffel because the leader's spirit spread to his pupils. We trusted his leadership. It never occurred to us that anyone would be left behind. And so we went after our enemies boldly and cheerfully.'

'You were so confident in Boelcke that you would follow him anywhere. In any weather, too?'

'Of course. Once we were flying with him during stormy weather and still felt safe because we were with him. There was only one Boelcke! Most other airmen would not go up on such a day, only the fighter pilots. It was not long before we saw some daring Englishmen, apparently also having fun in the bad weather. There were six of us and two of them. Even if there had been twenty of them, Boelcke's signal to attack would not have astonished us.'

Sensing that the conversation is going in another direction, I interject and ask bluntly: 'You flew with Boelcke on the day he was killed, 28 October 1916. Can you tell me what happened?' Richthofen pauses for a moment, as if pulling a long string of memory from some secluded part of his mind.

'It began as a peaceful Saturday. Then, in the late afternoon, we were called up to the Front to disperse enemy fighters attacking our infantry. Once there, we saw several English fast single-seat fighters and the usual battle began. Boelcke went after one and I the other. But then I had to pull away because I was distracted by another one of our own. I looked around and saw that, about two hundred metres from me, Boelcke was pressing towards his opponent.

'Again, it was the usual scene. Boelcke was firing away and I could only watch. A good friend of his was flying close to him. It was an interesting fight. Both were firing and at any moment the Englishman was sure to go down. Suddenly, there was an unnatural movement in both German planes. All I could think was: Collision! I had never seen a collision in the air but, like many others, had imagined what it must be like. It had not been a collision;

rather, it was more of brushing against each other. At a plane's great speed, though, a light brushing is like a violent concussion.'

'News accounts said only that Boelcke died in an accident. I have since heard that the accident also involved Leutnant Erwin Böhme. If so, what happened to him?' Then I let Richthofen ramble on, as I know that he revered Boelcke and is friends with Böhme.

'Nothing. Böhme made it to the ground. Immediately after the two planes touched, Boelcke pulled away from his intended victim and headed for the ground in a great spiralling turn. I did not think he would crash, but as he glided down I noticed that a section of his top wing was broken. I could not see what happened next, but in the clouds Boelcke lost the entire top wing. His plane became uncontrollable and fell … accompanied most of the way by his faithful friend. Boelcke died instantly. His skull was crushed on impact.
'When we got back home, the the news had already arrived: "Our Boelcke is dead!" We could not believe it. The news was most painful, of course, to the one who survived the accident. Of all of us, he was perhaps closest to our leader. Boelcke's death affected all of us very deeply … as if a favourite brother had been taken from us.'

'You were Boelcke's most successful protégé. Why were you not given command of his Jagdstaffel?'

'Because Leutnant Stephan Kirmaier was the senior officer and he had shot down ten enemy planes. He was in line to receive the Pour le Mérite. He was the obvious choice for many reasons.'

'But your successful role in Jasta 2 was recognised?

'At the funeral. Yes, I was given the honour of carrying the velvet pillow bearing the dead hero's medals. The service for Boelcke was like that for a reigning prince.'

'What were the after-effects of Boelcke's death?'

'It is hard to say. During the following six weeks, we lost six pilots and one was wounded. Two others were washed up because of their nerves.'

'How did Boelcke's death affect you, personally?' I am always impressed by Richthofen's self-discipline. In this instance, he pauses for a moment and then, looking at me with an air of detachment, he says in measured tones:

'A week to the day later, I shot down my seventh. My nerves have not suffered as a result of the others' bad luck.'

Once again, I feel intrusive. I sense that he feels he must put up a barrier, which will not help the candour I hope for. Time to switch subjects. Trying to stay as calm as he seems to be, I say: 'Clearly, Boelcke contributed most to your success. Who was the first pilot to influence you and when did it happen?' Now, he flashes the warm smile that inspires the listener to accept what he says without question. His voice is much more cheerful as he says:

'Georg Zeumer, in the summer of 1915. At the time, I wanted to get through training as fast as possible because I was afraid I might get to the Front too late. It would have taken three months to become a pilot. By then, we could have been long at peace ... so that was out of the question. I felt that as a cavalryman, I would make a good observer. To my greatest joy, two weeks later, I was the first in my class to be sent to a front-line unit. And, at that, to the only place where there was still an active war: Russia. I felt a bit out of place as a beginner at Feldflieger-Abteilung 69, but my pilot was one of the unit's "big guns" and he was very active. We had a wonderful time together. It was very much like the cavalry. We were in completely mobile warfare. We made reconnaissance flights almost every day – morning, noon and all afternoon. Zeumer, the pilot, "drove" in the back seat while I "rode" in the front seat. I had a good view of the ground and gathered material for many good reports. Flying was so much more fun for me than being an assistant adjutant on the ground back in France. After a few weeks, unfortunately, Zeumer was transferred back to the BAO in Flanders.'

'I take it that was when you met your second pilot?'

'Yes. It is very important for an observer to find a responsive pilot. One fine day it was announced that Count von Holck was on his way to join us. He was a well-known racing car driver before the war and so my first thought was: "That is the man I need."'

'I suppose it helped that he also came from a cavalry unit?'

'No, Count von Holck was not merely a sportsman on the green grass. He was a pilot of rare ability and, most importantly, he was in a class far above the enemy. We made many splendid reconnaissance flights – who knows how far? – into Russia. I never felt the least bit insecure with him. On the contrary, at critical moments he inspired me. One look at his determined face and I had even more courage than before.'

'Can you recall a particularly memorable flight with Holck?'

'They were all memorable, but especially the last one. It was in August and we were nearly killed.'

I exclaim: 'That's the one I want to hear about!'

'We had received rather undefined orders to fly that day ... which is one of the nice things about flying. We are masters of the air and very much on our own. So, when we were ordered to fly to a forward airfield, we had to determine which meadow was the right one. On our way to Brest-Litovsk, we saw Russians in full retreat, burning everything. It was a horribly beautiful sight. Trying to determine the size of the enemy troop columns, we came over the burning city of Wicznice. We were down to fifteen hundred metres' altitude to see the ground conditions. Then an enormous pillar of smoke, reaching up to perhaps two thousand metres, prevented us from flying straight ahead. I advised Holck to fly around it ... a detour of perhaps five minutes. But he would not consider it at all. On the contrary: the greater the danger, the more attractive it was to him. So, right into it! What fun to be with such a plucky fellow! But our carelessness soon cost us dearly. Barely had the tail of the plane disappeared into the cloud when I noticed we were swaying. I could see nothing more, the smoke stung my eyes, the air was much, much warmer. Beneath me I saw only an enormous sea of fire. Suddenly the plane stalled and went spiralling downwards. I grabbed on to a strut to brace myself and not be tossed out. I looked into Holck's face and regained my courage from the sight of his steely confidence. My only thought was: it is so stupid to die a heroic death in such a needless way . . . '

Richthofen pauses and, frustrated by this digression, I prod him: 'What happened? What happened?'

'We dived to about five hundred metres over the burning city. Whether it was through Holck's skill or Divine Providence – perhaps both – suddenly we dropped out of the smoke cloud and the good Albatros started up again and flew on as though nothing had happened.

'We'd had enough of changing airfields and just wanted to get back to our own lines posthaste. We were still behind Russian lines and at low altitude. Then about five minutes later Holck yelled out: "The engine is packing up." I was convinced that a horde of Russkis was coming after us. We could hear bullets hitting our plane. They sounded like chestnuts popping in a fire. Then, the engine quit. We dropped into a long glide over a forest, as Holck headed towards an abandoned Russian artillery base. As soon as we landed, we jumped out of the old crate and ran for the forest, to defend ourselves.'

'What kind of weapons were you carrying?'

'Holck had nothing and I had a pistol and six rounds. It looked as though the situation would become worse when we saw men in fur hats running towards our aeroplane. They looked like Russians. One of them approached us and, as he came closer, Holck recognised him as a Prussian grenadier guard. Later, the commander of the unit, Prinz Eitel Friedrich of Prussia, had us provided with horses. Once again, we old cavalry airmen were on "hay-burning engines", but we got back to our airfield later that evening.'

'How long did you fly with Count von Holck?'

'Not long enough. The third week in August, I was transferred to the BAO in Ostend. On the way to my new posting, I stopped at Schweidnitz to see my parents for a few days.'

'So now you flew with a third pilot?'

'No, when I arrived at the railway station in Brussels, I was greeted by my old friend Zeumer, who drove me to Ostend. I was intrigued when he told me that we would be flying a big aeroplane with two engines. These small flying fortresses could haul a lot of bombs. I hoped we would go into action against England.'

'I have read of aeroplane bombing flights over England – in addition to the Zeppelin raids – did you take part in any of those missions?'

'Unfortunately, no. I had a nice time in Ostend, but it had little to do with the war. We flew a lot, seldom had any combats and never any successes. But our regular life was delightful. We had taken over a hotel on the beach at Ostend and every afternoon we went swimming. Unfortunately, the only other guests at this place were soldiers. We sat out on the terraces at Ostend, wrapped in colourful bathrobes and drank coffee.'

'But you were right on the North Sea coast. Surely, the English must have initiated some hostile activity.'

'Well, yes. One time an English naval squadron appeared and many of us went up on to the roof to get a better look at them. There was a whistling sound and then an enormous explosion … a shell hit the beach right where we had been in the water. I never ran so fast to the bomb shelter as I did that time. The British ships fired perhaps another three or four times and then turned toward the main points of Ostend, the harbour and railway station. They hit nothing, but they gave the Belgians a good scare.'

'Did the BAO react to this incursion?'

'That evening we flew out, looking for the culprits. We were somewhat far out when I saw a ship below us, not on the surface, but – as it appeared to me – beneath the water. I pointed it out to Zeumer and we went down to take a closer look. It was a submarine, but we could not determine the nationality. While we pondered what to do – whether to bomb or not to bomb – I suddenly noticed that one of our radiators was losing water. I pointed it out to Zeumer who pulled a long face and headed for home. We were some twenty kilometres from the coast and now had to make that distance. Shortly thereafter, the engine began to quit and I prepared myself for a cold bath. But we made it. The big old barge managed with one engine and we were able to reach the coast and make a nice landing at our field.'

'I imagine the "cold bath" would have been the least of it. Tell me, during your many flights have you ever been wounded or injured?'

'Not really wounded. At the decisive moment I always ducked my head or drew in my belly. But I <u>have</u> shed my blood for the Fatherland. One day, Zeumer and I were over British lines dropping bombs and I wanted to see the results. But, while our big barge was well suited for carrying bombs, it was hard to see the explosions … as, just after the bombs were dropped, the plane passed over the target and obscured it with its wings. This time, after the drop, I signalled Zeumer to fly at an angle so the wings were off to the side. As he banked, I forgot that our old barge had two propellers, one on each side of my observation "pulpit" up front. I was pointing out to him about where the bomb had exploded and – whack! – a propeller tip nicked my finger. It was not a serious injury, although I was not allowed to fly again for a week. Now, there is only a slight scar on my finger, but at least I can proudly say: "I, too, have a war wound." A short time later, we had our first serious combat … I did not receive so much as a scratch.'

'You and Zeumer were involved in an air fight? When was that?' Again, Richthofen refers to his logbook and says:

'On 1 September 1915, I spotted a British Farman, blithely making his recon-naissance. My heart pounded madly as Zeumer approached him. Before I knew what was happening, the Englishman and we were storming towards each other. I had got off, at the most, four shots when suddenly he got behind us and fired the whole works at us. Time and again, we circled each other … then the Englishman turned away and flew off. I was greatly disappointed, as was Zeumer.

'We arrived home, both of us in a very bad mood. He blamed me for being a poor shot and I blamed him for not getting me into a good firing position. Our rapport, which was so splendid before, had suffered badly … as had our plane, which had taken a respectable number of hits.

'Later the same day, we flew a second patrol. It was also without results. I was very unhappy, for I had imagined that life in a combat unit would be quite different. I always believed that when I fired, the enemy would fall. But I soon learned that a plane can sustain a lot of damage.'

'Do you think that episode spoiled your relationship with Zeumer?'

'Oh, no. We are still good friends and, as I told you, later he taught me how to fly. First in a two-seater and then in a single-seat fighter. Two weeks later, the BAO was sent to the Champagne Sector, where I believe Osterroht and I <u>did</u> shoot down an enemy plane, even though we received no credit for it.'

'You mentioned that, despite the big bomber training you and Osterroht received at Döberitz, both of you remained with Kampfgeschwader 2 and eventually went on to become fighter pilots. How did either or both of you manage to avoid remaining with bomber units?'

'Just luck, I guess. It was after I returned to Kagohl 2 that I was able to rig my two-seat Albatros with a machine-gun and shoot down a Nieuport in April 1916, which was acknowledged but not added to my list of victories.'

'Did you have any other fights with your modified Albatros two-seater?' Again, *he opens his logbook, and says:*

'Not directly. But four days after I shot down the Nieuport, we saw a fight going on east of Fort Douaumont. One of our Fokkers was attacking three French Caudrons. Unfortunately, there was a strong west wind and we could not get to him. I pointed out the scene to my observer, who thought the lone German must be a very daring guy. We wondered whether it was Boelcke and tried to get there to find out. Then, to my horror, I saw that the attacker had become the defender. The Frenchmen, who had been joined by at least ten more planes, forced the German lower and lower. I could not help him, as I was too far away and my plane could not move fast against the headwind. The Fokker pilot defended himself desperately. Now the enemy had driven him down to about six hundred metres. As his pursuers pressed the attack harder, he disappeared into cumulus cloud. I breathed easier, for I thought that manoeuvre could be his salvation.

'Back at our field, I reported what I had seen and learned that the German pilot was Count von Holck, my old comrade in arms from the Eastern Front, who had become a fighter pilot just before the Verdun offensive.'

'Did you find out what happened to him?'

'Yes. Witnesses said that he had shot down one of the Frenchmen and then, apparently, had a jam in his gun. As he headed for our lines, a whole swarm of Frenchmen were after him. He was hit – one shot through the head – and went down from three thousand metres. It was a beautiful death.'

Being familiar with the works of Nietzsche, who used almost the same phrase to describe death in combat, I feel compelled to relate the philosophical to the real, and so I ask: ' How could a death be beautiful? Holck was married and had children!' Richthofen seems surprised by the question and looks at me suspiciously. Then he says simply:

'For Holck, life with only one arm or one leg would have been unthinkable. He was a healthy and vigorously powerful man. Unlike Boelcke in his final plunge, knowing what would happen, Holck did not suffer. I flew to Sivry in a Fokker single-seater for Holck's funeral. I was ready to become his successor.'

Once again, the conversation ends on a sombre note. Now, Richthofen says he will nap for a while and, as if he has willed it, he falls asleep in a short time. I begin to work on the white burgundy (after pocketing the cigars) and review my notes.

At some point I have drifted off and am awakened by a steward as the train arrives in Berlin. It is time for me to return to a normal life in Berlin, while Manfred von Richthofen remains on the train. He is off to visit his family – this time as a highly decorated national hero. He actually blushes when I use that phrase. Fame and honour have not yet spoiled him.

3

MODERN TEUTONIC KNIGHTS

D uring the rest of February, I follow Richthofen's successes in War Ministry announcements and various news stories. According to one report, in the third week of March he gains an early promotion to Ober-leutnant [First Lieutenant], giving him seniority over all of his cadet school class-mates. I wonder how many of them are former bullies who learned very early of this smaller boy's resilience and determination? And what must they think when, just two weeks later, he is promoted to Rittmeister? Or, on 11 April, when he raises his score to level that of the great Boelcke!

Upon receiving news of Richthofen's fortieth victory, my editor sends me back to the Front, anticipating that Germany's new master of the air may well have shot down fifty by the time I arrive at his airfield. During the long train ride from Berlin to Douai, I review a sheaf of war news reports, clippings and other back-ground material.

* * *

Saturday, 14 April 1917: I arrive at La Brayelle airfield in the morning only to find that Jagdstaffel 11 is in the process of moving to Roucourt, south-east of Douai. The pilots and aeroplanes have already departed. There is snow on the ground and the weather is chilly – so I am happy to be back in the warm car, although my young escort is agitated about not being informed of the move. He grumbles about it during the long, round about ride to the new field.

As it was during my first visit, Jasta 11 has the same energy-charged atmos-phere at Roucourt, generated by this leader of a new cadre of air warriors – including such emerging heroes as Carl Allmenröder, Karl-Emil Schäfer, Kurt Wolff, Sebastian Festner, and, of course, Richthofen's younger brother, Lothar. Clearly, Jasta 11 is becoming a modern-day Grand Lodge of Teutonic Knights. Despite being punctuated by the thunder of artillery from the Battle of Arras, raging only thirty kilometres to the west, the mood is sky-high among the airmen and ground crew. I speak to an enlisted man pushing one of the red Albatroses into a hangar and ask about the Rittmeister's current score, and he snaps back at me proudly: 'Forty-four as of this morning! But yesterday was truly the big day.'

He points to the Army Daily Report tacked to a notice board next to the hangar. I pause to read it and learn:

'The enemy lost twenty four aeroplanes in aerial combat, of which thirteen came down on our side of the lines. The Jagdstaffel led by Rittmeister Freiherr von Richthofen destroyed fourteen aeroplanes; in the process Freiherr von Richthofen himself shot down his forty-first, forty-second and forty-third opponents. Leutnant Wolff shot down four enemy aeroplanes and thereby raised the number of his victories to fourteen. Leutnant Schäfer defeated three, Leutnant Freiherr von Richthofen, Leutnant Klein, and Vizefeldwebel Festner each shot down two opponents.'

I can hardly wait to talk to The Man himself, but now I find that I must wait, as I am redirected by my staff officer companion, with the news: 'I'm sorry, but at the moment Herr Rittmeister is on the telephone to Headquarters. It may take some time. In the interim, would you like to speak with his brother? He shot down his sixth enemy plane this morning and can certainly testify to the Rittmeister's effectiveness.' Making the best of the situation, I accompany my host to the Officers' Mess in the nearby château, which has been taken over by the Staffel. Like a tipster at a horse race, my guide hands me a sheet full of notes about the younger Richthofen's military career.

You would never know the battlefront is so close from the sight of the white-jacketed steward bringing coffee and cakes *as I settle into an elegant chair* beside *a long dining-table. I am inspecting the fresh linen* cloth *on the table when in comes my host, accompanied by a taller man with soft, pleasant features. This must be Leutnant Lothar Freiherr von Richthofen; the family resemblance is obvious, even though the younger man looks to stand half a head taller than his brother. I am curious about the number of red aeroplanes out on the airfield, and, after some pleasantries, ask him why the other pilots imitate his brother's distinctive colour scheme.*

'Because the English know that my brother flies a red plane, and we want to make him less conspicuous. Manfred consented because red signifies a certain arrogance and, through our victories, we have proved ourselves worthy of the colour. Of course, only my brother's crate is <u>all</u> red. The rest of us have our own distinguishing marks. For example, Schäfer's elevator, rudder and rear fuselage are black. Allmenröder has the same arrangement, but in white. Wolff has green and, as a former dragoon, I have yellow. From a distance, it looks as though all of us have red planes, but the different second colours enable us to recognise one another in the air.'

After looking at my notes, I say: 'I understand that you arrived at Jasta 11 early in March. What was it like, being a brand-new fighter pilot assigned to such a famous Staffel? Did your brother initiate you into the art of aerial combat?'

'No, I had made combat flights when I was an observer with Kampfgeschwader 1. When I arrived as a novice fighter pilot at Manfred's Staffel, the only advantage he gave me was the use of one of his old planes. He had scored ten victories in it. He also gave me a pair of old leather gloves, which he had been wearing when, often at just the right moment, he pressed the machine-gun triggers.'

'Do you think of them as "good luck charms"?'

'Yes, I suppose I do. When I first joined the Air Service, I met one of our oldest pilots. He always tied a little bear, a child's toy, to either the radiator or a strut of his plane. This bear accompanied him on many record-setting flights and brought the pilot home safely. The bear was richly decorated with medals and mementoes, and the old chap flew only with this talisman. At the time I laughed at it. But then, after I became an observer, I got into the habit of carrying my old riding crop with me. I tucked it into my compartment before every flight and it became my talisman. On the three occasions when I neglected to bring it with me I paid a penalty. The first time, the main support strut and the most stable parts of the plane were shot up. On the second and third times I also paid dearly. Both were night flights that became foggy, which is the greatest danger for airmen. It was a miracle that I came back alive. Wintgens also carried a riding crop with him . . .'

'Kurt Wintgens? The Pour le Mérite fighter pilot?'

'Yes, and the one time he left it at home was the day he was killed in combat. So I am glad to have a talisman from Manfred.'

I make no further comment on Lothar von Richthofen's superstitions, but, before I can turn the conversation back to my original question, he adds:

'Wolff is never without his nightcap. Manfred has worn the same old leather jacket while scoring all his victories. And having one's photograph taken just before take-off is sure to bring misfortune. Boelcke allowed that once. He did not come back alive from that flight . . .'

Now I must interrupt: 'But, surely, you and your comrades feel secure when you fly with your brother, don't you?'

'Yes, of course. He fills us with confidence.'

'Tell me about your first combat flight with Jasta 11. When was it and what did you learn during that flight?' As methodical as his brother, Lothar pulls out a small logbook for the precise information.

'It was on the morning of 25 March. We were alerted that enemy planes had crossed the lines and, soon after take-off, we saw two Nieuport fighters escorting a big lattice-tail reconnaissance plane. Manfred led us up to the last plane in the formation and, and over Douai, he shot him down within our territory. I fired at the other one and must have hit him in the fuel tank, because as we say, he "stank" – leaving a ribbon of fuel behind him. But he did not fall.'

'In general, how are these interceptions organised and carried out?' After another look into his logbook, he responds:

'The Staffel is divided into two groups, so that half the Staffel always flies together, and my brother flies as Staffel leader first with one group, and then with the other. During the flight on 2 April that I have just described, for example, my group was led by Schäfer, and included Wolff, Allmenröder and Lübbert.'

'Who is Lübbert? I don't recognise the name.'

'Leutnant Edi Lübbert. He was one of the original members of Jasta 11, and a very brave pilot. He was shot up so many times that we nicknamed him bullet- catcher. He fell in combat about two weeks ago. He was our first casualty. Poor old bullet-catcher showed great promise and only death could keep him from receiving the Pour le Mérite.'

I jot down Lübbert's name to remind myself to inquire about him when I am back in Berlin. There may be a story in his brief time in Jasta 11 and his early

death. Turning to Lothar – and almost instantly I feel comfortable about
addressing him by his first name, as he seems to have a warmer side to him than
does his brother – I ask: 'How did the flight on 2 April begin?'

'On that day, we were up very early, between four and five o'clock. We sat in
our little hut at the field, waiting for the orders. It did not take long for the
telephone to ring and the message was brief: "Six Bristols coming from Arras
towards Douai. We ran to our planes and took off to intercept them. I noticed
that my brother's red bird was ready for take-off. His mechanics were there,
but he was nowhere in sight.

'There was broken cloud cover at about three thousand metres and we
could see the Englishmen flying below it. We went after them, but they flew
so skilfully in the cloudbanks that none of us could shoot one down. Whenever we got within firing distance, they disappeared into the clouds above or
below. I was very proud that at least I had hit one of them with my machine-
gun fire. I think I must have hit his fuel tank, but he disappeared into the
clouds. Most machines have a reserve tank and he must have switched over
to it. I was, of course, very sad that he did not go down. But, as my brother
said later, it is too much to expect victory in one's first fight.

'We landed about an hour later. There stood my brother's red bird, but
even from a distance we could see mechanics working on it and it was obvious
by the condition of the machine that he had already been up.'

'What had happened?'

'We were told that Manfred was still in bed when the report came in. Quickly,
he put on his flight suit over his pyjamas and took off about five minutes after
we did. About twenty minutes later he came back, having shot down an
Englishman on this side of the lines. Now, he was back in bed and sleeping,
as if nothing had happened. Only some hits in his machine and reports about
the plane he shot down gave any evidence of his flight.
'We were all a bit ashamed of ourselves. There had been five of us, we had
taken off earlier, landed later and had nothing to show for it.'

'Did he say anything to you about it?'

'No. As we gathered for the second flight, at eight o'clock, my brother
appeared. He complained only about the Englishmen … calling them "night-

time disturbers of the peace who drummed peace-loving people out of their beds in the middle of the night". Of course, we congratulated him, and told him our experiences. Then he told us his: He had just got to the Front when, a few kilometres ahead, an Englishman broke through the clouds right in front of him. In a few seconds the battle was decided. The Englishman went down on fire. The wreckage fell to the ground on our side.'

'That is interesting – but when you do fly into battle with your brother, what is it like?'

'First, I stay close to him; flying no more than fifty metres away so that I can be the first to fire at the enemy. But it doesn't always happen like that. On one occasion a lone British trench-strafer was flying over the Front. I had enough to do with my machine and other things, which is the way it is with beginners, and had seen nothing of the Englishman. But my brother had missed nothing. Quite suddenly, Manfred put his machine into a long dive, and in a very short time he was behind the Englishman … at the same moment the English plane broke up in the air. The machine-gun burst just collapsed one wing. The rest of the plane looked as though someone had emptied a bag of scrap paper in the air. I watched the scene from about a thousand metres away. Although I wanted to keep up with my brother, I had not succeeded. We flew the same type of machine, with the same engines, so it must have been my fault. Flying fast must be learned correctly and I had yet to do that.'

'How does your brother teach new men to become effective fighter pilots?'

'After a fight we usually discuss what we have just experienced. It is very funny to watch someone describing an aerial combat, with his arms waving around. He speaks with his hands in order to instruct us and to tell us what was done right and what was done wrong. But my brother has another way to achieve his objective. When he took over the Staffel, he had only Wolff, Allmenröder, and a few others. At that time they had no experience at all and, in aerial combat, beginners have more fear than love of the Fatherland. In the first days, my brother flew with them, attacked numerous English planes, and his machine received an enormous number of hits, without successes to make up for it, and they did nothing to help him. Of course my brother came back somewhat annoyed, but he did not reproach them; on the contrary, he didn't say a word. As Wolff and Allmenröder later told me, his silence influenced them more than the harshest dressing-down. After the discussion, they realised that he had only the greatest concern for them.'

'What happens after you fly with your brother?'

'We usually take about a half-hour's rest, or as much of a rest as the air situation allows. During the busiest times of the ground war in our area, we often fly from five to seven times a day. In order to maintain that pace, there is one basic rule: eat and sleep, but do not touch a drop of alcohol.'

'Yesterday was Friday the thirteenth. Despite that ominous date, your brother achieved a triple victory over enemy bombers. I realise that such a feat is more skill than luck. What part of that action remains uppermost in your mind?'

'The last one. Towards evening, he shot down an English lattice-tail two-seater. The plane made a normal descent, even though the crewmen had already been fatally hit by many bullets. The plane continued down and glided right into the roof of a house near Noyelles-Godault. It was completely demolished. I was well within our area, so I went with my brother in a car to the crash site to get the serial number of the plane and other information.'

'Was there anything left of the aeroplane?'

'When we got there, it was not a pretty sight. Half of it was hanging off the roof and the rest of it was in the street. As the Englishmen had dropped bombs in the area, many people had seen the fight. Later, a bunch of infantrymen came to look at the wreckage. After we had determined some information about the crash, we got under way to our airfield. Meanwhile, the soldiers had recognised Manfred, and we left the place amid a thundering "Hurrah!" '

Just then the Rittmeister enters the room and Lothar is obviously relieved. Lothar does not impress me as being a shy man by any means, but I sense that he is glad he does not have to recount any more stories about his famous brother. After a brief exchange of pleasantries, he leaves the room.

The Rittmeister *makes himself comfortable at the head of the long table and I say: 'To bring your story up to date since our last interview, I would like to discuss recent events.'*

I begin with an item from my file: 'According to the Kriegs-Echo magazine, your Staffel had a very successful day with the new Albatros fighters on 9 March. The article notes that an English pilot who was shot down that day, Lieutenant G. J. Haeseler of the 40th Squadron, said that his and eight other F.E. single-seaters were overwhelmed by four Albatroses. The magazine says the new aircraft were from Jagdstaffel 11 and quotes another pilot shot down, Lieutenant D. B. Hills, also of the 40th Squadron, as saying: "Two months ago the squadron could have flown over German lines for hours without being attacked or disturbed. Since the appearance of the new Albatros fighters, the situation has changed to such an extent that, on 6 March, pilots of the 40th Squadron protested against an assignment to make an offensive patrol over German lines because of the inferiority of their machines . . . The F.E. single-seaters have completely insufficient climbing ability against their opponents." Has there really been such a dramatic shift in air superiority for our side?'

'Yes, now we have clearly superior aircraft, even though in the incident that you mention, I was shot down.'

I cannot believe my ears! Richthofen – shot down? Then I see that he wears a mischievous smile and I wonder: was he truly shot down in an air fight or is this a joke? After I catch my breath, I say as calmly as I can: ' Shot down? This is the first I have heard of it. Please tell me more about it?'

'Well, "shot down" is probably the wrong way to describe what happened to me. In general, I call it "shot down" only when one plops to the ground. This time I began to fall, but came down intact. I was in a formation and saw an opponent, flying in a larger formation over our artillery positions in the Lens area. It is the most exciting moment, when you see the enemy and know that in a few moments the battle will begin. I believe that I then pale, but, unfortunately, I do not bring a mirror with me to see it. I find this moment to be beautiful, for it is so thoroughly stimulating and I really love it.'

'A "moment of truth", so to speak?'

'Yes. You observe your opponent from afar, count the number of enemy machines, and weigh the unfavourable against the favourable things that could happen. For example, wind direction plays an enormous role in battle, whether it blows me towards or away from my side of the Front. On one occsion, I put the fatal shots into an Englishman on his side of the lines and he plopped down near our forward tethered observation balloons. The wind had carried him so far over the lines.'

'I see. Well, perhaps we can discuss that fight another time. At the moment I would like to hear about the fight on 9 March, when you said that your smaller flight attacked a much larger enemy force.'

'Yes, there were five of us and they were three times as strong. The Englishmen were as thick as a swarm of gnats. But this swarm was so well coordinated that it would not be easy for one machine to scatter them ... and it would be extremely difficult for a larger group. Especially when the difference in numbers was so unfavourable, as it was in our case. But, you feel so superior to your opponent that you do not doubt the certainty of your success for a moment. Having the attack spirit and going on the offensive is the main point of combat in the air, as it is elsewhere. But, scarcely have our opponents seen us, when they turn towards us. For the five of us that means: pay attention! If one of us breaks ranks, it will get messy. We close up our formation and let these gentlemen come closer. I watch for one of them to break ranks. There – one is so stupid. I am after him with a roar. He must be nervous, because he opens fire at me. I think to myself: you can fire, but you won't hit me. He fires tracer ammunition that I can see going right past me. It is like water streaming from a watering can. It is not pleasant, but the Englishmen almost always fire this stuff; therefore, you have to get used to it.

'Now, I am fifty metres away. A few good shots and then success is inevitable. So I thought. Suddenly, there is a big bang; I have barely got off ten shots when again there is a smack on my machine. It is clear that it has been hit. At the same moment there is a terrible stink of fuel, and the engine slows down. The Englishman notices this, and redoubles his fire. I must break off immediately.

'I go straight down. Instinctively, I switch off the engine. Just in time. If the fuel tank is punctured and the stuff squirts around my legs, there could be a fire. In front of me, an internal combustion engine of more than a hundred and fifty horse-power is glowing hot. One drop of fuel on it and the whole machine will catch fire. I leave behind me a trail of white mist. I know it very well from having seen it in opponents ... often just before an explosion. I am three thousand metres up and have a long way to go to reach the ground. Thank God, the engine stops running.'

'How fast were you going?'

'I could not calculate the airspeed. But it was so great that I could not stick my head out without having the rush of air push it back in.

'Soon I am rid of my opponent and, before I come down to earth, I still have time to see what my four gentlemen are doing. They are still locked in battle. I can hear their machine-gun fire. Suddenly, a rocket comes down. Is it an enemy signal flare? But no, it is too big for that. It is getting bigger and bigger. A plane is burning. But what kind? It looks like one of ours. Thank God, it is an opponent. Who could have shot it down? Right after that, a second plane falls from the fight, and, like mine, it goes straight down, spinning, continuously spinning – and then – it recovers. It flies straight towards me. It is an Albatros. Undoubtedly, the same thing that happened to me has happened to him.'

'And you are still diving towards the ground?'

'No. By now I am flying level and have several hundred metres' altitude to look for a place to land. I find a meadow, just big enough if one is careful. The location is good for me, alongside the road to Hénin-Liétard. I land smoothly. Now, my first thought is: where is the other man? He landed some kilometres away from me.'

'In what condition was your aeroplane after this encounter?'

'It took some hits, but the one that made me break off combat went through both fuel tanks. I did not have a drop of fuel in them and, likewise, the engine was shot up. What a pity. It ran so well.'

'How did you get back to your airfield?'

'After I inspected the plane, I sat on the edge of the cockpit, with my legs dangling over the side, probably looking foolish. Immediately, a big crowd of soldiers gathered at the site. Then an officer came along. He was completely out of breath. Very excited. Certain that something terrible had happened. He rushed up to me, gasping for breath and said: "I hope that nothing has happened to you. I observed the whole event and am very upset about it. Good Lord, it looked terrible!" I assured him that there was nothing wrong with me. Then I jumped down from the plane and introduced myself to him. Obviously, he did not catch a syllable of my name. But this nice fellow – an engineering officer – invited me to go with him in his car to the nearest field telephone location, and then to Hénin-Liétard, where his quarters were.'

'*You say that he did not catch your name – meaning he did not recognise you?*'

'Yes. We sat in the car and drove along. He still had not calmed down. Suddenly, with a start, he asked: "Good Lord, where is your driver?" At first, I was confused and did not know what he meant. Then it became clear that he took me for the observer of a two-seater and was asking about my pilot. Quickly, I composed myself and said to him: "I drive alone." We in the Air Force despise the word "driving". We don't "drive"; we fly! As he thought I "drove" alone, I had lost esteem in the eyes of this fine gentleman. The conversation became a bit reserved.'

'*He thought he was "chauffeuring" an enlisted man, who "drives" the aeroplane, rather than the officer observer, who gives the orders?*'

'Exactly.'

'*When did you disabuse him of that notion?*'

'Not until we reached his quarters. Along the way, he besieged me with endless questions. He was more excited about the subject than I was. When we got there, I still had on my dirty, oil-stained leather flying jacket and a heavy scarf. He urged me to lie down on his sofa, reasoning that I must be flushed from my recent combat. I assured him that I had already fought in the air many times, but he could not get that into his head. Certainly, I did not look very warlike.

'After some conversation, he came to the famous question: "Have you already shot one down?" As I said, he had not heard my name. "Oh yes," I said, "now and then." "Is that so?" he responded. "Have you already shot down two?" "No – twenty four." He laughed and repeated his question, clarifying that by "shot down" he understood that to mean it fell down and stayed there. I assured him that was also my understanding of it.'

'*What was his reaction?*'

'From his expression, it was clear that he took me for a big braggart. He left me sitting there and said that lunch would be ready in an hour and, if I wanted to, I could join him. I accepted his offer and slept soundly for an hour. Then we went over to the Officers' Mess, where I took off my jacket, and, as luck would have it, I was wearing my Pour le Mérite. Unfortunately, I was wearing only a vest and not my uniform jacket. I asked to be excused because I was not properly dressed.'

'Did your host notice your Pour le Mérite?'

'Oh, yes. Immediately. And he was utterly speechless. He assured me that he did not know who I was. Once again I told him my name and it seemed to dawn on him that he had, in fact, heard of me. Now I was offered oysters and champagne, and really did very well. Finally, Schäfer came with my car to fetch me, and, when I told him the story about being a "driver", he laughed all the way back to Roucourt.'

We are having an enjoyable time, whiling away the afternoon, with Richthofen telling me the 'driver' story at least twice more. The descriptions of his host become funnier each time. Unfortunately for me, the pleasant chat is interrupted by Leutnant Schäfer, who says he must speak to Richthofen about organising the late afternoon patrol. 'Not to worry, sir,' Schäfer says, looking at me, 'we will bring back some good stories for you.'

* * *

Shortly after seven o'clock, the pilots enter the dining-room. There is much to celebrate, as the patrol just concluded claims four victories: two for Schäfer and one each for Kurt Wolff and Lothar von Richthofen. My staff officer host is quick to point out that these latest triumphs bring the Staffel's total victory score to ninety-two aircraft since the unit began operations in January. Fortunately, many people – including my talkative escort – crowd around the victors, to hear the details of their success, and I am able to slip away to a small table at the back of the room, where Manfred von Richthofen joins me. He is in such high spirits I cannot believe he has not had a little 'something' to drink. While he is so mellow, I resume our earlier conversation by asking: 'Getting back to the events of 9 March and your being "shot down", what happened after you and Schäfer returned to La Brayelle?'

'I went up in another machine and shot down my twenty-fifth enemy plane. This one was a Vickers single-seater, not far from where the others were shot down.'

'Was there anything especially noteworthy about this victory?'

'No. With three of my planes I attacked several of the enemy and singled out a machine. After I fired about a hundred rounds, he went crashing down.'

'Were our people able to salvage anything from it?'

'No. It was almost completely burnt out and too close to the front lines. But, that evening, I had the pleasure of calling my host in Hénin-Liétard to inform him that I had completed a quarter of a hundred victories that day.'

'And I see by the reports that one of your friends from Jasta Boelcke, Leutnant Werner Voss, has attained almost that number. Is he a rival?' Richthofen's good humour this evening seems to bubble over. He laughs as he responds:

'If so, he is a very friendly one, to be sure. I like Voss. He is a very tenacious fellow. Last month, when our ground forces withdrew to the Siegfried Line, we did not relinquish the air to the Englishmen. Jasta Boelcke saw to that. During one fight, Voss forced an Englishman to land in no-man's-land. The British pilot probably assumed – and with some justification – that the ground had already been occupied by his side. But Voss had a different opinion. Shortly after the fight, he landed near the abandoned enemy machine and hastily removed the machine-gun and other useful parts from it and loaded them into his own plane. Then, as he later told me, he put a match to the plane and within a few moments it was a mass of bright flames. A minute later he was up in his aerial steed, waving cheerfully to the English troops below, streaming to the spot from all sides.'

'Do you see Voss often?'

'Occasionally. After my thirty-second victory, he visited me and we had a nice long conversation. The day before, he had scored his twenty-third victory. By now, he has twenty-eight to his credit and is ranked right behind me.'

'And I read that, recently, Leutnant Voss was awarded the Pour le Mérite. That raises the question: have Germany's two highest-scoring fighter aces been in action together?'

'Yes. In fact, the last time he visited me, I accompanied him part of the way back to his field at Lagnicourt and we went by a roundabout way over the Front, looking for opportunities. But the weather became so bad that we gave up hope of finding more game. Beneath us were dense clouds. Voss did not know the area and I could see that he was becoming uncomfortable. Then, over Arras, we came upon my brother, who had got lost from his formation. He recognised my red bird and joined us.

'Soon, we saw an enemy formation approaching from the other side. Immediately, "Number Thirty Three" flashed in my mind. Even though there were nine of them and they were over their own territory, they withdrew to avoid combat. But we caught up with them. It is important to have a fast machine in combat.

'I was closest to the enemy and attacked the one farthest back. To my great delight he also wanted to fight … and with even greater pleasure I noticed that he had been abandoned by his comrades. Soon I had him all alone.'

'What kind of aeroplane was he flying?'

'A two-seater, like the one I fought with in the morning. But this pilot did not make it easy for me. He knew what he was doing and, most of all, he was a good shot. I learned that to my sorrow. Then the favourable wind came to my aid and carried us both over our lines. He noticed that the situation was not as simple as he had thought and disappeared in a dive into a cloud. That was almost his salvation. I dived after him, came out beneath him and, on my first try, found that by some miracle I was right behind him. I fired and his observer fired, but there was no tangible result. Then, finally, I hit him. I could tell by the white fuel vapour that trailed after his plane. He had to land because his engine had packed up.'

'In a case such as this, in which you have your opponent cornered, is it possible to surrender in the air? Just as ground troops do? Can he indicate that he will land peacefully, asking you, in effect, not to kill him?'

'Yes, that is possible, but it did not happen this time. The observer was very stubborn. He must have recognised that the game was over. If he fired again, I could shoot him dead immediately, as, meanwhile, we were down to only two hundred metres altitude. But he defended himself as tenaciously as the fellow I had shot down that morning, right until he landed.'

'I take it that, once on the ground, the crew realised further resistance was fruit-less?'

'Oh, no! After they landed, I flew over them at about ten metres to determine whether I had shot the observer dead. And what did the chap do? He used his machine-gun to shoot up my plane!'

'I see from the record that you received credit for shooting down this Sopwith two-seater. Did Voss also shoot down an aeroplane in that fight?'

'No. Voss and my brother were unable to catch any of the others. But, after-wards, Voss said that if he had experienced what had happened to me, he would have flown back and shot him dead on the ground. In fact, I should have done just that, because the Englishman had not surrendered. He was lucky to remain alive. I was quite satisfied to fly home and celebrate my thirty-third.'

I do not contradict Richthofen, but I have copies of his combat reports in my portfolio, to provide me with additional details he may not mention, and in his report for Number Thirty Three, he wrote that even as the British machine 'was on the ground, he kept shooting at me, thereby hitting my machine very severely when I was only five metres above the ground. Consequently, I attacked [the aeroplane] on the ground once more and killed one of the occupants.' I do not know why he changed the story. Perhaps after so much action, all these fights become a jumble in his mind. But another remark he made prompts me to ask him for details of another fight:

'You mentioned that this crew fought as hard as did the Englishmen you shot down the same morning. Your brother has already told me how you took off after the others and returned first with a confirmed victory. From his description, however, it sounded as though you surprised your opponent and shot him down. Can you recall that fight?' Richthofen pauses for just a moment. He does not have his logbook with him, but, from the way his expression hardens, I can tell

that details of the first fight on 2 April are etched into his memory. Slowly, he begins to speak:

'No, I did not surprise him. In my haste to catch up with my comrades, this impudent fellow surprised me. He came down on me and tried to force me down. I let him come on ... then we began a merry dance. My opponent flew on his back. He did this, he did that. He flew it like a two-seat fighter. But I was better than he and soon I realised that he could not get away from me. During a lull in the fight, I looked around to be sure that we were alone. In this situation whoever shoots better, remains the calmest and has the best position at the critical moment, will win.

'It did not take long for me to get beneath him and open fire, without being fired at seriously by him. We were at least two kilometres from the Front and I thought he would want to land, but I misjudged my opponent. When he was but a few metres above the ground, suddenly he flew straight ahead to get away from me. That was too much for me and I attacked him again. We were so low that I feared we would graze the houses in the village below us. The British observer defended himself to the last moment. Almost at the end I felt a hit in my machine. I could not let up; now he had to fall. He crashed full speed into a block of houses in Farbus.'

'Surely, you admire the Englishman's daring, to fight to the very end like that.' This becomes one of those times when I wonder how well I know my subject, as I am surprised when Richthofen's animated demeanour changes instantly to a look of disdain, as he replies:

'It was a case of splendid daring. He defended himself to the last. But in my view it was, in the end, simply more stupidity on his part. It was just at the point where I draw the line between daring and stupidity. He was going down, in any event. So he paid for his stupidity with his life.'

'He might have been better off by landing and allowing himself to be taken prisoner?'

'Exactly.'

I am tempted to compare the aeroplane that flew into a house on 2 April with the event of the evening before my arrival, when Richthofen sent his forty-third victim crashing into a house. Perhaps I don't need to. Perhaps he has already made the comparison in his mind. It is difficult to pry secrets from Richthofen. Like so many successful people – in business, in government or the military – he has developed a knack for insulating himself from certain matters. After noting to myself that his thirty-fourth, thirty-fifth and thirty-sixth victories resulted in English airmen being taken prisoner, I had to assume that those opponents had seized opportunities to survive. Or perhaps they were simply lucky.

Changing the subject slightly, I ask: 'As you have become so well known, do you think that now you are a special target for the British? Were they trying to eliminate you during their night raids on airfields in this area last week?'

'No, it is more likely that our dear Englishmen were especially active during the Battle of Arras and took advantage of the full moon nights earlier this month. On Holy Thursday, we were sitting in the Mess when the telephone rang and we were informed: "The Englishmen are coming." That brought a great cheer from us. We already had shelters prepared; Leutnant Simon, our construction chief, had seen to that. So we went to the shelters and heard, faintly at first, the sound of aircraft engines. The anti-aircraft and searchlight batteries seem to have received the news at the same time and they slowly came to life.'

'What did you and your men do during the attack?'

'We defended ourselves from the ground. The first Englishman seemed to fly very high. First, once around the entire airfield. We thought he was looking for another target. Then all of a sudden he switched off his engine and dived down. "Now it's getting serious," Wolff said to me. Each of us had fetched a carbine and we began to fire at the Englishman, even though we could not see him. Just the noise of our own shooting calmed our nerves.

'Then the searchlight beam caught him. Almost everyone on the airfield opened fire. We recognised it as quite an old crate. He was at most a kilometre away from us. He flew right towards our airfield. He came lower and lower. Then he switched the engine back on and came flying right at us. Wolff said: "Thank God, he is looking for the other side of the airfield." But it was not long before the first bomb and then others began to rain down. It was quite a fireworks display that they put on for us, but not effective. Only a frightened rabbit would have been impressed by it. I find that, in general, bombing at night affects only morale. If someone fills his pants, then it is very embarrassing for him, but not for the others.'

'I understand that the following evening – Good Friday – you were better prepared when the Englishmen returned. What did you do?'

'Earlier that day, we had men drive poles into the ground near the Mess and the Officers' Quarters … captured British machine-guns were mounted on them and ranged to hit incoming aircraft. Each of my gentlemen had a battle station. Again, we sat in the Mess. The topic of conversation, of course, was night flyers. Then one of the batmen burst in and cried out: "They are coming! They are coming!" and disappeared into the next shelter. Each of us rushed to his post. Some of the enlisted men, who were good shots, also had battle stations. They had carbines, too. The Staffel was armed to the teeth.

'The first Englishman came over, just as on the previous evening, at very high altitude. Then he came down to fifty metres and, to our great joy, this time he aimed for the side of our barracks. He was right in the searchlight beam – and, at most, three hundred metres away from us. One of our men began firing at him and then everyone opened fire. A massive assault could not have been better warded off than the attack of this cheeky fellow at fifty metres. A raging burst of fire greeted him.'

'What was his reaction?'

'He could not hear the machine-gun fire over the sound of his own engine, but he must have seen the muzzle flashes and I think he was very daring in not veering off, but, rather, for staying on course. He flew right over us and then away. At the moment when he flew over us, of course, we quickly jumped into the shelter. To be hit by a stupid bomb would be a foolish hero's death for a fighter pilot. Scarcely had he gone over us when we were at our guns again, firing away at him.'

'Did anyone hit him?'

'Schäfer said that he did. He is a very good shot, but, in this case, I don't think he did. Besides, everyone else had just as good a chance. At the very least, we made the opponent drop his bombs without effect. One landed a few metres from my petit rouge but did no damage to it.'

'After you thwarted their plans, did the Englishmen return?'

'Yes. This fun was repeated several times more that night. I was already in bed and asleep, when, as if in a dream, I heard anti-aircraft fire. I woke up to find that the dream was happening. One artful fellow flew so low over my quarters that I pulled the covers over my head in fright. At the next moment there was a tremendous noise near my window and the panes fell victim to the bomb. Quickly, I leaped into my shirt to get a few shots off at him. Outside, everyone was firing at him. I had overslept.'

'That was some solemn Good Friday! I know that on the following day you were promoted to Rittmeister – did you have any other good luck?

'Yes. The next morning we were surprised and highly pleased when we found that we had shot down no fewer than three Englishmen. They came down not far from our airfield and were taken prisoner. For the most part we had hit their engines and forced them down on our side. So, perhaps Schäfer had not been mistaken. All in all, we were very satisfied with our success. The Englishmen were somewhat less pleased and they have not attacked our airfield since.

'Later that afternoon, four of my gentleman and I attacked an enemy flight of six Nieuport fighters south of Arras, behind enemy lines. The plane I had singled out tried to escape by various manoeuvres. I hit him, the engine began to smoke and he headed down, twisting and twisting. At first I thought it was another manoeuvre, but then I saw the plane smash into the ground near Mercatel.'

'According to my information, that victory on Holy Saturday was credited as your thirty-seventh and, the next day, you shot down two more.'

'Yes, that is correct. Late in the morning, four of us attacked a flight of Sopwith two-seaters over Farbus. The plane I singled out made a right-hand curve downward. The observer stopped firing and I followed the plane down and saw it dashed to pieces. After that, I could not see much, as the area was under heavy artillery fire.

'Later that afternoon, while flying over this side of the lines, I surprised an English B.E.2 artillery spotter. After a very few shots, the plane broke up in the air and fell near Vimy.'

'What is it like to see such a sight? Aeroplanes falling apart or crashing down?'

'Sometimes, from a distance, it looks almost harmless and unreal. I have gradually become accustomed to the sight, but I must say that the first Englishman I saw go roaring down, burning like a rocket, made a frightful impression on me and I dreamed about it for a long time.'

The sound of laughter from the other side of the room draws my attention to the celebrants of today's victories. Particularly full of life is Vizefeldwebel Sebastian Festner, twenty-two years old and, as of this morning, the victor over eleven enemy aeroplanes. I point to him and say to Richthofen: 'I understand that Festner's new Albatros also began to break up during one of your Easter Sunday fights. How did he survive?'

'That was a different matter. He was in normal flight at over four thousand metres' altitude when his lower left wing simply broke.'

'I thought the Albatros structural problems had been resolved?'

'So did I! Fortunately, despite the fact that the wing was torn to pieces and lost more than a third of its surface, Festner managed to land without incident.'

'What happened?'

'We don't know yet. Festner has submitted a detailed report and the machine was sent home, as it is useless for warfare. When I looked at it, I saw that most of the lower wing was folded upwards and all the wing ribs were broken. And this break occurred on the forward part of the wing, where the factory had applied special rib-supporting braces. The fabric covering of the wings was torn to pieces by the air current through the broken parts ... the wing was battered by the wind, forcing it backwards and forwards. Of course, this was too much strain for the V strut holding the upper wing. Festner was lucky to be able to land.'

Now the festivities reach a high pitch. Richthofen must leave our cosy table and, like a tribal chief, spend time with his warriors. As the meal is being served, the chief steward announces that the evening's wine comes 'with best wishes from 'a certain factory at Johannisthal'. There is loud hooting and raucous comments.

Festner stands and, very theatrically, demands to see the bottle, to be sure it has no cracks in it. Another pilot whispers to me that the wine is a gift from the Albatros factory, a typical gesture from the manufacturer, which is now under suspicion due to Festner's episode.

The Staffel leader gracefully leaves centre stage to his brother, who now has seven victories to his credit and, as the elder brother points out, Lothar needs to be seen in the light of his own accomplishments. When I ask: 'How did he become a pilot?' the Rittmeister grins with pride, pauses, as if to sum up all that has led to this moment, and responds:

'Lothar began as a Leutnant with Dragoner-Regiment Nr. 4 and began the war as I did, as a cavalry officer. I don't know what heroic deeds he has accomplished, as he never talks about himself. In the winter of 1915 he followed my advice and became, as I had, an aviation observer. Just a year later he was a pilot. Training to be an observer certainly is not difficult, nor is becoming a fighter pilot. Last month he passed his third examination and immediately came to my Jagdstaffe*l*.'

'What kind of a pilot has he turned out to be?'

'At first he was very green and cautious. He never thought about looping and other such tricks, but was satisfied when he took off and landed all right. Two weeks later I took him with me for the first time into action and told him to fly close behind me, to observe the situation.

'After the third flight, he suddenly broke away from me and dived after an Englishman and finished him off. My heart leapt with joy to see this! It was further proof of how little art there is to shooting down a plane. It is only the personality or, among other things, the energy of the person doing the job.'

'So, you are satisfied that he has the spirit needed to be a successful fighter pilot?'

'My father distinguishes between a hunter – a sportsman – and a shooter who only fires a gun for fun. When I shoot down an Englishman, my hunting passion is calmed for the next quarter of an hour. It is not necessary for me to shoot down two Englishmen, one right after the other. When one falls I have a feeling of absolute satisfaction.

'It is different with my brother. I had the opportunity to observe him when he shot down his fourth and fifth opponents. As we attacked a flight, I was the first to open fire, and my opponent was soon dispatched. I looked around and saw my brother sitting behind an Englishman whose machine erupted into flames and then exploded. Near this Englishman flew a second. Lothar did nothing further to the first one, which had not yet fallen and was still in the air. He turned his machine on the next one and immediately opened fire after he had barely finished with the first. But the second one also fell after a short fight.

'After we returned to our field, he asked me proudly: "How many did you shoot down?" I said quite modestly: "One." He turned his back to me and said: "I got two" – whereupon I sent him up to the Front to look around. He had to determine who the fellows were and just where they fell. Late that afternoon he came back and said he had found only one. The inquiry was difficult, as it usually is for such shooters. It was not until the next day that ground troops reported where the other lay. They confirmed that the other had fallen, as all of us had seen.'

'So, is it fair to say that your brother is a shooter and you are a hunter? Not in a derogatory sense, of course. Merely as a comparison of methods of operation.'

'Yes, in that context, you could say that.'

'To be sure, I will place it in context. But I cannot help remarking that, for one who is satisfied with one clear victory at a time, you seem to have outdone your-self yesterday, when you shot down three in one day.' Richthofen's face lights up in self-satisfaction as he replies:

'And this one – my most successful day thus far – had a humorous ending to it. One of the Englishmen we shot down was captured and we talked to him. Of course, he asked about the red aircraft. It is known even to the troops down in the trenches and is called le diable rouge. He said that in his squadron it is rumoured that a girl flies the red machine. A German Joan of Arc. He was very surprised when I assured him that the alleged girl stood right before him. He was not trying to be funny. He was convinced that only a young maiden could sit in such an oddly painted crate.'

'This reminds me of the conversation I had with your brother. He told me about various pilots carrying good-luck charms with them. And now it seems that this Englishman is trying to account for your success in supernatural or legendary terms. What do you think of talismans and other such inexplicable things?'

Richthofen pauses to consider the question. Is he wondering whether Festner had a lucky charm with him when his new Albatros almost lost a wing due to as yet unexplained circumstances? Slowly, he answers:

'Every so often we find that wonders never cease. Once, for example, I saw a British plane going down burning. At five hundred metres altitude, it burst into flames that engulfed it. As we flew home, we saw one of the crewmen jump out of the plane at fifty metres' altitude. It was the observer. At fifty metres' altitude! The highest church tower in Berlin is not much higher. Imagine what would happen if one were to jump from the tip of such a tower! Most people would break their necks jumping from the second floor of a house. In any event, this good man jumped out after his plane had been burning for almost a minute and received nothing more than a fractured ankle. Right after this happened, he even made a statement to the effect that he had not suffered physically at all.

'Another time I shot down a British machine ... and the pilot had a fatal head wound and the plane plunged out of control, vertically, from three thousand metres. Quite a while later, I glided past the site and saw nothing more than a deserted heap. To my astonishment, I learned that the observer had only a fractured skull and that his condition was not life threatening. He must have been lucky.'

I am about to interrupt with a question and then think better of the idea, as it is apparent that Richthofen is in a talkative mood and might tell me some delightful story that has not been heard before. I let him go on.

'Yet another time, I saw Boelcke shoot down a Nieuport fighter, which fell like a stone. Later we drove to the spot and found the plane half buried in soft soil. The pilot was unconscious from a stomach wound and he had wrenched his arm when he hit the ground. But he did not die.

'On the other hand, once I watched a good friend of mine make a landing and one of his wheels went into a rabbit hole. The machine was just rolling along and went slowly up on its nose, as if pondering which way to tip, and then fell on its back. The poor fellow inside broke his neck.'

Once again, Richthofen's men are calling to him, waving him over to join them in celebrating this remarkable day. I let him go, as I have a good supply of notes for my next article. Tomorrow is Sunday, which promises to be a good day for more questions.

4

FIFTY-TWO DOWN AND GLORY

I had begun to settle in to a degree of comfort at Jasta 11's new airfield, making progress with my interviews, enjoying a quiet Sunday as the Staffel completes its move to Roucourt. The following morning, however, a French offensive opens in the south. My colleague assigned to that area is back in Berlin for a rest, so my editor sends a telegram directing me to cover developments at 7th Army Headquarters. It is a fruitless journey. By the time my associate returns, the French advance has failed and, in the north, the forces of Crown Prince Rupprecht of Bavaria, which include Richthofen's unit, continue to pound the English on the ground and in the air. I am glad to head back to Roucourt.

* * *

Thursday, 26 April 1917: In the ten days that I have been away, many changes have occurred at Jagdstaffel 11. Schäfer was shot down behind enemy lines and escaped, and Lothar von Richthofen was nearly shot down. Good-natured little Festner, shot down on the other side of the lines, was not so lucky. He is presumed dead. Also we learned that Richthofen's old friend Paul Henning von Osterroht was lost the same day as Festner. The good news is that, on the day I left, Richthofen was presented with the Kingdom of Saxony's Knight's Cross of the Military Order of St Henry. The award is for his thirtieth victory and now he is among such recipients as Max Immelmann. My staff officer host whispers to me that, for unknown reasons, the Saxon native Oswald Boelcke had not been so honoured.

When I meet Richthofen, it is again in the Officers' Mess for another celebration dinner. There is no talk about his Saxon decoration, which would lead only to an invidious comparison with Boelcke. A touchy subject with him. This evening, all eyes are on Leutnants Karl-Emil Schäfer and Kurt Wolff, who have received an even higher Prussian decoration: the Knight's Cross of the Royal Order of the House of Hohenzollern with Swords, which almost always precedes the Pour le Mérite. Further, Schäfer, has been named commander of Jagdstaffel 28. He is to carry the legacy of Boelcke, nurtured by Richthofen, to yet another band of air warriors.

With a wave of his hand, Richthofen dismisses my attempt to ask about today's other news: by Imperial decree, Jasta 11 is to be called Jagdstaffel Richthofen. So I try another approach to spark a response: 'The news about Schäfer must be a nice surprise, since it was feared that he had been killed on the 22nd. I know that you shot down your forty-sixth that morning and Schäfer his twenty-second that evening, but what happened after that?'

'We were coming back late and Schäfer drifted away from us along the way. Of course, everyone hoped that he would reach our field before darkness. It got to be nine and then ten o'clock and still he had not returned. By then he would have run out of fuel, so he must have made an emergency landing somewhere. No one would dare say that he had been shot down, but everyone feared it. The front-line telephone network was set in motion to inquire about airmen landing in various areas. No division or brigade had seen him. It was an unpleasant situation. At last, we went to bed, firmly convinced that he would be located. At two in the morning I was awakened by the telephone orderly, who, beaming, told me: "Schäfer has made his way to Sailly and asks to be picked up."

'At breakfast that morning, the door opened and there stood my good friend, ... looking as filthy as an infantryman who had lain among corpses for two weeks. He was greeted with a rousing cheer! Schäfer was very pleased with himself. He was as hungry as a bear, and after a good breakfast he told us the whole story.

'He said he had been flying homeward along the Front when he saw an enemy ground support plane at quite low altitude. He attacked it, shot it down and was starting to head back home when Englishmen down in the trenches opened up on him. He was saved only by the plane's speed, as the ground gunners fired <u>at</u> him instead of <u>ahead</u> of him. He said he was at about two hundred metres when one lucky shot hit his engine and it quit. He had to land, of course, but he did not know whether he was still over enemy territory. The British troops continued to fire like mad at him, even as he landed. Before the machine stopped, it was targeted by machine-gun fire from a nearby emplacement. Schäfer leapt out of the crate and dived into a shell hole. Despite the heavy fire – he had come down about fifty paces from an enemy position – he managed to crawl to our lines. Our advance troops led him back to safety. Later, he found a telephone and called for a "chauffeur" to fetch him.'

'The last time you and I talked, you mentioned that luck is important to survival in war. Considered another way, how were you so lucky as to find a good man like Schäfer?'

'In point of fact, he found me. He began as a pilot in my old Kampfgeschwader in Russia and, after being transferred to France earlier this year, he shot down a French plane. I heard about it and so, when he sent me a telegram asking whether I could use him, I wired back: "You have already been requested."'

'Is it that easy for you to obtain the quality of people you need?'

'Occasionally. After I was assigned to Jasta 11, an old friend from pilot training, Bodo von Lyncker, wrote to me, seeking transfers from Macedonia to the Western Front for himself and his comrade Otto Brauneck. Each had already shot down several enemy planes. Just the kind of men I need. Unfortunately, Bodo was killed in February, but Brauneck has since joined us. I sent a telegram to the Officer in Charge of Aviation at his Armee-Korps, as well as to the Office of the Commanding General of the Air Force. It was up to Brauneck to pressure his superior to be released from there.'

'Did you request that your brother be sent to your Staffel?'

'No, he was assigned here.'

I wonder about that point, because Manfred von Richthofen keeps a good eye on his brother. Then it occurs to me that the Higher Ups in Berlin may have their reasons. It is widely rumoured that Richthofen was urged to stop his flying after he had equalled Boelcke's score. Perhaps having another 'red baron' in reserve was a strategic move. There is no point in pursuing this line of conversation with this (or any) Richthofen, so I switch to a safer question: 'I understand that Schäfer saved your brother's life yesterday. How did that happen?'

'Schäfer was leading a flight of three others, including Lothar. After some time, Lothar saw a lone Englishman about a thousand metres below him and, typically, dived on him. But the Englishman was too fast for him and slipped away, meanwhile leading Lothar some kilometres over the other side. Wisely, he broke off and headed back for the Front. Then another Englishman got behind Lothar and began firing at him. At first Lothar laughed, because the enemy plane was too far away and could not hit him at that range. With luck, the Englishman would exhaust his ammunition by the time he caught up with my brother. But then the Englishman got lucky and hit one of Lothar's main control wires.

'He was still over enemy territory, so there was plenty to worry about. With that wire gone, Lothar could not make a sharp turn to slip behind his opponent. If he did, the wings might come off. He could only go straight ahead, even as the Englishman came closer and streams of incendiary bullets flew all around him. Lothar knew that his machine could not stand the strain of evasive manoeuvres … he told us later that he could imagine his plane catching fire at any moment. But then he looked back and saw the English plane was ablaze – and behind it flew a German plane. It was Schäfer, finishing off his twenty-third!

'When they got back, you never saw a more thankful person than Lothar. At dinner last night he gave Schäfer a really good bottle of champagne that he had been saving for a special occasion. And that was it!'

'You must be very grateful to Schäfer for saving your brother's life. Now that Schäfer has received the Hohenzollern medal, will you recommend him for the Pour le Mérite?'

'There is no need to do that. The recommendation went in some time ago. I am certain Schäfer will hear from the Kaiser at his new Staffel. As for saving each other's lives, we do that on a regular basis. A few days ago, for example, Lothar saved me from certain destruction.'

'I have not seen that in any of the reports. How did it happen?'

'We saw a British plane cross the Front to his own lines near Cambrai and, as we were not fired on from the ground, we followed him. Suddenly, five British fighters came down on us from a very high altitude. At first they seemed to be taking practice shots at us. Then one became bolder and pounced on Lothar, who quickly turned the tables on his overly eager opponent and went right after him. Meanwhile, the other four came at me, each trying to get into a favourable position. It was a wild mêlée of twisting and turning as I looked for an advantage. I was overjoyed when Lothar reappeared and stormed right into the middle of them, scattering them in all directions. They headed for home and so did we.'

'Did he return after shooting down the enemy fighter he went after?'

'No. Later he told me that, even though his opponent began to stink, as we say when a plane begins to leave an oil or fuel vapour trail, he had to break off as his machine-gun had jammed.'

'He came back to the fight with a useless machine-gun?'

'Yes. He knew I would be dealing with the other Englishmen. At that point I had given up on both of us until his mad dash into the fray saved us.'

'Did you give him a special reward, as he had done when Schäfer saved him?'

'No.'

'But I understand that you did give him a signed photo of yourself after he shot down his tenth enemy.'

'I do that for every pilot in the Staffel who has ten victories to his credit. And late this afternoon Lothar shot down Number Eleven to prove that his mishap of yesterday was due to a defect in his machine and had nothing to do with his flying abilities.'

'I don't think anyone questions the capabilities of any member of your Staffel. If anything, you and your men are achieving victories faster than Headquarters can count them properly. I am told, for example, that another one of your protégés, Leutnant Wolff, scored his twentieth and Jasta 11's one-hundredth victory on the day that Schäfer went missing. But the weekly information report of the Commanding General of the Air Force states the number of your victories incorrectly. It says, and I quote: "In the time from 23 January until 22 April 1917 Jagdstaffel 11 has shot down 100 enemy aeroplanes. I am pleased to be able to announce this singularly unrivalled success to the aviation forces. Here a small band of brave pilots has been trained and led into battle by an outstanding leader, Rittmeister Freiherr von Richthofen, who alone has contributed 39 of these 100 aircraft, for the benefit of the hard fighting troops on the ground, and accom-

*plished feats which redound to the highest honour of the German air service."
Didn't you shoot down your forty-sixth on the 22nd of this month?'*

'Yes, I shot one down early that morning. But you must remember that I already had sixteen victories when I arrived here. So, the arithmetical error in the report is that, at that point, only thirty of Jasta 11's victories were mine. All twenty of Wolff's victories and all but one of Schäfer's twenty-three belong to our Staffel's tally.'

I do not even try to do the maths in my head about the leading airmen of Jasta 11. It has been a long day for me. The cheering and loud voices in the Mess have given me a thumping headache. Richthofen excuses himself from my company to spend time with his men and so I am left to enjoy a light supper in the relative solitude of the back of the dining- room. A helpful steward leaves a bottle at my table. 'A sleeping draught,' he says with a wink.

* * *

Monday, 30 April 1917: During the past few days Manfred von Richthofen has been a veritable one-man aerial destruction force. He shot down one enemy plane on the 28th and four on the 29th. The latter achievement is a new record, even for him. It was impossible to discuss those events with him at dinner last evening, because his father, Major Albrecht von Richthofen, and several of the Rittmeister's old friends were here to celebrate the event. Today, he is completing administrative matters prior to going on leave tomorrow and so, while the after-noon patrol is out, he and I have time for post-lunch coffee and cakes, over which we discuss recent events. I knew that his father had been recalled from retirement to active duty, but I was unaware that he was stationed so close by and ask about it. With that certain charm he exudes when something really pleases him, the Rittmeister responds:

'My father is the local commandant of a small town near Lille, not very far from here. At times I come in low and can spot him from the air. Every so often he comes here to visit. Usually, he arrives in Douai by train at nine o'clock and, by nine-thirty, he has been driven to our field.'

'From what I saw at dinner last evening, your father seems sanguine enough about you and your brother – that is, about your contribution to the war effort.'

'The old gentleman is not one of those fathers who frets about his sons. On the contrary, it seems he would just as soon go up in a machine himself and shoot down an Englishman.'

'Forgive me for stating the obvious, but this is war.'

'He has seen that aspect, too. The last time he was here, Lothar and I had breakfast with him and then flew off on patrol again. After we returned, an air fight took place over our field. An English flight had broken through our defences and was being attacked by some of our reconnaissance aircraft. My father observed it with great interest. Suddenly, one plane flipped over, recovered and then came down in a normal glide. It was a German machine that been shot up but was making its descent under control. The pilot attempted to land, but our airfield was rather small for a big plane. He was unfamiliar with the territory and his landing was anything but smooth. We all ran to the wreckage, where we saw with regret that one of the crewmen, the backseat man, had been killed. The sight was new to my father and it made him more serious.'

'But, surely, your four victories yesterday must allay any fears he has?'

'Yes, that was a good day for us. The weather was wonderfully clear. The anti-aircraft guns could be heard constantly, so obviously there was considerable flying activity. Late that morning my brother, Wolff and I flew to the lines, hoping to find some opponents. After about twenty minutes, the first arrived and attacked us. This had not happened to us for some time ... the English had abandoned their celebrated offensive tactics ... They were too costly.'

'What type of aeroplanes were they and how did they compare with your Albatroses?'

'They were three SPAD single-seaters. Excellent machines. We were three against three ... the way it should be. Almost from the beginning, however, their offensive became defensive. I went after one opponent and my brother and Wolff went after each of the others. The usual waltz began, circling around one another, and then a favourable wind carried the fight away from the Front and behind German lines.

'My man was the first to fall. I must have hit his engine. I attacked him a second time and his whole machine broke into pieces while in a turn and plunged, burning fiercely, into a swamp near Lécluse, less than ten kilometres from our airfield.'

'He was your forty-ninth. Were you able to learn his identity?'

'No. After he fell into the swamp, it was impossible to dig him out. He had disappeared. Only the end of the plane's tail was visible to mark the spot where he had dug his own grave.'

'What happened to the other two SPADs?'

'Wolff and my brother brought them down a short distance away.'

'And your father witnessed all this from the ground?'

'Yes. When we returned from the flight, Lothar was first to jump out of his crate and greet the old gentleman with: "Hello, Papa, I have just shot down an Englishman." After which I hopped out of my machine and said: "Hello, Papa, I have just shot down an Englishman."
'That afternoon, my brother and I started out twice more with Schäfer, Wolff and Allmenröder. The first flight was unsuccessful, the second flight much better. Together with five of my gentlemen, I attacked a flight of five Vickers two-seaters. After a long, curving flight, during which my opponent defended himself admirably, I got behind him. It took three hundred shots, but his plane caught fire. On the way down, both crewmen fell out.'

'And that was your fiftieth victory. Were you able to learn anything about the occupants of <u>that</u> aeroplane?'

'I have no details about the plane. It burned to ashes. While I watched where the debris fell, I looked over at my brother. He was barely five hundred metres away from me, in the midst of fighting with his opponent.'

'Did you fly over to help him?'

'There was no need to. As I watched him, I must say that I could not have done better myself. Lothar had circled behind his opponent and taken him by surprise. Suddenly, the enemy plane reared up … a sure sign of being hit. No doubt, Lothar had shot the pilot in the head. The plane went into a steep dive and its wings came off, one after the other. The wreckage fell near the one I had shot down. I flew over near my brother and waved "congratulations" to him. We were satisfied and flew off. It is nice when you can fly with your own brother.

'Meanwhile, our comrades had been nearby and had watched our little drama. They could not help, as they know they should shoot only when they are busy with their own opponents.'

'Just as you could not intervene to help Lothar?'

'Precisely. The others can only watch and cover the planes in action, to ensure they are not attacked from behind by a third plane. We flew on and saw another enemy flight coming towards us. Unfortunately, they were higher than we were and we could do nothing. We tried to reach their altitude but failed. We had to let them go.

'Then I saw two B.E. artillery observation aircraft approaching our Front. I signalled to my brother and he understood. We flew close together and increased our speed. We felt superior to the enemy and, more than anything else, we knew that we could count on each other. My brother approached the first one and I went after the second.'

'I take it your comrades were nearby?'

'Yes, but I still looked around quickly to make sure a third English plane was not nearby. We were alone: one on one. Soon I got on the favourable side of my opponent, fired a short burst and watched him lose his wings and go down. When the plane hit the trenches near Rouex, it caught fire.'

'And that was your fifty-first. But in all of this activity, where were the British fighter 'planes? Should they not have been there to intercept you and your comrades?'

'Of course and, after I shot down that B.E. two-seater, we regrouped with our comrades just in time. While climbing to higher altitude, our flight was attacked by a strong force of enemy Nieuport, SPAD and triplane single-seaters. We were

Above: Manfred Freiherr von Richthofen (centre), who entered the Cadet Institute at Wahlstatt at the age of eleven, looked every bit the future officer when he came home on leave. He is seen here in the garden of the family home in Schweidnitz with his youngest brother, Bolko (left), and his younger brother Lothar.

Right: Upon completing his studies at the Main Cadet Institute at Gross-Lichter-felde, outside Berlin, Manfred von Richthofen was commissioned Fähnrich [Ensign] in Ulanen-Regiment Nr. 1.

Left: Leutnant Manfred Freiherr von Richthofen shed his 'first drop of blood' for Germany during a flight on 4 September 1915, when he reached out of his observer's cockpit in a two-engine A.E.G. G.II similar to the one seen here, and a propeller blade nicked the tip of his right little finger. Later, screens were added to the sides of the observer's cockpit to avoid such accidents.

Opposite page, bottom: Richthofen's bandaged fractured finger is evident in this photo taken a few days later when he posed with comrades (from left) Rittmeister Hans Freiherr von Könitz, Leutnant Hans Reichsfreiherr [Baron of the Holy Roman Empire] Haller von Hallerstein and Leutnant von Katte at the Brieftauben-Abteilung Ostende's airfield at Ghistelles, Belgium.

Below: Richthofen flew in early Albatros two-seaters, which offered considerable firepower and commensurate in-flight risk, as demonstrated in this ground-level view of an observer's battle station.

Opposite page, top: Manfred von Richthofen's fondest dream was realised when he occupied the sparse but effective cockpit of a Fokker Eindecker.

Above: Christmas 1916 was a joyous occasion for Major Albrecht Freiherr von Richthofen (seated among members of Jagdstaffel 2). Standing from left: Leutnant Erwin Böhme, Leutnant Diether Collin, Leutnant Lothar Freiherr von Richthofen (still an observer, as evident by the badge worn below his Iron Cross award), Leutnant Manfred Freiherr von Richthofen, (unidentified), Leutnant Hans Wortmann and other unnamed Jasta 2 comrades.

Left: Richtofen's mentor, Hauptmann Oswald Boelcke, victor in forty combats, lay dead in a heap of wreckage after colliding with one of his own pilots while fighting with British aeroplanes on 26 October 1916.

Opposite page: Richthofen being suited up for a flight in his Albatros D.III from Roucourt airfield in early spring 1917.

Above: Manfred von Richthofen and his Great Dane, Moritz, which he raised from a puppy and kept with him until the ace was killed in air combat on 21 April 1918.

Münchner Illustrierte Presse

A popular German magazine cover featured Manfred von Richthofen in the seat of his Albatros D.Va fighter and some of his victory trophies. In the centre is the Cup of Honour presented by the Air Force after his first confirmed victory. He ordered the smaller silver cups from a jeweller to commemorate his victories and milestones (from left): large cup for his twentieth victory; smaller cups for his seventeenth, eighteenth, twenty-second, twenty-third and twenty-fourth victories; large cup for his thirtieth victory; smaller cups for his twenty-fifth, twenty-sixth, thirty-sixth and thirty-fifth victories; large cup for his fortieth victory; and smaller cups for his thirty-fourth and thirty-third victories. More information about the air combats that led to these victories is in the appendix of this book.

During his invited visit to Kaiser Wilhelm II in May 1917, Richthofen (centre) posed with then Oberstleutnant Hermann von der Lieth-Thomsen, Air Chief of Staff (left) and Generalleutnant Ernst von Hoeppner, Commanding General of the Air Force.

Left: Noted German artist Arnold Busch created this portrait from life just prior to Manfred von Richthofen's near fatal crash on 6 July 1917. The inscription reads: *Im Felde – Juli 1917* (In the field – July 1917). Richthofen's signature appears at the foot the illustration, which became the subject of a popular postcard.

Below: Richthofen's Albatros D.V (serial number 4693/17) following his crash on 6 July 1917. The aircraft was repaired and Richthofen flew it in subsequent combats.

Above: Albatros D.V 4693/17 was the only original Richthofen aircraft to survive the First World War intact. Displayed in a museum in Berlin, this historical artifact was destroyed in an Allied bombing raid during the Second World War.

Below: Wounded but obviously glad to be alive, Rittmeister Manfred Freiherr von Richthofen posed with Hauptmann Wilhelm Reinhard , who succeeded him as Kommandeur of Jagdgeschwader I. Richthofen is seen holding the Geschwaderstock made from a British propeller and a symbol of the Kommandeur's authority. Eventually, the famed walking stick went to the last wartime leader of JG I, Oberleutnant Hermann Göring, and has since disappeared.

Above: The last family portrait of the Richthofen family, taken before the famed ace's return to active duty following the 7 July incident. From left: Manfred (with a slender cord attaching a bandage to his head; his mother, Kunigunde Freifrau von Richthofen; his brothers Lothar and Bolko, and his sister, Ilse. Seated is his father, Major Albrecht Freiherr von Richthofen.

Below: The Richthofen family home at 10 Striegauer Strasse (later renamed Manfred-von-Richthofen-Strasse) in Schweidnitz provided a refuge for the celebrated ace while he was alive and became a shrine to his memory after he was killed in combat.

Above: Manfred von Richthofen (with hands in pockets) posed by the wreckage of his sixty-first aerial victory, a Sopwith Pup B.1795, brought down on 3 September 1917. To the ace's right is Leutnant Eberhard Mohnike and to his left is aircraft builder Anthony H. G. Fokker, seen wearing the captured British pilot's flying helmet and flight coat.

Right: In his near fatal crash on 13 March 1918, Lothar von Richthofen received serious head injuries and required a brace during his convalescence.

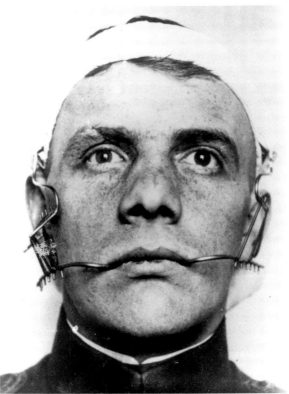

On the day Lothar was shot down, Manfred visited Jasta 5 and is seen here conferring with its leader, Ober-leutnant Richard Flashar.

Although he seldom smoked cigarettes, Manfred von Richthofen was caught by a photographer having a few puffs with his protégé Oberleut-nant Erich Loewen-hardt (left).

Right: Looking drawn near the end of his life, Richthofen posed by his Fokker Dr.I triplane wearing a heavy fur coat to keep warm in the cool spring air over the Western Front.

Below: Groundcrew (foreground) inspect engines and prepare Fokker Dr.I triplanes for flight while a technical officer and a pilot (background) discuss maintenance problems caused by poor-quality lubricants.

Above: Manfred von Richthofen was shot down and killed while flying Fokker Dr.I 425/17, seen here. He scored his last two victories in this aircraft, which was torn apart by souvenir hunters after Richthofen's death.

Right: The last photograph of Manfred von Richthofen was taken as his corpse was examined at the Australian airfield at Poulainville, some fifteen kilometres from where he crashed after being fatally injured on 21 April 1918. His body was buried with full military honours – twice in France before being returned home for a national hero's funeral in 1925.

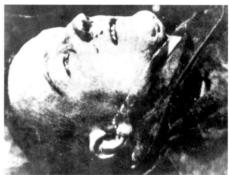

Below: Cappy airfield as it looked on the morning of 21 April 1918 when Manfred von Richthofen took off on his last combat flight.

easy to recognise, as the sun from the west illuminated our planes and let their beautiful red colour be seen from far away. We closed up tightly, for we knew that we were dealing with "brothers" who pursued the same trade we did. They were higher than we were, so we had to wait for their attack. I much prefer to have the clientele come to me than to have to go after them.

'One of them finally got up his courage and dropped down on the last man in our formation. Of course, we accepted the challenge, even though it was unfavourable for us . . . '

'How so? You said that you like to have them come to you?'

'Yes, but the pilot who attacks first has the advantage. In any event, we must accept what comes along. Therefore, my men and I turned towards the enemy. The Englishmen noticed this and broke off immediately. But the battle had begun. Another Englishman sought me out as an opponent, and I greeted him with bursts from both machine-guns. He did not seem to appreciate this gesture and tried to escape by diving away. That was his undoing. Now I was above him. Anything beneath me, alone and over our territory is as good as lost ... especially if it is a single-seater, which cannot fire from the rear. My opponent had a very good machine . . .'

'One of the new British triplanes, according to reports . . .'

'And very fast. But it was not his luck to reach his lines. When we were over Lens, I began to fire at him. I was too far away, but that was a trick I used to rattle him. He fell into the trap and made banking turns, which enabled me to get closer to him. Quickly, I did the same thing again and then a third time. As my "friend" tried to escape, my shots got closer and closer to him. Now I was quite close – at most fifty metres away from him. I took aim, waited a moment, and then pushed the buttons of both machine-guns. At first there was a faint trail of smoke, a sure sign that he had been hit in the fuel tank, then a bright flame and then he disappeared below. He was my fourth of the day . . .'

'And Number Fifty-Two and your first triplane . . .' Still talking, Richthofen said:

'... and my brother got two. Between the two of us, we shot down six Englishmen in one day. That is an entire flight of a British squadron. Apparently, we had invited the old gentleman to a feast. Our joy was boundless!'

'I believe that fight was also your first encounter with the new British triplanes. Recently, I saw an advisory that said, and again I quote: "The number of enemy triplanes sighted has increased. They are said to surpass the Albatros D.III in manoeuvrability and above all in climbing ability." Do you feel that the British aeroplanes are better than yours?'

'The famous Triplanes and SPADs are new machines, but it is not a matter of the crate as much as who sits in it … these "brothers" were wary and had no spunk. I don't understand why they show off when they are in squadron strength and then, when they come close to us, their hearts fall into their shoes.'

Despite his euphoria and because I have heard about concerns for Richthofen's personal safety, I must ask: 'It is no secret that the Higher Ups wanted you to go on leave right after you equalled Boelcke's score. Why have you persisted in continuing to wage a one-man battle against the British Royal Flying Corps? Do you have a personal vendetta against the British?'

'No. I am simply doing my duty. I wanted to reach a total of fifty enemy planes shot down and, then, when I had the opportunity, I shot down two more the same day. In fact, originally, I was supposed to shoot down only forty-one .'

'One more than Boelcke?'

'I am no record keeper. Here at the Front, records are far from our thoughts. If he had not had the fatal accident, by now Boelcke would have shot down a hundred. Many other good fallen comrades would have achieved higher numbers, except for their sudden deaths. But it was nice to attain the fifty I was allowed before being sent on leave.'

For one so young, Manfred von Richthofen has become very adept at manoeuvring the Prussian administrative structure. That makes me wonder about someone who was at the celebratory dinner last night. He was not an officer from Richthofen's old Uhlan regiment. A discreet inquiry revealed the name of Oberleutnant Erich-Rüdiger von Wedel and so I ask: 'Is he to be a future protégé in your Staffel?' Richthofen laughs, surely perceiving that I am trying to determine the extent of his 'powers' and replies:

'Wedel is a good old friend. Many people want to come here and there are a number of people I would like to have here. Recently, I visited Böhme at Jasta 2 and asked him to lead Jasta 11 when I go on leave, but he feels he must stay there. He has an obligation to Boelcke and I understand that. As to who will come here – only time will tell.'

In an instant, Richthofen becomes cool and distant. He has a mound of paper-work to finish – a real chore for someone who is not a 'pencil-pusher' by nature – and he seems to be irritated by my questions. I was about to ask him about his long-rumoured leave, but I take the hint and excuse myself.

* * *

Saturday, 1 May 1917: At breakfast, I learn more about Richthofen's leave. Feeling awkward at our last parting, I did not attend dinner in the Mess last evening. I missed the news of Lothar von Richthofen's fifteenth victory, placing him about five short of qualifying for the Pour le Mérite. The festivities were inter-rupted by a telephone call for the Rittmeister from Supreme Headquarters, summoning him to a meeting with our Supreme War Lord, Kaiser Wilhelm. Richthofen is to leave for the meeting today and he comes over to my table to give me the good news. I summon my courage and greet him with a cheery question: 'So, how does it feel to receive a call from the highest level of the Empire?' With a wide smile, he responds:

'It was the greatest fun to talk directly to the Great Office. I received the delightful news that His Majesty wishes to speak to me personally.'

'When and where?'

'Tomorrow at the General Staff Headquarters in Bad Kreuznach! It is not possible to get there in time by train, so today I will fly there.'

'Surely, you will not fly all the way to Germany in a small fighter plane?'

'Oh, no. I will "ride" in a two-seater flown by one of our pilots, Leutnant Krefft, who is going on leave. This way he will arrive home even quicker.'

I assume that Leutnant Kurt Wolff, the Staffel's second-ranking pilot, will be the acting leader of the unit in Richthofen's absence. Without being asked, Richthofen clarifies the point:

'My brother will take command of the Staffel and continue to make progress until I return to the company of these fine fellows.'

I wish him well and the, knowing that my work is done here for the moment, I return to my room in the château to pack my belongings in anticipation of using a more prosaic mode of transportation to return to Berlin.

5

HIS MAJESTY INVITES ...

Due to various wartime interruptions, it takes me three days to get back to Berlin by car, lorry and train. When I arrive at the Anhalter Railway Station, I see copies of my newspaper with a big headline: 'British Price on the Head of a German Flyer'. I buy one and, without looking at a word, I know whom the story is about. I read it to learn:

'The English have assembled an aircraft squadron of volunteer airmen that is said to seek exclusively the annihilation of the most successful German fighter pilot, Rittmeister Freiherr von Richthofen, who has already shot down fifty-two enemy aeroplanes. The airman who succeeds in shooting down or capturing Richthofen will receive the Victoria Cross, a promotion, the gift of his own personal aeroplane, £5,000 and a special prize from the manufacturer of the aircraft he uses. A special motion-picture cameraman is supposed to fly with the British squadron to record the entire event for the purpose of later use in a British Army film'

I dismiss the story as a British propaganda fantasy and head for my office to try to convince my chief to send me to Bad Kreuznach to write a story about Richthofen's meeting with the Kaiser. But my editor's superiors have received word that there is to be no mention of Manfred von Richthofen while he is on leave. A few days later, however, reports circulate that Lothar von Richthofen has shot down the leading British fighter pilot, Captain Albert Ball. Then a pall is cast on that triumph when we receive 'confidential' information from the War Ministry that Lothar was shot down on 13 May. He is in hospital and, knowing of his superstitious nature first-hand, I know that he will not want to comment on a misfortune occurring on the thirteenth of the month.

Another 'confidential' message, which is totally useless because I cannot publish its contents, is that Manfred von Richthofen has been sent on a good-will tour of Austria and Turkey beginning on 1 June. Obviously, the Empire is trying to preserve its legendary air warrior. The reason for this becomes quite clear when news is received four days later that his protégé Karl-Emil Schäfer has been killed in action. Further, we are informed that Richthofen flew from Vienna to Schäfer's home town for the funeral. After that, his whereabouts are a mystery.

Then, in mid-morning on 13 June, comes a complete surprise: Richthofen is in Berlin and telephones, inviting me to dinner with him at the Continental Hotel, near the Friedrichstrasse Railway Station. Before returning to the Front tomorrow, he promises a long evening of free time to answer all my questions – and he knows there are many.

* * *

Wednesday, 13 June 1917: I arrive in the lobby a few minutes early to observe the stately hotel's guests. Stories have circulated about parties and 'accommodations' made for airmen by aircraft manufacturers who maintain suites at the more exclusive Adlon and Bristol Hotels. Quite in keeping with Richthofen's stoic nature – or perhaps shyness – the Continental seems to offer only a pleasant atmosphere and, of course, the elegance that befits a national hero such as Manfred von Richthofen. A chorus of polite hand- clapping interrupts my reverie as Richthofen is recognised walking across the lobby. He is beet-red and not from exposure to sunlight as he shakes my hand and leads me at a brisk pace to a private reserved dining-room. Richthofen informs me that he has ordered his favourite pheasant dish for us, accompanied by a lovely Pomerol wine. I am less interested in his culinary expertise and, I am no sooner seated, when I begin: 'That was quite a nice reception.' With a nervous laugh he responds:

'It has been like this ever since I left the Front. Everywhere I go. At first it was beautifully calm, sailing through the sea of air over Liège, Namur, Aachen and Cologne. The weather was splendid. It was so peaceful. There have not been such clear skies for a long time.'

'And if you had not left?'

'With weather like that, there would have been much to do at the Front! But it was good to get away … soon even our observation balloons faded from sight. The din of the battlefield was even farther back. We passed over steamboats sailing on the rivers, and easily overtook an express train, whistling through the countryside. Everywhere we looked it was perfectly flat … even the beautiful mountains of the Meuse Valley did not look like mountains at all.'

'It must have been a very enjoyable trip for you. How far did you go that day?'

'It was wonderful. We landed at Cologne about midday and knew that we would reach Supreme Headquarters by dinner-time. Our arrival in Cologne had been expected. This was the first leave I had taken wearing the Pour le Mérite and the first time I had come home since making a name for myself. So it was quite strange to have so many people looking at me. My fifty-second victory had appeared in the newspapers the day before and people gazed at our machine as if it were a miraculous thing.'

'As I recall from watching you and Krefft leave Roucourt, even your Staffel's Albatros two-seater used for routine chores is painted all red. Do you suppose the people in Cologne thought that it was your red Albatros fighter?'

'That could be. I did not think about it, as I am quite used to the old crate and it is fine for me. In any case, Hauptmann Otto Zimmer-Vorhaus, a fellow Silesian whom I know from my bomber training days, had organised a nice reception for us. After the usual pleasantries, when I told him I had a headache from the three-hour flight, he arranged for me to be excused to take a short nap before setting out for Bad Kreuznach.'

'I have met Zimmer-Vorhaus in Berlin. He is very highly regarded. I am told that his former unit – Flieger-Abteilung 18 – is a training ground for good fighter pilots. Have you drawn on that resource? Or on Zimmer-Vorhaus himself?'

'Oh, yes. Festner and Krefft came from "18" and I have my eye on others. And from the Hauptmann himself I have learned – and instructed my men – that everyone must show absolute trust in the leader in the air. If this trust is lacking, success is impossible from the outset. The Staffel gains trust by the leader's exemplary daring and the conviction that he sees everything and is able to cope with every situation.'

Despite the elegant meal being set before us, I plunge right into an unpleasant subject: 'What do you think about the so-called "Anti-Richthofen Squadron" that, according to news reports, the English have organised to kill or capture you?' He does not seem to be bothered by the news, as he says calmly:

'I do not want to over-react, but I have a feeling that the proper English gentlemen will not be able to settle the matter according to their plan. For example, what would happen if I were to shoot down one of them and were so unlucky as to hit the film cameraman? What then? The British Army film would be interrupted, the gentlemen involved would be in the gravest predicament and, of course, blame me for it.

'How would they like it if a number of our gentlemen went up to shoot down one of them and their man were filmed being shot down? I believe that if that were the case, their man would first shoot down our cameraman. So, I want only to shoot down the cameraman who is supposed to film me being shot down. I would love to do that!'

It is clear that Richthofen is fit and well rested. Indeed, I have not seen him so cheerful as to take a serious question and turn it into such a response. He must have had a wonderful time at the Imperial Advance Western Command Post in the lovely old spa city of Bad Kreuznach. I ask him: 'What can you tell me about your arrival at Supreme Headquarters on 1 May, which I believe was a day before your twenty-fifth birthday?' His face becomes flushed again and he rolls his eyes upwards at mention of his birthday, during which he was fêted by no less a personage than His Imperial Majesty. After some self-conscious throat-clearing, he responds with a big smile:

'Krefft and I arrived at Supreme Headquarters later that afternoon. We were greeted by personnel from the staff of the Commanding General of the Air Force with bouquets of flowers and a thundering cheer. I knew all of them by sight; for the most part they came from the BAO or the BAM . . .'

Richthofen seems not to mind when I interrupt him for clarification, so I ask: 'What is the BAM? I know that, earlier, you flew with the Brieftauben-Abteilung Ostende, but I have not heard about the BAM.'

'It was a similar unit, based at Metz – the Brieftauben-Abteilung Metz – and, like the BAO, it produced many fine airmen.

'In any case, I became better acquainted with other comrades who work in the "great office". I feel sorry for these "pencil pushers", as they experience only half the fun of war. Nevertheless, I got the feeling that those up in the great administrative "factory" live with each detail and each success, and do not simply push them back and forth like numbers in a calculator.

'Krefft was soon on his way home and I was taken to General von Hoeppner.'

'The air chief himself! Can you tell me what you discussed with him?'

'Mostly, he talked and I listened. It was all very flattering. In his concluding remark, he said the spirit of Boelcke lives on in me, which, as you know, has very special meaning for me.

'The next morning, I was presented to Generalfeldmarschall von Hindenburg and then to General Ludendorff. As usual, Hindenburg was swamped with appointments with civilians and uniformed people, and so I was able to speak with him only a bit.'

'I suppose everyone wants to talk to the Chief of the General Staff. What was it like with his top man, Quartermaster-General Ludendorff?'

'As I sat in Ludendorff's waiting room, I had the opportunity to observe how busy this man is. There were a lot of important personalities in that room. I saw Ballin [General Director of the Hamburg-American Shipping Line], near him a high-ranking General Staff officer with a fat bundle of papers, and then [Foreign Minister] Zimmermann. [Chancellor von] Bethmann-Hollweg was there, as well as Helferrich [Secretary of the Imperial Treasury] and many generals, all waiting for an audience. And then there was me.

'After an hour, an adjutant motioned to me and pushed me through the door. Ludendorff stood up, shook my hand and said: "So how are you? You look well-fed and cheerful." He directed me to a chair and asked: "What is the air situation like at Arras?" I began to tell him, right down to the smallest details, which were of little military importance. Then he simply cut me off and began to tell me about the things I had just told him. He went on at some length. After he elicited everything he wanted to know about the air situation at the main battle front at Arras, I was abruptly dismissed. I must say that I was quite satisfied to be let go, as this serious, dispassionate-thinking person seemed a bit odd to me. It was a strange feeling to be in the room where the destiny of the world is being decided. I was quite happy when I left the "great office".'

'What was your next appointment?'

'At midday, I was summoned to have lunch with the Kaiser. Someone must have told His Imperial Majesty that it was my birthday and so he congratulated me – first for my success, then for the twenty-fifth year of my life. And he surprised me with what he called a "small" birthday present.'

'May I ask what it was?'

'Yes. A handsome bronze and marble bust of the Kaiser himself in his parade uniform. It is beautiful, but too heavy to carry back to the Front with me and so a staff officer arranged to have it sent to my home.'

'What was it like to meet the Kaiser?'

'He was exactly as I imagined him to be. After lunch he spoke to me for about half an hour. The conversation was very one-sided. He talked only about anti-aircraft guns.'

'Did the Kaiser say anything about the aeroplanes that those guns shoot down, affecting pilots such as you?'

'Yes, in a way. In a light moment, he said to me: "I have heard that you are still flying. You be careful that nothing happens to you!" Then he turned to an aide-de-camp and asked: "How could that be? Have I not forbidden him to fly?" The aide answered: "Majesty, in the interests of the entire situation, we cannot do that. We need Richthofen as an example and as a Geschwader-Kommandeur [Wing Commander]. We need him as a fighter pilot."'

'What do you think he meant by that? That you might become a Geschwader-Kommandeur?' I ask, suddenly sensing the reason for his quick return to Berlin. I press further: 'Would they transfer you from your fighter pilot duties to command a Kampfgeschwader of bombers, like the ones you flew in Russia?' My first thought is Kampfgeschwader 3, which is much in the news for its raids over England. Richthofen seems surprised by the question and snaps back:

'I don't know yet.'

I do not question him further on that point, although I wonder whether the Higher Ups are dissatisfied with the current deployment of their Jagdstaffeln? In any event, it is clear to me that Richthofen is important to the future of the Air Force and only time will tell how it will all sort out. Returning to the earlier theme, I ask: 'What happened after your meeting with the Kaiser?'

'That evening the Air Chief invited Generalfeldmarschall von Hindenburg to a dinner in my honour.'

'*Alone?*'

'Oh, no! Ludendorff was also there. And, sitting together at one table, were no fewer than eight Knights of the Orden Pour le Mérite. I would never again see so many in one house unless the war were to last so long that the Pour le Mérite would became as common as the Iron Cross Second Class.

'Hindenburg's speech was very flattering. Indeed, never would I have dreamed that on my twenty-fifth birthday I would sit at Hindenburg's right hand and be mentioned in a speech by him.

'Then, in the course of the conversation he asked in a good-natured, calm way: "Now tell me, Richthofen, were you also a cadet?" I told him that I had begun my military career in the 2nd Company at the Cadet Institute at Wahlstatt and, in fact, in Barracks 6. Then the old gentleman said: "Well, look at this, I also began to play soldier in Barracks 6 at Wahlstatt and have presented the barracks with my photo as a memento." '

'*When did you leave the Supreme Headquarters?*'

'The next day, but not before I had flown up to Bad Homburg vor der Höhe with Fritze von Falkenhayn.'

'*The son of the General? Hindenburg's predecessor?*'

'Yes. We had flown together in the BAO and now he is on the Air Chief's staff. I had been forbidden to fly during this leave and, with Krefft gone, someone had to take me where I was going. I had been invited to have breakfast with the Kaiserin Auguste Victoria. She had such interest in aviation that she appeared at the airfield when we arrived. During the flight I had worn the old leather jacket in which I had achieved all my victories. As soon as we landed, I went off immediately to join her. I had left the Front hastily and had no formal dress uniform and so, in order to justify to some extent why I was dressed in my flying- jacket for this ceremonious occasion, I told Her Imperial Majesty that I had won all my fights while wearing it.'

'*What did she say?*'

'She simply stroked the jacket and said: "The good jacket, you have gone through fifty two victories with it.' I didn't know what to say to her. During our brief time together I had the same nice feeling that I'd had when I was with Hindenburg. I felt I was in the presence of a charming lady; it was just as nice as being with a favourite old aunt or my own grandmother. I could almost forget that she is the Empress.

'I felt very honoured when she also presented me with a belated birthday gift … a gold-and-white enamelled cigarette case inscribed with her name.'

'Later, Falkenhayn and I made a dramatic exit when we went whistling down the long green lawn in our plane, and headed south for Freiburg. We had been granted a state permit to hunt wood grouse in the Black Forest. That is where we were when word came about Lothar's great defeat of the English pilot, Captain Ball, who is said to have shot down more than forty of our planes.'

'That event must have been as important as your victory over Major Hawker. How did you learn about it?'

'Even when I am on leave, the Air Chief's office keeps me informed of events. In this case, the weekly Air Force news bulletin made special mention of Lothar's nineteenth and twentieth victories, and that the former resulted in the death of Captain Ball. Further details came from one of our men, Leutnant Wilhelm Allmenröder, whose brother Carl also shot down a plane in that fight.

'Willi told me that he thought the fight would end because it had become dark. But Lothar and the Englishman turned and rushed at each other several times, firing like mad. Finally, Lothar's opponent dived to the ground and Lothar also went down in a steep turn and disappeared in the mist. Ball was killed. Fortunately, Lothar was uninjured. Later, he received some souvenirs from the wreckage of Ball's machine and sent them home to Schweidnitz.'

'What happened to the British pilot's body?'

'Ball was buried in a village cemetery nearby and photos of the grave were dropped over English lines. Our people informed them that Ball fell in a fight with a pilot of equal prominence.

'As you may know, a few days later, Lothar received the Pour le Mérite.'

'Yes, I saw the bulletins announcing the awards for him and for Kurt Wolff. But then we received word that, on 13 May, Lothar had been shot down in a fight. We were given no details – can you tell me what happened?'

'I had been on leave for a week when I received the message: "Lothar is wounded, but not life-threatening." Not a word more. After making direct inquiries, I learned that he and Carl Allmenröder had been in a fight with the enemy.

'Below him, somewhat far on the other side over Arleux Forest, Lothar saw an Englishman buzzing around. It was one of the enemy ground attack planes that our troops find troublesome. My brother was at about two thousand metres' altitude and the Englishman at a thousand. Lothar stalked him and then, at the right moment, went into a dive and was on him in a few seconds. The Englishman also went into a dive and, without hesitating, my brother was after him. He did not care whether it was on their side or ours. Lothar's only thought was: he must go down. If my brother does not get at least one victory on every flight, he has no fun at all. Lothar caught up with him just above the ground and blasted away at him. The Englishman plunged straight down into the ground. There was nothing more to it.

'After such a battle, especially at really low altitude, in which one twists and turns so often, flying once around to the right and once around to the left, a normal person has no idea where he is. On this day the weather was bad. It was rather misty. Quickly, Lothar regained his orientation and noticed that he was quite a way behind the Front. He was behind Vimy Ridge, about a hundred metres higher than the rest of the area. To the ground observers, my brother seemed to have disappeared behind Vimy Ridge.

'Until you reach your own position, the flight home is not very pleasant. You can do nothing about it when the enemy fires at you. They seldom hit you, but at such a low altitude, you can hear every shot ... it sounds like chestnuts snapping in a fire when individual infantrymen fire at you.

'As Lothar approached our lines, his plane was hit. He felt a pain in his right hip and he felt blood trickling down his leg. Meanwhile, the firing from below continued. When it finally stopped, he knew he had crossed our lines. He saw a forest and then a flat meadow. He had to land there. He switched off the engine and, at that moment, he lost consciousness and simply glided in for a landing. He was completely alone in his plane, with nobody there to help him. When he woke up, he was in a field hospital. Later, he was transferred to the Bavarian War Hospital in Douai.'

'Thank goodness some of <u>our</u> people found him. Despite that incident, he had achieved quite a record of success. Twenty-four victories in a little over six weeks . . .' Now, Richthofen taps his fork on his dish as a way to interrupt me and interjects:

'Had my brother not been wounded, I believe that after my return from leave, he would have gone on leave with fifty-two enemy planes to his credit.'

I do not want to digress into another conversation about Lothar and so I ask: 'How was the rest of your leave? Were you able to go home?'

'It was all very nice. Falkenhayn and I stayed in Freiburg until the day after Lothar's misfortune. Eventually, I got home, but first we headed for Berlin to look at new planes – but, due to the weather, we almost did not make it!'

'What happened?'

'I was a passenger from Freiburg to Nürnberg, but we changed positions during our refuelling stop. A thunderstorm was coming and I was in a great hurry to get to Berlin. All manner of interesting things awaited me there, so we flew on despite the coming storm. The weather became beastly and the rain came in buckets. Then there was hail, which beat up the propeller and made it look like a saw blade.'

'It seems that you enjoyed the challenge of flying through the storm.'

'I did. In fact, it was so much fun that I lost track of where we were. I tried to orient myself, but hadn't the foggiest idea of our location. It was a fine mess! Being lost over my own country!

'As it turned out, I had been driven about a hundred kilometres off course. Using the sun and my compass, I flew on in what I thought was the direction of Berlin. Cities, villages, rivers and forests rushed beneath me, but I could not recognise anything.

'After about two hours, Falkenhayn and I decided to make an emergency landing. That is always unpleasant, especially when it is not at an airfield. You don't know what the surface is like and, if a wheel goes into a hole, the crate is finished. At first, we tried coming in low to see the name of a railway station – but the sign was so small that we could not make out a letter of it. In any case, we had to land. There was nothing else to do. We spotted a meadow that looked quite nice from the air and tried our luck. The appearance was deceiving, as we realised later from our slightly bent undercarriage. We had come down in the vicinity of Leipzig and had to make the rest of our journey to Berlin by quite ordinary means, an express train.

'A few days later I was back home in Schweidnitz, also by train, I might add. It arrived about seven in the morning and I expected the usual quiet scene one finds at that time. But there was quite a crowd of people there and they gave me quite a welcome.

'It was very nice, but even nicer to get away from the crowds and go into the quiet forests, where the only sounds were made by my quarry.'

'Where did you go to hunt?'

'First I went to Stanowitz, not far from home and then to the Pless estate, also nearby.'

I bolt up at the sound of the name. My young friend – if I may call him that – is now moving in some very high society! The Princes of Pless are from one of Europe's oldest noble families, dating back to the twelfth century, if I recall my history correctly. I thought only emperors and kings were invited to Pless, unless the invitation policy became more liberal when it served as Supreme Headquarters from 1915 until the recent move westwards to Bad Homburg. Still amazed at the access that Richthofen has gained in his new role as a national hero, I interject: 'Pless? Why did you go there? And when did you go there?'

'During my visit to Supreme Headquarters, the Prince himself invited me to hunt "aurochs" with him. The true aurochs is extinct, of course, but the bison is the next best thing. On the whole earth they are found in only two places – at Pless and at the game preserve of the former Tsar in Bialowicz Forest. Therefore, it is through the kindness of the Prince that shooting such a rare animal is allowed today. In about a generation there will be no more of these animals, as they will be exterminated.

'I arrived at Pless on the afternoon of the twenty-sixth. I was driven directly from the station to the game preserve, and I brought down a big bull that evening. We travelled along the famous road through the Prince's enormous wildlife preserve, on which many crowned heads had travelled before me. After about an hour, we got out of the car and walked for another half-hour to reach the spot where the beaters were in place, waiting for the signal.

I stood on the high spot where, the head gamekeeper told me, the Kaiser had stood numerous times and had bagged many a bison.

'We waited for some time. Suddenly I saw, in the high timber, a giant black monster trundling along straight towards me. I saw this even before the forester, got ready to shoot and, I must say, I had hunting fever. It was a mighty bull. At two hundred and fifty paces away, he sniffed the air for a moment. I was too far away to shoot. Perhaps I would have hit the monster, as one generally does not miss something so gigantic. But if I had missed him, searching for him would have been unpleasant, as well as a disgrace. He must have noticed the beaters, for suddenly he made a sharp turn and came directly toward me at remarkable speed for such an animal. It was a bad angle for a shot. Then he disappeared behind a stand of thick spruce trees. I heard him snorting and stamping, but I could no longer see him. Perhaps he had got wind of me. In any case, he was gone. I saw him once again from a great distance and then he disappeared.

'Whether it was the unusual view of such an animal or who knows what ... at the moment when the bull came at me, I was gripped by the same hunting fever that I feel when I am in a plane ... I see an Englishman and must fly along for five minutes to come at him. The difference is that the Englishman defends himself.

'It did not take long before a second bull came along. He was also a mighty fellow and made it easier for me. About a hundred paces away from me, he sniffed the air and turned his whole shoulder to me. I hit him with the first shot. A month earlier, Hindenburg told me: "Take many bullets with you. I used half a dozen on mine, as such a fellow does not die easily. His heart is so deep within him that most hunters shoot past it." And that was the case this time. I had not hit the heart, even though I knew precisely where it was. I fired again. Then a third time until, finally, he stood where he was, mortally wounded, about fifty paces away from me.

'Five minutes later the beast was finished. The hunt was over and a member of the Prince's retinue sounded his horn to indicate that the quarry was dead. All three bullets were over his heart – the sign of good shooting.'

Richthofen continues in great detail about the huge animal's final moments. These comments are of little interest to a non-hunter such as myself. While he talks, I have before me a statement from Erwin Böhme, which I had planned to read to Richthofen to get him to compare his love of the forests with his success in aerial combat. The question is now meaningless and the statement remains among my notes, simply as commentary: 'Hunting is Richthofen's whole passion and for him the ultimate. And, primarily, he has to thank his hunter's eye for his incredible success. Watching like an eagle, he spots the weakness of his opponent and like a bird of prey he dives on his victim, which is inescapably in his clutches. As for flying itself, I believe he does not care very much for it. Most likely, he has never performed a loop for the sheer joy of it, and above all he has strictly forbidden his Staffel to do any "acrobatic tricks", as he calls them.' Richthofen continues to talk about this (apparently his greatest) hunting experience:

'On the way back, we drove past the Prince's beautiful hunting lodge. Every year during the hunting season the Prince's guests stay there while shooting red deer and other game. We stopped to see the inside of his house at Prom-nitz, located on a peninsula with a marvellous view. There is not a single human being within five hundred kilometres. This is not only a hunting-preserve; it is a wilderness. We did not reach the main house until shortly before dark.'

I can only imagine the sumptuous dinner that awaited the hunting-party and the long night of hunting stories. But I interject: 'Then, I gather, you had a pleasant time back in Schweidnitz?'

'Yes. But not for long. I was informed by telephone that, a few days later, a plane would land on the parade ground near my home. My leave was coming to an end and I was to fly to Berlin for further duties. As it turned out, an old two-seater and a new single-seat Halberstadt showed up . . .'

I was surprised by the choice of the fighter-type aircraft he was assigned to fly to Berlin this time, as I knew he had test flown a sleek-looking LFG Roland D.III as a potential replacement for the trouble-plagued Albatros D.V series. I ask: 'Was the Halberstadt a test machine or simply a means for you to become accustomed to flying single-seaters again?'

'Both. In any event, after breakfast, my mother and my sister saw me off. Before we left Schweidnitz, the Halberstadt factory pilot assured me that his plane was so easy to fly that I would not need to fasten my safety belt. After my experience with thunderstorms, I told him: "I buckle up for every overland flight." And it was good that I did. Halfway between Schweidnitz and Breslau I let go of the control column for a moment. Normally, the machine flies on.

At the Front when everything is calm, from time to time, I like to put my hands on the fuselage sides and admire the view. The plane flies itself, so to speak. I should have remembered that I was flying a machine entirely new to me, as, suddenly, I was flying upside-down … held in only by the seat harness!'

'So much for good advice from a company pilot. What went wrong?'

'The Halberstadt was so nose-heavy that the moment I let go of the controls, it went over on me … if I had not fastened the harness, I would have fallen right out. Quickly, I regained control of the plane and rolled it back over to the normal position. I was shaken by the experience and flew carefully to our next stop, at Militsch.

'There we had more bad luck with the Halbertstadt. As I was preparing to take off again, the engine simply quit and could not be restarted. Not even by the factory pilot. Then a bad storm blew up and with it came hail and gale-force winds. There were too many bad signs, so I travelled the rest of the way by train.

'When you returned to Berlin, what new duties did they have for you?'

'Only one. I was scheduled to tour the other battlefronts in the Balkans and elsewhere, beginning in Vienna.'

Much like the 'grand tour' arranged for Boelcke after Immelmann's death, I thought to myself. Richthofen was being sent out of harm's way. I ask: 'How long was the battlefront tour to last?'

'I don't know. My orderly, Menzke, and I left Berlin for Vienna by train on 1 June and were still in Austria a few days later when I received news of Schäfer's death. I cancelled my appointments and returned to Berlin. Then I flew to Krefeld for Schäfer's funeral.'

Richthofen pauses for a moment, searching for words in a moment of emotional turmoil. It is the first time I have seen him so upset. Slowly, he begins to speak:

'It had been harder and harder for me to be away from my Staffel.'

'Were you "homesick" for it?'

'You could say that. In any event, the continual flow of reports about British numerical superiority in the air was very distressing. Quite simply, I could have no peace as long as our comrades were threatened by enemy air units.'

I learned from my growing network of Air Force *sources in Berlin that a Richthofen cousin on his mother's side of the family, Leutnant Oskar von Schickfuss und Neudorff, a pilot with Jasta 3, was reported missing the same day that Schäfer was shot down. No doubt this loss has also weighed on Richthofen's mind. I ask him: 'Do you know what happened to your cousin?' Regaining his composure, he answers:*

'I have determined with certainty that he is dead. He fell or jumped from his plane at fifteen hundred metres. He lies near the Front, but on the other side. We have dropped notes to the British, trying to learn whether they were able to recover his body. The Royal Flying Corps people are very noble in this regard.'

Although Richthofen's cousin and Schäfer were most likely flying the now much criticised Albatros D.V fighters, I am curious as to how much aerial superiority the British and French have attained. From my valise I pull out an article that appeared in Norddeutsche Allgemeine Zeitung shortly after Schäfer's death and ask Richthofen about this quote by General von Hoeppner: "The superiority of our aeroplanes and their first-rate weapons play a role of course. However, one must not forget that a heated competition is taking place between German and enemy aircraft manufacturers that again and again will lead to a settlement one way or the other. The French with their new 200-horsepower SPAD and the English with their Sopwith Triplane have excellent combat aeroplanes. That a number of our fighter pilots have succeeded in shooting down a substantial number of both types offers splendid proof of their keenness and skill." With a sense of recognition that turns to defiance, Richthofen responds:

'Yes, that is true. At the moment, the enemy enjoys a certain superiority . . . But, as the Air Chief said, the fighting ability of our pilots . . .'

He seems to have become very tense. I rephrase the question: 'Do you know what kind of planes Schäfer and your cousin were fighting?' I catch myself before naming the terrible events. 'Were they new SPADs or Sopwith Triplanes?'

'I understand that Schäfer's adversary was an English F.E.2 – a very dangerous opponent. The observer has two gun positions. Apparently, Oscar was attacked by an English Nieuport, which is similar to our Albatros fighters.'

I recognise the designation F.E.2– the so-called 'Vickers' two-seater type – that brought down Immelmann and some of our other best air fighters. There is nothing to be gained by pursuing this point, so I move on: 'How was your second visit to Supreme Headquarters?'

'Interesting in its own way. I reported to the Air Chief on 10 June. I was informed that my Staffel moved from Roucourt to Harlebeke, north-east of Courtrai, the day before, so they would need time to settle in.

'The day I arrived at Bad Kreuznach, King Ferdinand of Bulgaria was there and I had the opportunity to speak with him. The King is a tall, stately gentleman with an angular eagle-nose and a very intelligent face. Everything that he says is substantive. He spoke with me for quite a while, asked me about this and that in aerial combat and I must say I was astonished at how broad an insight he had into my business. Seldom have I found such aware-ness in Regular Army officers who are not airmen.

'The King's second son was also there and I was impressed by him. He still looks very boyish; he is only seventeen or eighteen. He has great interest in machinery and knows quite a bit about the Albatros D.III.'

'How was your meeting with the Kaiser?'

'The official state dinner was as usual. We sat at two long tables. I was at the Kaiser's table, next to the Prince of Pless and had the opportunity to thank him for the recent hunting invitation. I spoke with him almost the whole time. He told me that he wanted his son to become an airman. I find this quite a decision for a Prince to let his oldest son take up such a dangerous trade of war.

'General Freiherr von Lyncker, the Chief of the Military Cabinet, was especially cordial to me. He resembles his son . . .'

Although he has barely touched his wine, Richthofen drifts off again, as if savouring – ever so briefly – the memory of his fallen friend, Bodo, whom he came to know during fighter pilot training at Döberitz and who later wanted to transfer from the Macedonian Front to Jasta 11.

'. . . or I should say that the son resembled him so much. Every movement and facial feature was exactly the same. Even though I knew Bodo a relatively short time, he struck me as being the ideal soldier. He was his father's son.

'After dinner I spoke briefly to the King and then he went on to take care of his political business. The following day, I was presented by His Royal Majesty with his kingdom's Bravery Cross.

'The old Prince of Pless presents himself very well. One thing especially impressed me about the old gentleman: that at the age of seventy-five he sat in a plane with Fritze Falkenhayn and flew around the area for an hour and a half. He was so thrilled by it that, after alighting, he pressed twenty Marks into the hand of each mechanic. He would have preferred to take off again. That impressed me greatly; for there are no end of younger gentlemen who are knights without fear or reproach, but who would never be moved to climb into a plane.'

'You seem to have enjoyed the atmosphere and all that goes on at the Supreme Headquarters. Would you accept a staff position there? A post that would enable you to share your knowledge and experience with others?' That question got Richthofen's full attention and he quickly and clearly shared his view with me:

'No. Absolutely not! I spoke with several highly placed staff officers; for example, with Nikolaus Graf zu Dohna-Schlodien, who, after his latest voyage with the surface raider *Möwe*, was rewarded by being appointed as Naval Aide-de-Camp to the Kaiser. I asked him whether he is satisfied with his post. He gave me a very sly look ...'

'Meaning what? That he was cynical about it or that, having tasted glory, he was now resigned to a less active role in the war?'

'I am not sure, but I can tell you that this small, inconspicuous-looking man made by far the best impression on me. One could see that he was a fighter and no courtier.'

I want to know more about the great naval hero's reaction, but Richthofen has become very adroit in dodging finer points of questions. He simply continues to talk about other important people he met at the Kaiser's dinner party.

'Moreover, I was impressed by Count Frankenberg, who from time to time doffed his courtly bearing and showed that he is just a human being. He made a particularly apt observation to me: "The people around you are only people, from the most supreme to the lowest ranking, and all of them have basic human characteristics." True words well worth remembering.'

I am amazed at such egalitarianism among the aristocracy – on the part of both Richthofen and Frankenberg – and seize this unguarded moment to ask him whether he saw anything that evening to reinforce Frankenberg's contention. Quickly, Richthofen responds:

'Yes and, furthermore, we all passed the evening standing, as usual, while the Kaiser sat. That was awkward for the rest of us, especially the old gentlemen, such as Hindenburg, who with Ludendorff had been commanded to attend the dinner.'

While Richthofen is in such a candid mood, I spring the question I have long wanted to ask and which I am sure my readers will find of interest: As casually as I can, I ask: 'While I know you miss the comradeship of your men, is there perhaps "someone else" whose companionship you also miss?' Now he must tell me outright to mind my own business and not pry into his personal affairs or, if I am lucky, tell me about some Fräulein or Mademoiselle with whom he shares his innermost secrets. Detecting my trick, he blushes, then laughs and says:

'Only Moritz, the most beautiful creature ever created.'

Moritz! A man? Now I am truly shocked and wish I hadn't asked! People simply don't talk about these things. I have reached too far and am mortified. My discomfort is very apparent and Richthofen seems to be enjoying it immensely, as he laughs and laughs. Then, clearing his throat for added drama, he tells me:

'Moritz is my "little lap dog", a Great Dane that I bought for five Marks in Ostend. Zeumer took a second one from the same litter and called him "Max". Unfortunately, Max came to a sudden end under a car, but Moritz has thrived splendidly. Ever since Ostend he has accompanied me almost everywhere and has grown in my heart. But Moritz has grown bigger and bigger, and now my "little lap dog" is quite an enormous animal.

'I even took him up with me, as my "leading observer". He behaved very well and eyed the world with interest. My mechanics, however, were angry because, afterwards, they had to clean some unpleasant things from the aeroplane. But Moritz was very unconcerned by it all.'

Richthofen looks at me, awaiting my next question. I can manage only one: 'How old is your lap dog?' Still smiling smugly, my dinner host responds in a friendly tone:

'He is now more than a year old, but still acts like a puppy. He plays billiards very well. Unfortunately, many balls and in particular many billiard table cloths have suffered. He also has quite a hunting instinct and this makes my mechanics very happy, as he has caught many nice hares for them. But he gets a good thrashing from me for it ... I am little pleased by this passion.

'But, for all his faults, he is very protective. Back at Roucourt, I once left orders for some servants to clean my quarters. After we finished flying for the day, I returned to the place and found nothing had been done. I ordered one of the servants, a Frenchman, to come to me. Scarcely had he opened the door when Moritz greeted him with his teeth showing. It turned out that, even though he is Belgian, Moritz does not care for Frenchmen. Now I understood why the gentleman had not cleaned my quarters.'

I am galled by Richthofen's self-satisfied smile. Of course, I cannot say anything, as I went looking for trouble and found it. We have finished our meal and I decline an after-dinner drink, pleading that I must catch a late train and return to my apartment in Potsdam. He has an early departure and must prepare for it.

With that, I bid Herr Rittmeister a pleasant journey in the morning and hurry off to the Friedrichstrasse station.

6

THE NEW KOMMANDEUR

I was clear at our last meeting that Manfred von Richthofen was ready to
return to the Front with a renewed sense of purpose; perhaps even to avenge
his cousin Oscar, his protégé Schäfer and, more recently, the gallant Allmenröder, possibly a victim of the anti-aircraft guns that the Kaiser had inquired
about. The importance of Richthofen's quick return to Berlin became clear.
Although relatively junior in rank, he had gained enough prestige and access to
the Higher Ups to make a case for new and better fighter aeroplanes. And now I
understand why Richthofen pays his own hotel bills in Berlin and avoids the
'hospitality' offered by manufacturers. He is free to speak his mind and, as my
Air Force sources whisper to me, Richthofen is totally candid in pointing out
that even the improved Albatros D.V fighters are inferior to new English and
French fighters.

I learn that now Richthofen's Staffel is equipped with newer Albatros D.Va
fighters and that, following his return on 15 June, he used one to shoot down his
next five victims. The really big news, which – damn it all! – I cannot write about
yet, is that, on 24 June, Richthofen is assigned to command Germany's first
Jagdgeschwader [Fighter Wing], made up of four Jagdstaffeln and dedicated to
achieving supremacy over their battle sectors. As General von Hoeppner writes to
his staff: 'Due to his numbers and tenacity, the Englishman is our most
dangerous enemy and the British Front requires, as a matter of course, the main
force of German air strength. The ever-increasing number of aeroplanes that the
opposition deploys to reach a target makes it desirable for us to combine several
Jagdstaffeln into a Jagdgeschwader. In the personage of Rittmeister von
Richthofen, the Geschwader has a Kommandeur [commander] whose steel-
hard will in relentlessly pursuing the enemy will be infused into everyone under
his command. His gallant manner and military skill have secured for him in the
Army an unshakable trust that, despite his young age, is matched with great
respect.'

My editor no longer questions whether I will go to the Flanders Sector, where
Richthofen now flies, but only how soon I can make arrangements to get there.
En route to the battlefront, the ever-helpful Air Force press office makes sure that
I know about Richthofen's fifty-seventh victory, achieved on 2 July. I will learn

the details from the new Kommandeur himself. The promise made at Richthofen's first meeting with the Kaiser has been fulfilled and I am anxious to learn more about it.

* * *

Thursday, 5 July 1917: It is early on a brilliant summer morning when I pass through the Belgian town of Marcke and arrive at Marckebeke, an elegant baronial estate with broad green lawns and a collection of small buildings that make the place a first-class air operations centre. Of course, now a German baron – Manfred von Richthofen – is ensconced in the 'Castle,' which is actually a good-sized château, but quite nice, none the less. By now, most of his associates know me by sight and I am shown into a stately dining-room, which is much nicer than the one at Roucourt. I am glad that I called ahead before I left Courtrai for the short ride here, as a marvellous breakfast has been prepared. All manner of meats and cheeses, marmalade and rolls – and real coffee, not the ersatz devil's brew that shows up in most German restaurants. Oberleutnant Karl Bodenschatz, formerly of Jasta Boelcke and now the new Geschwader's adjutant, introduces himself and makes small talk for a short while. Bodenschatz tells me that he accepted Richthofen's telephoned invitation to join the Geschwader and was out of Pronville and off to Marcke even before all of the paperwork was finished. He is just explaining to me how the four Jagdstaffeln are clustered around the Marckebeke estate when in walks the Kommandeur, who surveys the array of plates and silverware that Bodenschatz has laid out to show how the units are close but dispersed. 'This looks like something from your cavalry days,' I say. He responds:

'I must be close to my units. It is not feasible for me to have my quarters somewhere in the rear and communicate by telephone to my men. The orders received from the strategy planners back in the support area must be given more directly.'

'So, you are here, right in the middle of it all.'

'Yes, I want to be in close contact with my Staffel leaders and even get to know the abilities of each pilot in the four units. I must be able to separate the wheat from the chaff. I can only do that when I am constantly with the men I command.'

With a wink to Bodenschatz, Richthofen continues:

'Flying against the enemy is not as easy as arranging things on a table. I must be sure that each of my pilots attacks our enemies when he sees them. He must be capable of engaging in combat at all times ... without thought to whether he may be lying on the ground in his shattered machine at the end of the battle.'

To draw attention away from Bodenschatz, whom I will cultivate as a source of information about his new Kommandeur, I say jokingly: 'Oh, so your new assignment is not just a desk job. I understand from prisoner reports that some British wing commanders stay on the ground, but I take it that you will be in the thick of it.' He laughs at my comment, but answers seriously:

'The Jagdgeschwader-Kommandeur must be a fighter pilot and a successful one, at that. He must fly with his men to observe how they fight. He must know which men to place together by understanding which ones will fight well together in the air. Successful fighter units contain comrades who are well coordinated. And they know that no one will leave the other in the lurch when the situation becomes precarious.'

'But you are bound to have some personality differences among people ...'

'True, but comradeship is important. I will not tolerate a troublemaker ... unless, of course, I can find a way to make him useful against the enemy.

'The Kommandeur should not control his Staffeln too tightly. Each Staffel leader must have total freedom over his operational sector. During important moments the Staffel leaders should direct their main areas of battle without having to say who will do what and when. Such rigid orders are utter nonsense. The pilots should be assigned to certain areas in which they will cruise at will, but when they see an opponent, they must attack and shoot him down. Nothing else matters to us but the victory.'

'Are you developing a new strategy or is this a refinement of Boelcke's tactical dicta?'

'No, it goes back to Klaus von Clausewitz: "Nothing else matters in war but the destruction of the enemy."'

'I have read the old Prussian general's book, the "Bible" of warfare, but I have been told that, in this war, aerial reconnaissance and bombing are the key purposes of aircraft and the role of fighter aircraft is to deter the destruction of one's own reconnaissance and bombing planes, and to destroy as many of the enemy's aircraft carrying out those missions. Is that not so?'

'No, it is not! The mastery of the air is won only through battle. Moreover, that kind of order – fight only to protect your own territory – has a devastating effect on some fighter pilots … if their resolve is not strong and their will to fight is weakened easily. I have heard one such "careful" fighter pilot say: "You accomplish the same thing when you fly back and forth at the Front as when you attack and destroy the enemy." This rather questionable "fighter" pilot will be completely useless when the battle is joined. The outcome of the war does not depend on well-written battle orders. It is only in combat that the battle is won.'

'According to your report of 18 June, upon your return to the Front the first enemy aircraft you shot down was an R.E.8 two-seat reconnaissance plane. But I gather that you mean the type made no difference? It could just as easily have been a single-seat fighter?'

'Yes, that is correct. In the morning we encountered Nieuport fighters and Carl Allmenröder shot one down. A few hours later we came upon more Nieuports and they got one of our men. A very short time later, we saw the R.E. north of Ypres and went after it. I was closest to it and fired about two hundred shots into the fuselage and then zoomed up. As I passed above the plane, I could see that both pilot and observer were dead in their cockpits. Their plane did not fall immediately, but went down in uncontrolled turns to the ground. It fell into farmland and began to burn.'

'Which of your Staffel comrades was lost and what happened to him?'

'He was a new man, Leutnant Bordfeld. I had not flown with him before. He was killed, either in the fight or when he crashed.'

Richthofen seems detached when tells me about the inexperienced young man who fell in that fight. His mood changes quickly, though, when I refer to my notes and ask: 'Wasn't that the day after your old friend Zeumer fell while flying with Jasta Boelcke?'

'Yes. Poor old Zeumer was shot down. But perhaps it was best for him … for he knew the end of his life was just ahead of him . . .'

Perhaps unable to say the terrible word, Richthofen taps his chest and I understand instantly Zeumer's devil-may-care attitude: he knew he had tuberculosis.

'He was a splendid fellow. It would have been terrible if he were slowly tormented to death. So, his was a beautiful, hero's death and he was buried with military honours.'

There it is again, that frightful but so embraceable image from Nietzsche: the splendour of a warrior's death. It bothers me, but I must ask about the next casualty within Richthofen's sphere, his protégé Carl Allmenröder, his fourth acolyte to receive the Pour le Mérite. At that moment, I am looking at the most resolute person I will ever meet. His face beams with pride as he replies:

'When I went to Hamburg to visit Lothar in hospital, I had such complete confidence in Allmenröder that I named him acting Kommandeur and that evening he proved himself worthy by attaining his thirtieth victory. The following morning, unfortunately, he fell on the field of honour . . .'

'Shot down by one of the new Sopwith Triplanes, I am told.'

'Some say by anti-aircraft fire. In any event, I was informed that an English plane that was at least eight hundred metres away and fired just a few shots … the usual fighting distances are a hundred or fifty metres away, or even a plane's-length away. Carl's machine was seen making a left turn, heading for our lines. That was a sign that he was still in control of the machine. His comrades observed that he had switched off his fuel to minimise the danger of fire in his plane. Then he began to glide down. From the glide he went into a dive.

'I wrote to his father that I myself could not wish for a more beautiful death than falling in combat. I wanted to comfort him that Carl felt nothing at the end.'

'Is it true that he fell into no-man's-land and that a special patrol was sent out at night to recover his body?'

'Yes. He was a German hero and entitled to a military funeral and burial in his home soil.'

'And that the Commanding General of the 4th Army attended *the funeral in Courtrai?'*

'Yes, that is also true. General Sixt von Armin led the cortege. I was informed of this sad event, while I was in Hamburg with Lothar, and I called the Staffel and gave Leutnant Brauneck the honour of representing the Geschwader at the funeral, carrying Carl's orders and awards, and accompanying our fallen comrade back to his home town. It was the very least we could do for such a brave man.'

'And, on the fortunate side, I understand your brother is recovering from his wounds and doing well.'

'Yes, he is. During my visit to him, I found him to be getting on very well. He looked just fine, with a nice tan, lying clothed on a chaise longue, with the Pour le Mérite around his neck. He is standing up already and is recovering. He can go out and ride again. In about two months perhaps he will be back at the Front. But first he should be restored to health.'

'Meanwhile, you are organising the first Jagdgeschwader – all with top people, I am sure.'

'Among the best in the Air Force. Jasta 4 is led by Oberleutnant von Döring, who has been flying since before the war and has already shot down several planes. Jasta 6 is under Oberleutnant Dostler, who has a dozen planes to his credit. Jasta 10 is commanded by Oberleutnant von Althaus, a distinguished fighter pilot who already has received the Pour le Mérite; he succeeded Dossenbach, another Pour-le-Mériter, who was killed a few days ago. And Jasta 11, is now in the capable hands Leutnant Wolff, who, as you know, is a Pour-le-Mériter and has shot down some thirty planes. These fellows and their men will give our English friends much to think about!'

'If I may ask a very personal, social question: from my last visit I noticed that you use [the informal personal pronoun] "Du" when speaking with your brother and with Wolff – but with no one else. Do you – or do you plan to – extend that sort of comradeship to your Staffel leaders?' He gives me a very perplexed look, as though I am asking him to rearrange part of the German language. There is an apprehensive tone in his voice as he responds:

'My brother is my brother, of course, and our family relationship comes first. I think people understand that. Wolff and I have become very close and you know how these things occur in German society. Wolff is like a brother to me. As for what will happen to the rest of us, thrown together in the crucible of war – who can say how close we will become? We are more concerned with defeating our enemies and staying alive so that we may continue to do that.'

Once again I feel embarrassed for having probed too deeply into Richthofen's inner thoughts, which he guards jealously. Quickly I spit out a different question: 'And the four Staffeln – will their aeroplanes also be painted red?'

'No. To maintain order, each Staffel has its own markings and the Kommandeur's aircraft is very conspicuous. Jasta 4 machines have a black snake line along the natural wood-finished fuselage, Jasta 6 has zebra stripes, and Jasta 10 uses yellow. The machines of our Stammstaffel [core unit], Jasta 11, are mostly painted red, but only mine is <u>all</u> red. I must say that when the Staffeln are formed up at the airfield, twelve planes behind each Staffel leader, the Jagdgeschwader looks quite colourful.'

Bodenschatz has already told me that Jastas 4, 10 and 11 are based at Marckebeke and that Jasta 6 is at Bisseghem, which is visible just across the Lys River from here. But he did not tell me how such great air strength is to be deployed. Therefore, I ask Richthofen: 'How many aeroplanes will you take out at any one time and how will you use them as a fighting force?' He pauses from breakfast and leads me back to the table on which Bodenschatz had laid out utensils to represent the units. The white linen tablecloth becomes a sky map as he explains:

'When Boelcke began the first Jagdstaffel operations in autumn 1916, he divided his twelve pilots into two flights, of five or six planes each. In general, this combat strength is sufficient even today. The British have the greatest experience with massed – or at least Geschwader-strength – operations and for the most part they form up this way.

'When the British come over in very large numbers, however, we are forced to respond with stronger formations. Hence, from here I will be able to take off with thirty to forty machines in a Geschwader flight to compensate for any shortcomings in our fighter planes or the sheer numbers of their formations.'

'But how will you keep so many aeroplanes organised and in formation?'

'As Kommandeur, I will fly the farthest out front and at the lowest point so everyone can see me. I will have one Staffel to my left, one to my right, one about a hundred metres above me and one at the same altitude as the third, but behind me. The Staffeln will form up a hundred and fifty metres behind each Staffel leader, and all of the leaders will be behind me.'

'Isn't this arrangement of aeroplanes the way a cavalry unit would ride into battle?'

'In some ways. I led Jasta 11 as though riding on horseback across a field and it was of no consequence whether I turned, pushed ahead or pulled back. The Staffel has to keep up with its leader. A Geschwader flight, however, will be quite different. The Kommandeur must adjust <u>his</u> pace to that of the slowest member of his Geschwader. And the individual Staffel leaders should not fly so close to the Kommandeur that he cannot make a sudden turn. That would hinder him very badly during an attack and, in some circumstances, spoil the success of the entire Geschwader flight.'

Thinking only of two-dimensional paintings and other pictures of cavalry battles and even formations of medieval soldiers at war, I am struggling to envision armadas of aeroplanes in great swirling battles overhead in a third dimension: depth. Clearly, Richthofen's mind is far ahead of my comprehension and, when he detects that he has lost me in his verbal imagery, he pauses. I can only tell him: 'It all sounds so complex – how will you organise it? Right from the very beginning, assembling and coordinating all these forces?' With a knowing, patient smile, he answers:

'Of course, it will take greater preparation for a Geschwader operation than for a Staffel flight. Before every take-off, without fail, the Staffel leaders and

I will discuss what we will do, beginning with the direction in which we will fly. The discussion before take-off is just as important as the one after the flight.

'On the evening before an operation I will announce, for example, that at seven o'clock the next morning, the Geschwader should be ready for take-off. By that I mean that each pilot will be fully dressed and waiting near or in his machine – not sitting in a room without his flying-suit. The mechanics will be standing by their machines, each of which will be fully ready for take-off. Obviously, I cannot know whether the enemy will arrive at seven o'clock, and so the entire Geschwader, fully suited-up, may have to wait at the airfield for as long as several hours.'

'How will you know when it is time to take off and intercept or attack the enemy?'

'I will receive a telephone call from Army Corps Headquarters … after they have been alerted by a forward unit. Then I will call the Staffel leaders, when they are at different airfields, as is the case with Jasta 6 over at Bissegem. We can ring a bell to alert the Staffeln here. Then each Staffel will take off – the last person being the Staffel leader – and assemble at about a hundred metres over a previously designated point. Lastly, I will take off and fly to where the Staffel leaders have taken up their prescribed places … all at low throttle. While the Staffeln are assembling in the air, I will make no turns. I will fly as slowly as possible, mostly towards the Front. When I am satisfied that the Geschwader is closed up and no machines are straggling, I can begin to make good use of my machine's capability and lead my men into battle.'

'Once the Geschwader flight is under way, will the various pilots then spread out, up and down, like a great net to scoop up the enemy?'

'No. The Kommandeur sets the altitude at which the Geschwader must fly. In such a large formation – thirty to forty machines – the Kommandeur and the Staffel leaders must maintain their positions during the entire flight. Likewise, there must be an order of position within each Staffel.'

'What will happen if one of your men has a mechanical problem with his plane? Is there a procedure for him to withdraw in an orderly manner?'

"There is no turning back by any pilot whose engine misfires or some such thing. We must push on.'

'Just as your brother did when he returned to the fight with jammed machine-guns, to make a show of support for you and cause the enemy to flee?'

'Precisely.'

'What will happen when a battle of large formations begins?'

'When an enemy formation is sighted, the leading aircraft will increase its speed. Every individual in the Geschwader must recognise this moment immediately, to assure that our strong formation does not disintegrate. The moment the Kommandeur dives, the entire Geschwader must do the same. The planes will become an almost fluid force, turning together in long, wide lines downward. Tight spirals and unnecessary turns are to be avoided ... to keep the formation intact. '

'But at some point, as you have said, it is a matter of individual combats.'

'Yes, but the purpose of a strong Geschwader operation is to destroy enemy formations. After we scatter the formation, attacks on individual planes are our objective. So a Geschwader operation is warranted in good weather ... only when brisk enemy action is anticipated. In the most favourable situation, we will get between the intruding formation and the Front. We will cut off its escape, get above it and force it to fight.'

'And the best way to do that?'

'Continuous attack. When the Kommandeur decides to attack, he will fly towards the main body of the enemy formation. Shortly before the attack he must slow his pace so that the Geschwader, which through fast flying or turning may have become separated, is all assembled. Every pilot must count the number of opponents the moment he sees them so that, when the offensive begins, everyone knows where all the enemy planes are.'

'And when the enemy formation begins to scatter?'

'The Kommandeur will follow the opponent's main body. Some of the enemy will fall away ... and be destroyed by aircraft in our rear. The main point is that, by that time, no enemy will have flown past the Kommandeur's field of

vision. Speed can only be regulated by throttling back and not by turning.
'If, due to some unforeseen circumstance, the Kommandeur is put out of action, he will transfer the leadership to a previously designated deputy.'

'How?' I interject. He frowns momentarily, but, no doubt remembering that he is the Kommandeur who has planned all 3these details in his mind and not I, he responds:

'He will fire a flare pistol. We have a series of signals. The moment the Kommandeur dives on the enemy formation – under any circumstances –each and every pilot must engage the enemy. Through the brunt of the first attack and through the absolute will of each of us to give battle, the enemy formation will be torn apart. When this is successful, shooting down the enemy is only a matter of individual combats.'

'I know it is not possible to "assign" targets, but how will each of your men know which target is his?'

'I impress upon the Staffel leaders – rigorously – to instruct their pilots that the man who is closest to an opponent is the only one who shall fire at him. If two or more pilots are within the hundred-metre firing range of the same opponent, the others must wait to see whether the first attacker has a gun jam and has to turn away. If not and if he is pursuing his opponent, they must seek their own targets.'

'Why is it to so important for them to seek individual targets? Won't several attackers assure the destruction of an enemy aeroplane?'

'I have seen ten to fifteen planes following one Englishman down to the ground, while up above the enemy formation flew on undisturbed. That is wrong. A pilot is of more help to a comrade by waiting in reserve rather than joining the attack himself.

'Furthermore, in a fight with a large formation, an individual who loses altitude should not wait until an opponent comes spinning down or is forced down … and go after this already conquered opponent. He should climb, flying towards the lines and try to attack one of the enemy planes escaping toward the Front.'

'After your men have won the battle, how will you reassemble your to attack other enemy formations?'

'When such a large-formation battle succeeds and splits up into individual combats, the Geschwader will be scattered about ... and not easy to regroup. In most cases, it will be only by luck that scattered individuals are found, as the Kommandeur circles over the main battle-scene or over previously directed, determined points. At this point, individuals must join up directly with him. The fighter mission will continue only if he gathers sufficient strength.

'Individual Staffel members who no longer find the contact point must fly home. To avoid unnecessary casualties, they should not loiter at the Front separately.'

'You have told me before that, ideally, you attack from above and with the sun at your back. What will you if this is not possible?'

'Just as we do in a Staffel flight. It is helpful, but not absolutely necessary to get above the enemy. There are times when we can no longer climb above a very high-flying formation. In that case, we hold back and remain in the proximity of the Front. Sooner or later, the enemy will cross over on his return flight, and we will follow below it for a while. Then we will dive at full speed to gain momentum to get up to their altitude by pulling up vertically. Very often the enemy takes up the fight. Especially the plucky Englishman.'

'But, surely, the Englishmen know these tricks, too?'

'No doubt, but when one of our pilots is attacked in this way, he evades the attack by going into a turn at full speed, while his comrades try to get above the opponent at the same time. Someone in the Geschwader will attain the same altitude as the opponent, pull above him to gain superior altitude, engage him and send him crashing down.

'Often, such battles are minutes long. The Kommandeur must continually turn to keep track of the situation ... because the Geschwader can be thrown into confusion. Everyone should head for the Kommandeur and try to gain altitude by turning with his machine. Flying straight ahead at this moment is very dangerous ... the enemy waits at every instant to attack unnoticed from out of the sun.'

'How will you practise formation tactics without being observed by the enemy?'

'We won't. Practice flights in Geschwader strength in a forward area are not necessary when each individual Staffel flies well. Such flights provide no real training and, as you may guess, can be instructional for the enemy.

'For our own purposes, immediately after every Geschwader flight, the most important constructive activity will be to discuss everything that happened during the flight from take-off to landing. Individual questions can be very useful for clarification.'

I know that Geschwader-strength operations have not yet taken place. But I am perplexed about Richthofen's current air fighting role, as he is still flying with Jasta 11 – even though Kurt Wolff, the brightest star in Richthofen's galaxy, leads that unit. Just before I embarrass myself by asking how Richthofen functions during this planning stage, in my notes I spot a copy of the report for his fifty-seventh victory: 'I attacked the forward aircraft of an enemy formation. The observer collapsed under the first shots. The pilot was mortally hit shortly thereafter. The R.E. dropped. I fired some shots at the falling aircraft from fifty metres distance until flames came out of the machine and the opponent crashed burning./s/ von Richthofen Rittmeister und Kommandeur des Jagdgeschwaders I'

Of course, his current title tells the story, so now my only question is: 'When will the four Staffeln begin to operate as a Geschwader?'

'As soon as possible. I have been meeting the Jagdstaffel leaders to clarify take-off instructions. We cannot leave to chance the possibility that orders will be received by the command posts in a roundabout way. Information about enemy aerial activity must be communicated precisely. I have ordered that direct connections with the most advanced front lines be established immediately. I have a direct telephone line to the four Staffeln so that when I pick up the receiver, all four of my leaders will be on the line at the same time.

'Recent enemy breakthrough attempts are being conducted with a tenacity not previously experienced. Each new attack is more brutal than the last. Our infantry are enduring fierce assaults under almost ceaseless heavy bombardment. When there is a pause in the shelling, enemy single- and two-seaters come over and strafe our trenches and other installations. Meanwhile, high above, large bomber formations head for our rear areas.

'It is crystal clear that the mission of each member of Jagdgeschwader I is to annihilate enemy infantry-strafers, fighters, and bombers. Now we have the force and a coordinated plan to do so.'

In a second his mood changes from patient and explanatory to controlled anger. It is as if Manfred von Richthofen assumes responsibility for conducting the entire war -- or as much of it as his forces can touch. I sense a certain frustration that, for the moment, Richthofen must concentrate on having his units respond individually, even if in a coordinated manner, to interdict enemy aircraft along this sector.

We finish our breakfast and Richthofen relaxes and smiles at me to assure me he is not angry. But he says not a word – only a mumbled phrase as he excuses himself to attend to his duties. I cannot fathom – and do not try to understand – the inner forces that drive him. I go outside and look for Bodenschatz in the hope of learning more about the flight operations planned for the coming days. When I find the Adjutant, all he can tell me is that tomorrow is a 'special' day. Richthofen has issued Geschwader Order No. 1, which calls for a sequence of daily take-off readiness from daybreak onwards. There will be a steady rotation of Staffeln to bolster the Geschwader's presence in the air.

I spend the rest of the day walking about the castle grounds and the airfield. It is clear that everyone is too busy to talk to me, so I simply watch as the vari-coloured aeroplanes are rolled out of their hangars for final adjustments and maintenance.

* * *

Friday, 6 July 1917: It is a bright summer day with clear skies. Aircraft and pilots are on the airfield, waiting for the first alert to be sounded. Richthofen has a five-metre rangefinder and stereo telescope set up in front of Marckebeke Castle to assure that no enemy aircraft slips undetected into his sector. At mid-morning, he joins the Jasta 11 flight and I attempt to watch 'the show' through the stereo telescope. Soon the aeroplanes become a confusion of forms, moving about the sky and, even though they are less than fifteen kilometres away, my untrained eye cannot tell which are ours and which are the enemy's. I leave the instrument to more experienced people and stand by to listen to them recounting what they see.

When the flight seems to be returning to Marckebeke, Bodenschatz becomes very agitated. He counts only six planes. Where are the other three? The answer comes when the pilot of the first plane to land, Leutnant Wolff, jumps out of his machine and runs toward us yelling: 'He has been hit!' Who? 'The Kommandeur!' Where? How? No answers. Bodenschatz, Wolff and the other leaders have no time for my questions. Back in the Geschwader office, the telephone rings. The Staffel leaders surround it and, while Bodenschatz listens, they discuss some-thing I cannot hear. Then comes an excruciating hour of silence. The telephone rings again. More whispered chatter and then Bodenschatz, Döring, Dostler and Wolff dash out of the office, pile into a small car and speed away.

'I must go with them!' I yell at the sergeant in charge of the office. A good Prussian, the sergeant replies with a crisp 'Certainly' and has me in another car in a moment. It is easy to follow Bodenschatz, who is driving so fast, he leaves a tall trail of smoke on the road towards Courtrai. Thanks to the sergeant's driving skill, we arrive at St Nicholas' Hospital right behind the others. Without thinking, I run into the hospital entrance as if I know where I am going. All I know is that, apparently, Richthofen has been shot down. That is an event. Whether he lives or dies, I must write a story. Only a stern hospital administrative officer impedes my way and will not budge, despite all my protestations. 'Talk to Leutnant Schröder,' he says, pointing to a young officer in the waiting area. 'He was in the ambulance with Richthofen.'

I introduce myself to Schröder and ask him what he knows. He is a pleasant fellow and, as I see by the observer's badge he wears, also an airman. He volunteers:

'Richthofen was wounded, but he will be all right.'

'Were you in the air when it happened?'

'No. I am an air defence officer with Army Group Wystschaete and I saw it through a telescope. We ordered the ambulance.'

'What happened?' I ask, pulling out my pad and pencil to scribble down the story. 'How did you know it was Richthofen?'

'We recognised the red plane and watched as it and the others attacked eight F.E.2s. But the British "lattice tails," as we call them, knew their business. They remained in pairs and each pilot looked after his partner, protecting one another and attacking their German opponents.'

'How long did the fight itself last?'
'A good quarter of an hour. And none of our people was able to pry one Englishman away from his partner. They all flew around like gnats, rising and dipping continually, but remaining more or less in the same airspace. The

Englishmen remained steadfast and maintained absolute superiority. Our machines tried to break up their formation with a series of advances and retreats; they pirouetted and spiralled, which only exposed them to more risks. The Englishmen seemed to be invulnerable.'

'You could see all this through your telescope?'

'Of course. That is what we do. We watch aeroplanes. Ours and theirs. Overhead, all we could hear was the continual rattle of machine-guns. Then, suddenly, Richthofen's machine went on to its nose and roared right through the throng of combatants. My heart nearly stopped when I saw him go into a vertical dive.

'I kept my glass on him. There was no stopping him. He was done for. In a moment he would hit the ground.

'Then, about two hundred metres above the ground, he recovered and flew straight at me. I followed his course until he was about a kilometre away and watched him land and roll to a stop. Still looking through my glass I saw him climb out of the aeroplane, stagger and fall.

'I shouted to one of my men: "He is wounded! Bring a first-aid kit!"'

'And you went to help him?'

'Of course. He was at the bottom of the hill of our observation post. When I reached him, he lay on his back with his head resting on his leather helmet. A stream of blood was trickling from the back of his head. His eyes were closed and his face was pale. As my corporal and I bandaged his wound, I asked him if he was in pain. He answered: "I am feeling better, but I want to go to Courtrai at once." I sent the corporal to the nearest telephone to order an ambulance.'

'Did you come right here?'

'No, we stopped at a field dressing-station in Menin and a doctor had a look at him. But Richthofen was insistent that we push on to Courtrai. And here we are. They tell me he will survive – but will not fly for a while.'

The sergeant who drove me to the hospital returns and tells me that he has been ordered to take me back to Marckebeke. Obviously, they do not want a journalist nosing around at such a critical time. Leutnant Schröder mentions to the sergeant that he and his corporal need a ride back to their post outside Wervicq. We depart together. On the way back, Schröder startles me by saying:

'Dear God! I hope Richthofen makes it! Just three days ago I saw one of the other Big Guns die in a fight with those damned Englishmen.'

'Who?'

'Albert Dossenbach from Jasta 10. It was horrible!'

'What happened?'

'Dossenbach and I were friends in medical school before the war and he knew I was in his area, so he would call whenever he flew over the lines. I would look out and he would wave to me and I would wave back. The same thing happened on Tuesday afternoon as he and his men headed for Ypres.

'I watched as the flight spiralled upwards over Gheluvelt, heading for some big British two-seaters. Just as the battle was about to begin, flames shot out of Dossenbach's plane, which seemed to stand still in the air.'

'How high was he?'

'All of four thousand metres. The unfortunate fellow could never bring the plane down in one piece. But Dossenbach was a real man. Calmly, he swung himself over the side of the burning machine. There was no hope – and he jumped. Although still alive, his life on earth was over. But in those final seconds, he cheated death of the initiative by his own free will. He came down before the burning wreckage of his machine. I watched until he hit the ground, near Zonnebeke.

'That is how it is out here. Just two weeks before that I walked beside Dossenbach, following the coffin of an officer from Richthofen's Staffel . . .'

'Do you remember his name?'

'Yes. Walter Bordfeld, a new man. New man, seasoned veteran, it makes no difference. As Dossenbach said to me then: "Every one of us has to go sooner or later. We fighter pilots are all doomed to death. I only wish that I knew who would be next.'

120

7

UNSEEN BATTLES

It is confirmed that Manfred von Richthofen is not mortally wounded, but that he must spend the next few weeks recuperating. There is no longer a reason for me to remain in Marcke and soon I am on a train back to Berlin. Working out of my newspaper's main office offers the opportunity to become friends with Oberleutnant Fritz von Falkenhayn, General von Hoeppner's staff technical officer. He is an old friend of Richthofen's and, knowing that I have gained the Kommandeur's trust, Falkenhayn shares with me information that turns out to be quite sensitive. A great story I will not be able to report until after the war is over, but that provides insight for my next visit.

Falkenhayn tells me that, in addition to the physical challenge of recovering his health, Richthofen is in a bureaucratic battle with the top aviation officer on the staff of the commanding general of 4th Army. Richthofen complains that this Air Operations Officer is weakening the Jagdgeschwader's mission by deploying the Jagdstaffeln only to hinder enemy aeroplanes from crossing our lines, rather than making aggressive attacks on both sides of the lines. The contest of wills bedevils Richthofen more than his wounds, but supporters such as Falkenhayn press his case. The latest news is that Richthofen is to resume his role in the struggle against the ever-increasing aerial opponents. Thanks to Falkenhayn's timely tip, I am soon heading back to Belgium – in anticipation of Richthofen's triumphant return.

* * *

Thursday, 26 July 1917: I learn that Richthofen has already made a brief visit to his command post and, according to one source, he was even fêted by the citizens of Courtrai for protecting the city from enemy bombers. So now he is a young German Caesar of the air. I scribble down even such florid tributes for what I feel will be a glorious moment to be witnessed.

I arrive at Marckebeke Castle in the evening expecting a sea of joyous faces, but am greeted only by the sad countenance of Oberleutnant Bodenschatz. He confirms that the Kommandeur is back – but any joy is overshadowed by reports that a promising Richthofen protégé, Leutnant der Reserve Otto Brauneck, was *killed in a fight with a large British formation over Polygon Wood. Brauneck was one of the two pilots who protected Richthofen after he was shot down on 6 July. Bodenschatz shows me into the main dining-room, where the assembled pilots are waiting to hear whether Brauneck's mechanic and other volunteers have succeeded in retrieving his body. I wonder: what must Richthofen be thinking? Could his entire Geschwader have saved Brauneck by slaughtering the British horde? My abundance of questions must wait until morning.*

* * *

Friday, 27 July 1917: Richthofen and I are at a table on a sun-warmed terrace. Ever resolute, he gives no visible hint of being troubled by last evening's events as he settles down to breakfast. Apart from the white bandage around the top of his head, like a small turban, he looks well. He seems pale and thinner, but shows a lot of energy as he responds to my questions about events of nearly three weeks earlier:

'We zoomed around for quite a while between Ypres and Armentières without being able to find a real fight. Then I saw an enemy formation in the distance and thought they were coming our way. They approached the Front, saw us and turned back again. So I used some deception and flew away, but continued to observe the enemy formation. It did not take long for them to resume flying towards our Front.

'The wind – coming out of the east – was not in our favour, but I let the whole bunch fly over our territory. Then I cut off their return route across the Front. Once again, it was a flight of my dear friends, the big Vickers lattice tails, with the observers sitting up front.

'Slowly, we gained on our fast opponents. Most likely we would not have caught them if we had not been at a higher altitude from them. After some time I had the rearmost plane so close to me that I could consider all manner of ways to attack him. Wolff was flying beneath me. From the distinct sound of the German machine-gun I recognised that he was already engaged in a combat. Then my opponent went into a dive and took up the fight with me. But he was so far away that we were not yet fully engaged. I still had so much time that I had not yet cocked my machine-gun. I watched as the observer, in great excitement, fired at me. Calmly, I let him shoot, for even the best sharp-shooter's marksmanship is to no avail at a distance of three hundred metres. You simply cannot connect at that distance!

'Then the English pilot turned completely towards me and I hoped to get behind him in the next turn and burn his hide. Suddenly there was a blow to my head! I was hit! For a moment I was completely paralysed. My hands dropped to the side, my legs buckled inside the fuselage. Worst of all, the hit had affected my optic nerve and I was completely blinded. The machine went into a dive. For a moment the thought flashed through my mind: this is what it must be like when you go straight down just before you are killed. I waited for the moment when the wings would snap off from the strain of the dive.

'I was alone in the cockpit. I had lost consciousness for a moment and struggled to regain the use of my arms and legs so that I could control the plane. By reflex action I must have shut off the fuel and the ignition. But of what help was that to me? I could not fly without being able to see! My eyes were open, my goggles were off and I could not even see the sun. The passing seconds were an eternity. I noticed that I was still falling. The machine began to go to and fro, but always went back into a dive. At the beginning I was at four thousand metres and by now I must have fallen at least two to three thousand metres. Gathering all my energy, I said to myself: "I must see!" I don't know whether this helped me, but all at once I could distinguish between the black and white spots before me. I regained more and more of my eyesight. I peered at the sun and could see it without experiencing the slightest pain or other sensation. At first, it was like being blindfolded and then it was like looking through thick black glass. But it was good enough for me.

'The first thing I saw clearly was the altimeter. It showed eight hundred metres. I had no idea where I was. I restarted the machine, brought it to a level position and set it on a glide path. There was nothing but shell holes below me. I recognised a forest and, to my great joy I saw that I was already a good bit over our side. If an Englishman were following me, he could have shot me down without batting an eye. But, thank God, I was protected by comrades, who could not understand why I was falling and diving.

'I just wanted to land because I did not know how long I could hold on until I blacked out. So I went down to fifty metres, but among the many shell holes there was not a flat spot where it would be possible to land. I increased speed and flew in an easterly direction at low altitude for as long as I remained conscious. At first it went quite well. But after some seconds I noticed that my strength was weakening and gradually everything before me was getting dark. It was now or never. I landed and put the machine down smoothly, but took with it some poles and telephone lines. I still had enough strength to stand up and wanted to climb out. In doing so, I fell out and, with no more strength to stand, just lay there.'

'That must have been when Leutnant Schröder from the observation post at La Montagne came out to help you.'

'I don't remember who it was, but immediately there were people who had observed the entire incident and who recognised my red machine. They wrapped my head with bandages. What happened after that is hazy. I had not lost consciousness entirely, but I was in a drowsy, dazed state. I know only that I had been lying on a thistle and no longer had strength to roll off it.

'I had been lucky enough to land my machine near a road. It did not take long for an ambulance to arrive and, after what seemed like many hours, transport me to a field hospital in Courtrai. The doctors had been alerted and prepared everything; when I got there, they went to work on me.'

'How badly wounded were you?'

'I had quite a respectable hole in my head – about ten centimetres across. It could be drawn together later; but in one place clear white bone as big as a Taler coin remained exposed. My thick Richthofen head had once again proved itself. The skull had not been penetrated, but in the X-ray photos one could notice a slight swelling. It was a skull fracture that I was not rid of for days. It was very uncomfortable.

'I understand that at home it was reported that I was in the hospital with severe head and abdominal wounds, but otherwise all right.

'Most of all, I was curious as to who would be able to climb into the crate first, my brother or I. Lothar was afraid it would be me and I was afraid it would be he.'

I think the comment about his brother is a joke. I could imagine Lothar looking for an opportunity to eclipse 'big brother', but I sense that the Kommandeur is secure enough in his position not to worry about it. I turn to a weightier matter and ask: 'In any event, I gather there had been a smooth transition with the Staffel leaders now reporting to Oberleutnant von Döring, even though he was slightly injured that day.'

'Yes, Döring is a good man. After the doctors had finished patching me up, Bodenschatz brought Döring, Dostler and Wolff to see me in the hospital. I was still very weak and could only apologise for being out of action right in the middle of things, but I told them I would be back again, very soon.

'Later I learned that when they returned to Marckebeke, they were mobbed by the men, seeking news. Bodenschatz told me that they wanted to know how I looked, what I said, how I felt, whether I had to stay in bed or could sit up in a chair, and whether I was attended by a good doctor – or at least a pretty nurse.'

'And I understand that, a few days later, you were joined in the hospital by Leutnant Wolff.'

'Yes. He was wounded in a fight with Sopwith Triplanes. One of them hit him in the left shoulder and hand, and knocked out his machine-gun. He was able to make a safe landing.'

I have not mentioned my conversation with Fritz von Falkenhayn in Berlin, because I want to hear Richthofen's side of the story about the 4th Army staff officer. I begin by asking: 'So it was left to Oberleutnant von Döring to lead the first Geschwader-strength flights against the English?' Calmly, Richthofen responds:

'No. In my absence, he was directed otherwise by my immediate superior, who, by the way, is not a pilot. In fact, he is an observer. But he is a Regular Army officer – a career man – and he has a high staff position. So, he told Döring what to do and, as any good soldier would, Döring followed his orders.'

'And what happened?' I asked. With that, Richthofen exploded:

'What happened? I'll tell you what happened! The Geschwader's casualty rate went up because of this "master tactician" and his first "brilliant idea" that our fighters should be used at night.'

I did not understand and simply offered: 'But we send bombers out at night – so, why not fighters, too?'

'For one thing, the night bombers are specially trained and equipped. We are not. Secondly, when British aircraft take off in the late afternoon or evening, they advance with the sun against their backs, making them hard to see by our attackers. It is the same advantage we use by making early morning raids with the sun at <u>our</u> backs. As if that were not bad enough, Döring told me that he had been ordered to send up individual Staffeln, rather than a big Geschwader formation.

'Of course, Döring pointed out that single Staffeln are in no position to do battle successfully with large British formations, which appear mainly in the evening. He advised his "boss" that simultaneous deployment of Staffeln is the best use of the Geschwader. He emphasised that the Staffeln must fly together over the Front at high altitude – four to five thousand metres – and, as much as possible, attack together when striking at the strong British formations. Döring understands that the Staffeln must fly in ways that they support each other – and not during the evening hours.

'When Döring has come here to discuss these matters with me, I have told him over and over that, during the day, individual Staffels should attack mainly the artillery-ranging and reconnaissance aircraft that fly at the lowest altitudes. Those planes are – tactically – the most important and most troublesome for our ground troops.

' And "what happened?" you ask. The Acting Kommandeur's recommendations were disregarded and we lost precious resources of men and matériel! <u>That</u> is what happened!'

'Is there any way to change the situation – without being insubordinate?'

'Oh yes and I have worked like the devil to have changes made. I will tell you how I did it and I don't care if you print it!'

Richthofen thought about his exclamation for a moment. He knew that my newspaper could not publish a story about a clash in tactics between two officers in the same area. I looked him dead in the eye and said: 'Perhaps after the war.' He nodded and replied:

'Yes, after the war. Then you can tell your readers that, at this point, when we have sixteen Jagdstaffeln in the 4th Army sector, when enemy aircraft have been shot down recently, it has been done only by the Jagdgeschwader. You may well ask: what have the other twelve Staffeln been doing?

'This situation has nothing to do with individual pilots or Staffel leaders. The blame lies elsewhere: at 4th Army Headquarters! When I came to this sector, the Air Operations Officer told me: "It does not matter to me that enemy planes are shot down in my sector. You and your Jagdstaffeln will create such a presence at the Front that you will form a barricade in the air!"'

'He wanted you to return to flying defensive patrols?' I asked incredulously, having heard from Falkenhayn that this old tactic was ineffective in 1915 and 1916 – and, in fact, led to the development of the Jagdstaffeln by Boelcke and others as a more aggressive form of offensive and defensive actions in the air.

'Yes! This is an insanely great mistake. I explained to the Air Operations Officer that I have quite a different view of fighter deployment and gave him a copy of my report about what I think about deploying Jagdstaffeln in Geschwader strength, as well as what we have accomplished so far.'

'And he did not change his mind and take your advice?'

'No. He arranged all the Jagdstaffeln on a timetable whereby each Staffel has a set time, a set area, and a prescribed altitude to patrol for an hour and a quarter. It is quite clear, of course, that these flights could never be fighter sorties. They were only the old defensive patrols with newer planes. But in his view there were to no fighter sorties; only defensive patrols.'

'How did the leaders of the other twelve Jagdstaffeln feel about these new orders?'

'They were as unhappy about it as I ... but they followed his orders. From the beginning, I did not have my men fly routine defensive patrols. Consequently, the Jagdgeschwader became a thorn in the Army air chief's side. After 6 July, of course, he used the opportunity of my being incapacitated to issue idiotic orders about how the Geschwader should prepare for take-offs, fly, etc., as if he were the Geschwader-Kommandeur. He was prejudiced in such a way that it was absolutely impossible to deal with him.'

'Does that explain why Hauptmann Wilberg has been assigned to replace him?' Richthofen responded, with a wry look that in other circumstances might have been a smile:

'The lack of success became strikingly clear. The English were able to fly wherever they wanted and absolutely dominate the air. And not just over their lines. They ranged far over the countryside. Relatively few were shot down, at least in proportion to the masses of planes they deployed.'

'And now that situation will change?' His wry look broadened to the big smile I had grown accustomed to and he said:

'You see extracts from the Army Reports. Watch them in the coming weeks and then <u>you</u> tell me they demonstrate!'

He is so confident that I sense there is something he is not telling me. And there must be more to it than a slight personnel change in the 4th Army's staff. As all this conversation is just between us, I can afford to be bold and ask him: 'Does that mean you will receive a replacement for your Albatros fighters?' His face betrays no emotion and he answers only:

'Our aircraft, quite frankly, are ridiculously inferior to British types. The Sopwith Triplanes and new SPADs, as well as Sopwith single-seat biplanes, play with our Albatros fighters. In addition to having better quality aircraft, they have far more of them, which have accounted for many of our really good fighter pilots. The Albatros D.V is so ridiculously inferior to the British single-seaters that we cannot even begin to do anything with them. But the people at home have brought out no new machines for almost a year, only these lousy Albatroses ... not much different from the ones that I flew last autumn.'

'You are confirming what I have heard in Berlin, that the Albatros company is such a solid supplier of fighter aircraft that it has no competition. I have heard that the Dutchman, Fokker, has offered the government a fighter biplane that is faster and more manoeuvrable than the Albatros D.V . . .' Richthfofen interrupts me:

'But which still has not gone into production.'

'What about the Fokker Triplane? When I left Berlin, there was talk that the government was about to award a contract for some of them.'

'But it is only a small order – and every Jagdstaffel is full of Albatros fighters.'

Now I abandon *my subterfuge and ask bluntly: 'But, Herr Rittmeister, am I misinformed or have you not told your own men that they will receive the Fokker Triplanes? If so, what can you tell me about them?' His outburst of laughter answers my question and he knows it. He responds:*

'Yes, we are to be the first front-line unit to receive the newest fighters. How are they? I have it on good authority that they climb like apes and are as manoeuvrable as the devil!'

Richthofen holds up his hand to signal an end to discussing the sensitive subject of new equipment. But I know that he must have more to tell me and so I probe a bit: 'There have been so many changes in aeroplane development that I suppose nothing is impossible . . .' He ponders for a moment and then says:

'The biggest difference is the extremes in size between giant aeroplanes and fighters. You must see the captured British giant to believe it.'

'Do you mean the two-engined Handley Page bomber that was "delivered" to us as a New Year's present this year?'

'Yes, that's the one. It has very long range – so long that the crew flew it to one of our airfields by mistake. It is a colossus. It can haul a tremendous amount of bombs and fuel. The fuel tanks are like railway freight cars. Loads of three to five thousand kilograms are nothing for it at all. You do not "fly" in such a big machine ... you "travel" in it. Even controlling the aeroplane is no longer done by feeling, but by the use of technical instruments.

'Such a giant aeroplane is tremendously powerful ... with engines of many thousands of horsepower ... perhaps an entire division could be transported inside the thing. You can walk upright inside the fuselage. In one section, technicians have a wireless telegraph unit for communicating with the ground. In another hang those beautiful "smoked sausages", the notorious bombs that we fear so much. A gun barrel protrudes from every corner of the plane. It is truly a flying fortress. The wings and their struts are like porticoes extending from each side of the giant fuselage.'

'Would you like to fly such an aeroplane?'

'No, thanks. I flew in this one and I found it to be monstrous, clumsy and boring. I prefer a plane such as "le petit rouge", which allows me to fly straight up, lying on my back, or upside-down, or whatever other way I want to fly. A small plane flies like a bird, even though it is not "winged flight", but only a flying engine that you control.'

'Have you ever considered flying in a machine other than a single-seater?'

'If I were not a fighter pilot, I believe I would have become a ground-support flyer. It is a great satisfaction to give direct assistance to our hardest-pressed troops. The ground-support flyer is in a position to do this. He has a much-appreciated mission. During the Battle of Arras, I saw many of these excellent pilots, flying in all kinds of weather, at all times of the day, at low altitude over the enemy … all in support of our hard-fighting infantry. I can understand the impassioned roar of their cheers after a hand-to-hand battle … when our courageous infantrymen send masses of the enemy flooding back. On many occasions when returning from a patrol, I fire the remainder of my ammunition into enemy trenches. Even if it is of little help, it has an effect on their morale.'

'But you began your air combat career as an artillery spotter, ' I interject. 'I thought it was your great desire to become a fighter pilot . . .' Suddenly I sense that I have intruded on the rumination of a soldier who has performed all these perilous duties and is simply reflecting on them. No doubt, his head wound has given him pause for thought. Richthofen continues:

'In my time it was a new thing to direct artillery fire … we tapped out messages with the wireless telegraph. It takes a special ability to do it. I prefer to be more involved in the fighting.

'I have also flown reconnaissance missions, particularly during trench warfare in Russia. There I was once again a cavalryman, going out on my steel Pegasus. Days of flying with Holck over the Russians are among my fondest memories. But the thrill of it all does not seem to come back.

'On the Western Front, the view of the reconnaissance flyer is quite different from that of the cavalryman. The villages and cities, the railways and roads look so dead and silent. Often there is heavy traffic on them, but with great skill they are hidden from the air. Only a highly practised eye can observe them with accuracy from high altitudes. I have good eyes, but it is doubtful that, from five thousand metres' altitude, anyone can recognise precise details on a road. Therefore, what the eye cannot do is accomplished by photography. And so you photograph everything that you think is important. But if you come home and the photographic plates are spoiled accidentally, the entire flight has been for nought.

'When a reconnaissance flyer becomes involved in combat, he has more important things to do than fight. Often a photographic plate is more important than shooting down a plane and, thus, a reconnaissance flyer cannot be blamed for not fighting in the air.

'These days, it is a difficult task to carry out a good reconnaissance flight on the Western Front.'

'Yet, almost every day, reconnaissance and bombing flights are carried out by all sides,' I say, seeing an opportunity to pull out another story from him. 'And defensive measures are taken, as I understand happened recently when you were credited with defending the city of Courtrai from the Belgians' own people – and were praised for it. Can you tell me any of the details of this unusual turn of events?'

'We have been stationed in this area for some time and have seen many things. But the events of mid-July were quite something. The English and to a great extent the French flew over Courtrai at night and busied themselves with bombing the city. Courtrai has about thirty thousand inhabitants and is the city with the most millionaires. No fewer than a hundred and fifteen of these people live here. You would think that the city where so many "shabbily dressed people" reside would be quite impressive. But it seemed that our opponents derived a special joy from making nightly visits to these gentle people. They flew back and forth, but dropped most of their bombs on the Belgians. Once, I stood in front of a Belgian house that, due to French bomb hits, collapsed like a house of cards. In this house no fewer than fifteen Belgians were slain. Then there was a loud cry among the populace that gave little approval to the conduct of their dear comrades in arms. Many people lost their lives to these impudent bomb-flingers … and early one morning I shot down one of these nasty characters. The plane came down just outside Courtrai and according to the inhabitants caused considerable damage to that area. One crewman was dead and the other had been hit, although he was only lightly wounded. He was brought to a hospital in Courtrai.

'The following day the city residents found out that this prisoner was no Englishman, but, indeed, a Belgian who came from Courtrai and, from his great knowledge of his home town, greeted the finer citizens by dropping bombs on them. That caused a great uprising and for good reason. And so a large group of men dressed in silk top hats and long black frockcoats appeared before the civil authorities and asked that the wounded man be handed over to them. Of course, they were refused ... which only added to their rage. Then they requested permission to at least hold a celebration in honour of their saviour – namely, me – because I had shot down the fellow.'

I am stunned. What Richthofen has just told me could not have taken place. A week after he was shot down, he was still in hospital in Courtrai, enduring the 'tender mercies' of a most formidable nurse, one Kätie Otersdorf, who maintained strict control over her patient, irrespective of his standing as a national hero. Having met this very determined lady, I am certain that she would not have allowed Richthofen out for an encounter with any enemy. I cannot understand why he told me this story. I wonder whether his head wound is affecting his memory?

I dare not question his veracity, so, while he is in such a talkative mood, I turn back to the main point and ask him: 'Now that you have regained command, how are you preparing your Staffel leaders and their pilots for the real mission at hand: Geschwader operations?' Any thought of his having a mental impairment evaporates with his response, the product of a razor-sharp mind that continues to refine the subject of mass operations of aeroplanes:

'I am reinforcing everything I told them earlier. First, a Geschwader battle on our side of the lines is usually most successful, because we can force our opponents to land. Second, a Geschwader battle on the other side is the most difficult, especially if there is an east wind, which we must face on our return.

'So, rather than acting as a "barrier", your planes will be a <u>snare</u> and draw the enemy into a trap of your making?'

'Ideally, but, as long as we can be on the offensive, we can carry out a Geschwader operation far on the other side. Indeed, with well-coordinated Staffeln, we can attack a numerically superior enemy from above and on the other side. When an enemy single-seater is put on the defensive – if his guns jam, if he is separated from his unit, or his engine is shot up or is defective, if he has to come down low or something like that, or if over his own lines, he faces a superior opponent who attacks him energetically – he is defenceless.'

'Will your offensive tactics allow you to chase your enemy far over German lines?'

'There is no need to pursue intruding enemy formations. Anti-aircraft fire will take care of them. Instead, our Geschwader will bore through the air high up between the Front and our opponents until we have climbed above them and then cut off their retreat. If the enemy formation intrudes far over our territory there is the danger that we will lose sight of them and they will sneak back to their own lines. It is my concern that this does not occur. During the battle, I must maintain an overall view of my planes vis-à-vis the enemy formation. Such a state of perfection is achieved only after numerous Geschwader battles.'

'But, as you have told me, at some point these masses of aeroplanes will devolve into a series of individual combats. Will all your aeroplanes strike together or will you have others to "cover" you at high altitudes?'

'There is no timetable for individual elements of battle. As we dive on to a formation, whoever is first in position against the enemy has the right to fire. The entire *Staffel* goes down with him. A so-called "cover" at a higher altitude is a cover for cowardice. If the enemy are attentive and not caught by surprise they will go into dives or turns at the lowest altitude. Then, in most cases, pursuit does not lead to success; for example, I can never hit an opponent who is turning. Also there is no practical value in driving them off. In five minutes or so they can regroup and resume their mission. In thatcase I consider it better to let them go, regroup my own forces, fly back to the Front again and repeat the manoeuvre until we shoot them down. Our greatest strengths are surprise and the numbers of planes we can bring to bear.'

I form an observation and write it down: The person talking to me is a twenty-five-year-old Rittmeister, but he has command presence I have encountered when interviewing generals and admirals. The Higher Command has chosen wisely in making him responsible for Germany's first effort to deploy a massed force of fighter aeroplanes. Now, as Richthofen himself has suggested, "the proof of the pudding" will be the Geschwader's air combat success in the weeks to come.

8

AUTUMN PROBLEMS

I thought that Manfred von Richthofen's return to the Front would result in great waves of our fighters attacking the enemy with devastating success. I remain with Jagdgeschwader I in the hope of recording and reporting such events, but, unfortunately, the proposed massed flights prove to be as illusory as Richthofen's claim 0f having shot down a Belgian bomber over Courtrai. I see only small flights being sent out. Indeed, when bad weather comes at the end of July, I observe all manner of British aeroplanes coming overhead to hit our rear areas, with little defence put up by the Richthofen units. That news is not suitable for the Home Front.

On 30 July, when Oberleutnant Ernst Freiherr von Althaus is transferred to the Fighter Pilot School at Valenciennes, I ride with him as a means of making my way back to Berlin. The story I had hoped for is not to be found at Marcke-beke. And I learn nothing from Althaus, who is silent during the entire journey, no doubt dispirited about being replaced by the younger and far more successful Leutnant der Reserve Werner Voss as leader of Jasta 10.

In the weeks that follow, Richthofen's Staffeln regain momentum and the Kommandeur adds to his own victory score. But the High Up sense that he is burning himself out and order him to go on leave. One of Falkenhayn's people informs me that a reservation for Richthofen has been booked in at the Schloss Hotel in Gotha, where he plans to stay for some days. Quickly, I convince my editor that I need to order a room at the Schloss and set out to 'just happen to be there' with pencil and paper when he arrives.

* * *

Friday, 7 September 1917: I am sitting in the hotel lobby, thinking about lunch, when I spot a tired-looking Army officer and a porter heading toward the reception desk. My God! It is Richthofen, but he looks ten years older than when I last saw him. He smiles as I approach, surely knowing why I have tracked him down. He says only: 'Right now I need a hot bath and a rest. We can talk later.' 'Dinner at seven o'clock?' I respond. He nods and heads for the lift.
I learn that Richthofen is here as the guest of the Duke of Saxe-Coburg-Gotha,

which makes it easy for me to reserve a private dining room for us. In his usually thorough fashion, however, Richthofen calls down to choose the menu. When he arrives, he is unusually quiet. But he has his small logbook, and is obviously prepared to talk about his recent air combats, and so, as the waiters do their work, I begin: 'I regret that I left the day before the latest British-French offensive at Ypres, but I notice that your men did well, bringing down five of the six victories recorded for that day. All with the Albatros, I trust?'

'Yes. As I have told you, superior pilots can defeat supposedly superior planes. In most cases, that is. You may know that, on occasion, we have had to cancel flights when conditions were beyond the capabilities of our old machines.'

'No, I was not. Why would you cancel a mission?'

'British bombing and reconnaissance aircraft groups now fly over our lines at very high altitudes – forty-five hundred to five thousand metres – and it is pointless to take off against a group that has already broken through. Our machines do not have the climbing ability to reach the enemy in time. It is possible to approach such a group only when the ground observers report them forming up on the other side of the Front.'

'But I have read that you achieved your fifty-eighth victory, on the morning of 16 August, flying in an Albatros D.V.' He looks into his logbook and then answers:

'True, but four aircraft of Staffel 11 and I were already in the air when we saw a small flight of Nieuports. After a long chase, I attacked an opponent and soon shot up his engine and fuel tank. When the Nieuport went into a spin, I followed right after it until it was just above the ground. Then I gave it one more shot, so that the plane crashed into the ground south-west of Houthulst Forest. I was about fifty metres behind him and I passed through a cloud of gas from the explosion that made it hard to see for a moment.'

'And I understand that, the following evening, one of your new protégés, Leutnant von der Osten, achieved Jasta 11's two-hundredth victory – also flying an Albatros.'

'Yes, in fact, that was such a momentous event that I ordered a bottle of champagne. It was for von der Osten's achievement; not the Albatros. We drink very rarely in Jasta 11, as we always have to keep ourselves ready for action. But this was an exceptional occasion.'

'And, I would think such an exceptional performance would reinforce the value of the Jagdgeschwader with your new boss on the 4th Army staff.' The pained look on his face tells a different story. He turns grim and says:

'No. Not much has changed. I have complained to him that the Geschwader is being split into individual Staffeln for its operations. I have tried to impress upon him that on days of major combat it is necessary to have several Staffeln at the same time in the same place. Instead, Jagdstaffeln are being called to provide escorts for the two-seater low-level attack units and are being drawn away from the Geschwader formations for the greatest part of the day. A pilot who has already been deployed for protective flights, long-range missions and bombing flights can no longer completely fulfill his duty as a fighter pilot on the same day, as he must be quite fresh and alert if he is to be successful.'

'Did anyone respond to your complaint?' I ask, knowing that it probably went to his supporters on General *von Hoeppner's staff.*

'Yes, my complaint was "heard," but it was a mixed blessing. The Geschwader was relieved of having to provide escorts for bombers or trench-strafers. But when I received a telegram from General von Hoeppner, congratulating me on my fifty-eighth victory, it ended with a phrase that is now burned into my mind: "I expect that Rittmeister Freiherr von Richthofen . . . is conscious of the responsibility of the deployment of his person and, before the last traces of his wound are gone, he will fly only when absolute necessity justifies it."'

'That sounds as though you must operate on a rather short tether.' Pulling out a document from his logbook, Richthofen responds:

'Ha! That is an understatement. A short time later I received a communiqué from my "friend" at 4th Headquarters. Listen to this: "The opposition is obviously looking after its aviation forces. Similarly, whenever possible, we must do the same during the lull in the fighting. I refer to the Army Order of 12 August, subparagraph II and, if necessary, request notification in case this aspect is not being sufficiently taken into account." He practically invites anyone who has seen this message to keep an eye on me and report me if I misbehave!'

Richthofen's predicament is clear. His superiors are virtually preventing him from flying – for his own good – and he must decide when conditions are bad enough that he can risk some form of administrative procedure. They would not court-martial him, of course, but surely he fears a 'promotion' to some rear-area staff position. Therefore, I must ask: 'How did you justify going into combat on 26 August, when you shot down Number Fifty-Nine?'

'<u>That</u> was a provocation. Very early in the morning, a bunch of Englishmen came in over the Geschwader's airfields. We went after them and, some time later, caught one north of Ypres. I was with four gentlemen of Staffel 11, when beneath me I saw a single SPAD over a solid cloud cover. Apparently, he was hunting for low-flying artillery-ranging aircraft. I came at him from out of the sun. He tried to escape by diving away, but I got a good shot at him and he disappeared into a thin cloud cover. Following behind, I saw him below the cloud cover, diving straight down. Then, at about five hundred metres' altitude he exploded in the air. But, as a result of my own new, very bad incendiary ammunition, my pressure line, intake-manifold, exhaust manifold, etc., were so badly damaged that I could not pursue even a slightly wounded adversary. I knew I had to go into a glide as far from the Front as possible.'

'Despite the ammunition problem, it must have been exhilarating for you to be back in action and to be triumphant.'

'No, it was not like the old days. That was only my second combat flight since returning to the Front, but after each one I was completely exhausted. During the first flight I was almost sick. My wound is healing frightfully slowly; it is still as big as a five-Mark piece. Recently, the doctors removed another splinter of bone from my wound. I believe it will be the last.'

'Surely, the healing is a matter of time. And you must be finished with the old Albatros, now that Fokker Triplanes are being sent to the Western Front.'

'True enough, I will heal. But so far we have received only the two pre-production triplanes, which are flown only by Wolff, Voss and myself. Everyone else has the Albatros.

'After the English bombed our airfields again on the night of 31 August and early the following morning, I was justified in going after them. Flying the triplane for the first time in combat, I led four gentlemen of Staffel 11 against a British artillery-spotting plane. I approached until it was fifty metres below me and fired twenty shots, whereupon he went down out of control and crashed on our side of the lines.'

Now I check my notes and point out: 'According to the records, your sixtieth victory was over an R.E.8 two-seater, which, like the Vickers F.E.2, is a formidable opponent. Is the new triplane so superior that it can shoot down anything the English have?'

'I would like to think so, but, apparently, this crew mistook me for a British triplane … the observer stood up in his machine without making a move to attack me with his machine-gun.

'Two days later, however, we met a flight of Sopwith biplanes and they had no such illusions. Once again, I was with five planes of Staffel 11 when, at an altitude of thirty-five-hundred metres, I attacked an enemy machine. After considerable manoeuvring, I succeeded in forcing it to the ground near Bousbecque. I was absolutely convinced that I was up against a very skilful pilot, who even at fifty metres' altitude did not give up. He continued to fire and, even when flattening out before landing, he fired at an infantry column, and then deliberately steered his machine into a tree.

'But I can say that the Fokker Triplane is absolutely superior to the British Sopwith.'

'And that was Number Sixty-one. I understand that the English pilot – appropriately named Lieutenant Bird – was a guest of yours before being turned over to the military police. How was your visit with him?'

'He did not say much and, indeed, looked a bit chagrined. Lucky for him, he was only nicked by my machine-gun fire. Herr Direktor Fokker of the aeroplane factory was there also and used his ciné-camera to record our brief meeting.

'A few days later I went on leave – and here I am.'

'Yes, in Gotha of all places. Why here and not on to Berlin or home to Schweidnitz?'

'I was invited by Duke Carl Eduard to spend time at his hunting-lodge in Friedrichroda.'

'Of course, you could not decline an invitation from the first royal house to bestow a high award upon you. And, by now your passion for hunting is well known. So, this sounds like an ideal vacation for you. Pardon me for asking, but I wonder why you are not staying with His Highness at Reinhardsbrunn Castle?'

'They are having some big event in a few weeks and I gather there are many preparations to be made. In any case, I like the solitude of this hotel and I hope to spend some quiet time here.'

Well, that seemed to be as clear a signal as anyone could send to indicate he wished to avoid more questions. We finish our dinner and agree to meet again in a few weeks in Berlin.

* * *

Monday, 1 October 1917: I learn of Richthofen's return to Berlin in an unusual way. My editor knows a local man, Herr Glogau, who shared a train compartment with Richthofen yesterday and has agreed to talk about it. 'A good human interest story,' my chief thinks. And, to my mind, a good opportunity to gain another view of the complex person I have been following for some eight months. After a brief chat, I ask Herr Glogau how he met Richthofen.

'I was on the morning express train from Frankfurt to Berlin, when at the stop in Gotha, a young, agile Uhlan officer jumped on to the train as it was pulling out, dropped his hunting-rifle from his shoulder into the luggage rack of my compartment, pulled the collar of his overcoat up over his chin, settled into the thick seat cushions and in the next moment was fast asleep.'

'Without saying so much as a "hello?"'

'Not a word. That is what drew my attention to him. How could someone other than a character in a comic opera, put into a quick spell of hypnosis, be in the deepest state of rest and not move a muscle? Who could train himself so that in an instant he could transcend the borders of consciousness at will?

The young man must possess strong resolve, I said to myself, but his smooth youthful face seemed to contradict that notion.'

'Did you get a look at him before he went into this self-imposed dormancy?'

'When he got on, I noticed that the blonde young man was good-natured, had youthful blue eyes, was deliberate and determined in his movements, and vigorous in the way he handled his gun. It seemed to me that his squared-off skull and the firmly set jaw belonged to an eastern German aristocrat. But I wondered how worry lines got into this motionless face from cheekbone to chin? Had the war etched these wrinkles into this young officer? Just then I saw the two pips on his shoulder straps. A Rittmeister? At twenty, at the most twenty four years old, a cavalry captain? Then I thought I understood – he got on at Gotha, a Thuringian duchy – there was a high award under the collar of his overcoat – therefore, he must be a prince.'

"I take it that you did not recognise his face?'

'No, not immediately. Suddenly his eyes popped open, focused on my luggage rack and and seemed to sparkle with happiness. The "Prince" seemed to be hungry and asked: "Is there a dining car on this train?"

' "Unfortunately, not," I told him, "but may I offer you some bread and sausage? I thought I saw a hungry look in your eye and wondered whether I should speak to you." I removed my lunch-box from the overhead rack and, as I opened it to hand him some bread, out came a copy of the new book *The Red Air Fighter*, which I had purchased just before I got on the train.

'At the sight of it, he laughed like a rascal who had just been set free, turned red like an author who had been published for the first time and said:

"Oh no, there is the book. It amuses me very much, of course, that travellers buy such a thing."

'Then it dawned on me and I grabbed the book, opened it to the first photo page and knew then that I was sitting across from the Red Air Fighter in person, Manfred Freiherr von Richthofen.

"Have you read the thing?" he asked me. I said I had not and he responded: "That is just as well. I cannot write well. I can only fly and shoot, and talk a bit of nonsense, just speaking my mind."

'And so he told me about his adventures in the air until we reached Berlin. "I am only a fighter pilot," he said, "but Boelcke, he was a hero." With that,

140

Richthofen tucked the Pour le Mérite under his tunic so that the people would not stare at him.'

'Do you recall any of the anecdotes he told you?' I ask, anxiously hoping for some new insights?

'Oh, they would fill a book and most of what he talked about is already in his book.

'Wait! Now I remember. While we were talking, he pulled a telegram out of his pocket and said: "Look at this. Isn't it nice that the *Kaiser* wired me after my sixtieth victory? And then the Duke of Saxe-Coburg-Gotha invited me to go hunting. Now I am going to meet my brother Lothar in Berlin to stroll around a bit. Do you know Berlin? Yes? Splendid! Then you must show us a bit of Berlin, as we do not really know the city and have no relatives there. I was there only once, with the Kaiser, but he is not there now. I had a nice time: I was with a lady, as I am now with you, travelling together in a car assigned to me … due to the scarcity of transportation, I offered her a lift. I had my hunting-rifle, as always, slung over my arm. The lady had two sons serving at the Front and sneered: 'Yes, the gentlemanly officers can go hunting, but my fine sons must lie in the trenches.' I answered: 'I am always hunting, I do nothing else, day and night.' She replied that it was a scandal that I should boast about it. With that I dropped her off at her home, but before I departed I called out to her: 'I hope you will soon read about what I hunt. I am Manfred von Richthofen. You will have seen my face.' " '

I am dumbfounded. This is not the modest, shy Richthofen I have come to know. I press Herr Glogau: 'Did he really tell you that he spoke that way to the woman?' He answers:

'Those were his exact words, just as he told them to me. I did not know what to make of it.

'The train arrived at Berlin and, as we parted, he asked whether I would have free time at Christmas. He said he had a leave coming and he could meet me. "Oh, no," he interrupted himself, "I cannot really promise . . . as you know, I am already overdue. The English have long since put a big price on my head."

'With a click of his heels and a cheery wave of the hand, he surged into the mass of humanity.'

I thank Herr Glogau for his time and assure him that I will ghost-write an account of his meeting with the famous Red Aiur Fighter. Glogau will receive credit for the story and my chief will send him a (small!) cheque. It does not matter whether I believe this account. I know that Lothar von Richthofen cannot possibly be in Berlin, as the Air Force announced with a great fanfare that he returned to the Front last week and resumed flying as leader of Jasta 11. Therefore, my greatest interest is that Manfred von Richthofen is back in Berlin, where he has hardly been the stranger as represented to Herr Glogau.

* * *

Wednesday, 3 October 1917: Richthofen telephones the newspaper while I am out and leaves a message that excites my editor, who chuckles with excitement when he tells me: 'Richthofen is in town with other aviation people. He told me himself that they are at the Continental for meetings. I have booked you a room – get over there and see what's going on. Find out why he is staying away from the Front for such a long time.'

I practically run over to the Continental, only to find Richthofen seated in the lobby, watching for me and greatly amused when he sees me in a dishevelled state. After I regain my breath, I ask him: 'What's going on?'

'Nothing much.'

'My chief told me that you are here for some high-level meeting and that you might have something to tell me about it.' For a man in Richthofen's position, he has a maddeningly mischievous bent, as demonstrated by his cool reply:

'Well, I am on leave and away from my battle post and so I thought you might like a vacation from your "battle station", too. If you stay here for the next few days, I am sure we will have opportunities to talk about recent events. Then I have something else in mind.'

More mischief, I suppose, but harmless enough. With that, he gets up and leads me to the dining-room for a leisurely coffee and cakes to accompany our discussion. With no questions organised to pose, I can only think to ask: 'How was your hunting in Thuringia?'

'Oh, splendid! I got a big elk, three fine stags and a ram. I am rather proud of that "bag", as my father has shot only three stags in his life.'

'You did that for three and a half weeks?'

'No, most of it was in a little over a week. Then I had to come to Berlin. Sorry I did not call you while I was here, but I was in a hurry to get home to see my brother before he returned to the Front. After that I went to Gotha to finish up before coming back here for other matters.'

'It must have been a hectic time for you.'

'Yes, but at least I was given a plane and arrived in Schweidnitz at about six in the evening. That was better than a long train ride.'

'There is no airfield in Schweidnitz. Where did you land?'

'At the small parade ground near my home. I call ahead and the local authorities clear it out for me. Of course, that alerts the townsfolk and so I am assured of receiving a friendly reception. But this time I just wanted some peace and quiet.'

'And I take it you had an enjoyable time at home?'

'Not entirely. It was good that my father and Lothar were there, and my youngest brother, Bolko, came home from the Cadet Institute at Wahlstatt. My sister Ilse was there, too. It was the first time we were all together since Christmas 1915.

'But, as I unpacked my bag in my room, a telegram arrived from the Geschwader. It informed me that, two days earlier, Kurt Wolff had fallen in combat. What a blow! The "wolf cub" was one of our dearest and best comrades. Gone now at the age of twenty-two. Lothar was very upset by the news. He sat in silence the rest of the evening, saying only: "So young . . . became engaged on his last leave . . . no, he should not have done that . . . a fighter pilot may not do that." Wolff was orphaned early in life and no doubt his fiancée in Memel was his hope for a normal family life. Now she can only attend his funeral.'

'What about you? How are you holding up after this loss?'

'I am all right now. But then I needed to get away and went off to visit the Military School in Danzig … and then to a hunting-lodge in East Prussia. I got up early the following morning to begin tracking my quarry and became disoriented in the darkness. Finally, I came to a farmhouse in the forest and knocked on the window to get someone's attention. The dogs barked, a door flew open and two loads of buckshot whizzed past my ears. The farmer must have thought I was a burglar. We soon cleared that up and, shortly afterwards, I found the trail and bagged a buck.'

'You are lucky to be alive!'

'True enough, as I learned when I was back home, some days later. I received another telegram from the Geschwader. More bad news: "Leutnant Voss has not returned from a flight, probably fallen."'
'Then I got an earful from my mother. We went for a walk in the garden and she asked me: "Why don't you give up flying, Manfred?"'
' "Who would fight the war if we all thought that way?" I said. "Just the soldier in the trenches? When the professionals fail at leadership, it will soon be as it is in Russia."'
' "But the soldier is relieved of duty from time to time and goes to a rest area," she said, "while every day you endure – repeatedly – the most dangerous duels at five-thousand metres' altitude."'
'I could not help myself and became impatient. I said: "Would it please you if I were in some safe place, resting on my laurels?" I think she finally understood that I wanted to go back and to fight until this war ends.'

Of course, I cannot mention that I have observed his mercurial mood changes. So, as I am certainly old enough, I offer some 'fatherly' advice: 'Perhaps she feels that your wound and your fatigue are taking a certain toll on you.'

'Yes, that could be. One evening after dinner I had such a severe headache that I went to bed early. A short time later, well-meaning members of a local club stopped by to wish me well and my father came upstairs to wake me. I must not have been feeling well … my mother said I had a sour look on my face when I came to the door … and I was abrupt with the group.

'I tried to explain to her that I am little interested in the jubilation of this home town group. When I fly out over the trenches and the soldiers shout joyfully at me and I look into their grey faces, worn from hunger, sleeplessness and battle – then I am glad, then something rejoices within me. It is a sight to see. Often these brave men forget all danger, jump out of the trenches, swing their rifles about and wave to me. That means more to me than anything I receive at home.'

I should like to get to the bottom of Richthofen's self-imposed mission, but my facial expression must betray a lack of comprehension, because, suddenly, he seems to be annoyed with me. He jumps up from the table, saying only:

'We will speak again during the next few days. Right now, I must see someone out of town.'

* * *

Monday, 8 October 1917: The jangling telephone wakes me from a late afternoon rest. I am fully conscious in a second after I mumble something into the phone and my editor shouts back at me: 'What are you doing, napping at the Continental, while the man you are writing about is being married at the Duke's castle in Thuringia!' Married? Richthofen never mentioned having a lady-friend, much less a fiancée. 'I have today's Berliner Zeitung in front of me with a Page One story about Manfred von Richthofen marrying some official's daughter at a castle in Gotha. How do you explain this? How could you miss such a big event? The publisher will bite my ass off when he sees this!' he screams. My chief is so enraged that there is nothing to be gained by trying to reason with him. I can only assure him that I will be on the next train to Gotha, where I will track down my elusive subject. Of course, I am furious with Richthofen, who told me he was going out of town for a few days to see an old friend. Meanwhile, here I am, living like a prince and having a wonderful time. I pack my travelling bag in a few minutes and shuffle down to the lobby, feeling like a truant schoolboy.

As I hurry toward the foyer, there stands Richthofen, having an animated discussion with the doorman over a newspaper article. No doubt the one that set my chief on fire. I must say that Richthofen is dressed like a new bridegroom, resplendent in his full-dress Uhlan uniform and Tschapka dress helmet. His chest seems to be covered with medals. There is, however, no sight of a bride. I head towards him and feebly congratulate him, still wondering how to smooth over this breach with my editor. The problem is resolved in a second, as Richthofen says with a laugh:

'No, no. I am <u>not</u> married. Fritze Prestien, an old flying chum, was married today. Not me. I was invited to serve as best man at the ceremony … at the Court of Saxe-Coburg-Gotha, where his new in-laws live. The Duke let them use Reinhardsbrunn Castle.'

I remember meeting Hauptmann Prestien at the Inspectorate of Military Aviation. A career officer who had already served at the Front, he has a relatively safe staff job -– for now. I know he is one of Richthofen's inside contacts at the War Ministry, but learned only later that the two had served together on the Eastern Front. Made more secure by the good news, my mind is back on the job and, as we head towards the lift, I ask Richthofen about the wedding.

'The festivities at the castle were very nice, especially for a wartime wedding with fancy things so scarce. I spent some happy days there, but I am glad to be back for the rest of my vacation. I leave for Schweidnitz in the morning. Are you coming with me?'

This is an offer not to be refused. Getting the real story about Richthofen's so-called wedding and meeting other members of his family will prove to my editor that I have the situation well in hand. As we step into the lift, a porter and a group of happy young people recognise Richthofen and sing out in unison: 'Here's to your wedding!' His face becomes as red as his famous plane. All he manages to utter is:

'I am not married and not even engaged. I was only the best man . . . one of the guests . . .'

The young people get out of the lift, still cheering him. Richthofen is so shy in such situations that it seems he would like to melt into the walls. The porter is perplexed and so we ride up in blessed silence. Surely, he does not want to offend Germany's great hero of the air – but what about the newspaper story? Not another mention of it. As Richthofen and I leave the lift, he to go to his room and I to mine, he calls out:

'I am having dinner with Hauptmann von Salzmann at the place around the corner. Can you join us in about an hour?'

I nod and hurry to my room, eager to phone my editor with the good news. At the end of the conversation, he is much chastened and makes up for his earlier temper flare by giving me carte blanche to do whatever is needed to go to Schwei-dnitz. For my part, I am too excited to wait in my room and go to the restaurant early. There I am escorted to the specially reserved table occupied by Hauptmann von Salzmann, who, although retired, wears a new *cavalry uniform. Probably to impress the cadets at Wahlstatt, where he is help*ing *to mould the next generation of German officers. Following the usual pleasantries, I ask whether he has heard the latest 'news' about Richthofen. He laughs, but quickly becomes serious when I ask him how he knows the famous young* airman.

'I met him in Douai in 1915, when I was still on active duty. He and another fellow were coming down the street in a rickety little car when the officer with me hailed them so I could meet a man who was beginning to become well known. The two young men got out and introduced themselves. I have met many people in my life and I remember many of them and have forgot many more. At the time Richthofen was at the beginning of his rise to prominence, perhaps only one of many. Despite that, he caught my attention immediately.'

'How so?'

'He has a way about him that strikes me as being especially nice. Richthofen has a lot of self-confidence and poise that must be innate, that cannot be learned. For one thing, look at his face; it shows a quiet, determined and yet friendly manliness. That is a decisive trait that stands out in many of our young heroes.'

'I did not realise that he was already becoming known in 1915.'

'Oh, absolutely. Even as an Uhlan Leutnant, his name was being mentioned in Army reports. Yet he remained the modest officer from a good back-ground. At the time, to him I was the Hauptmann, the older comrade. On occasions when we went out together, he was always to my left and held the door so I could enter a room first. Later, I saw him, either with the unit or as my guest here in Berlin. He and I have sat together during regimental dinners. Wonderful events, complete with exquisite music. On those occa-sions, of course, there were drinks. In the good old Silesian tradition we clinked our goblets together and had a fine time.'

I knew this was a very personal question, but, in view of the recent confrontation with my editor, I must ask: 'Does he socialise with any one woman in particular?'

'I cannot say that there is any special one, but Richthofen has been with young ladies at my home in Berlin. There, too, he has the flawless manner, the naturalness that women like so much. He is not a ladies' man in the well-known sense of the word. Anything but that. He is almost the personification of modern manliness, and the ladies like him ... even though he does not go after them in every way ... as do many of the young cavaliers who have become famous.'

'Now that his photograph appears so often in the newspapers, do women seem to pursue him? How does he react to such forwardness?'

'Not in any ungentlemanly way. The last time he was in Berlin, we went to the races in Grunewald and for a while he remained unnoticed. That morning he had been at Johannisthal, test flying some new aircraft, and his "dress" was not really very elegant racecourse attire. In general, Richthofen is little inclined towards superficial appearances, although he does not neglect the way he looks. In any case, suddenly people recognised him. Then the photographers came. I have seen other young celebrities in such moments, putting on airs and posing. None of that for Richthofen. His complete self-confidence is obvious.'

'What happened on this occasion?'

'The young girls rushed towards him and asked him to sign their programmes as souvenirs. He simply shrugged his shoulders and asked me: "What else can I do?" Anyone else might have walked away. Not Richthofen. He stood there for some moments, signing calmly, patiently, always with the same friendly smile.'

To avoid being overly curious, I switch the topic to more mundane subjects, which take up quite a bit of time. So much, in fact, that it becomes clear that our guest of honour is late. Salzmann is about to go back to the hotel to check on him when our man arrives, this time in much more modest attire: trousers and a simple uniform tunic, but, as always, with the Pour le Mérite at his neck. He apologises for his lateness by noting that he had to take a telephone call from his father, who had returned home to Schweidnitz.

'News about my "wedding" is circulating all over the country and even at the Front. He called to ask me about it. There have been a countless number of calls at the hotel, but I spoke only to him and then hurried over here.'

'What did he say? What <u>could</u> he say? Certainly, you are old enough to get married if you wish.'

'He knows that, and he was very calm about the "wedding" report. He said something about "in these modern times fathers are no longer consulted" on such matters. In any case, I told him that I am in no position to get married now. He agrees and feels that it would be somewhat premature. I, myself, could imagine quite well enjoying my life as a carefree bachelor right up to the blessed end. I am in no hurry.'

'But, here in Berlin there are many nice young ladies who would like to meet you.'

'The girls will lose interest after reading the article about the wedding in Gotha. Besides, I cannot indulge myself in marriage as long as I could be killed any day. Look at what happened to Wolff. So, there will only be letters . . .'

'Letters? From anyone special?'

'That is for me to know and no one else.'

With that comment, Salzmann gives me a sharp look, as if to say: 'Stop right now, you fool!' And he is right, of course, but I am driven by the journalist's desire to know everything, even what should not be known. Oddly enough, Richthofen saves the day for me with a story:

'I understand your interest. It seems that everyone wants to see me happily married. Like my friend Prestien. A funny thing happened when I was home in May, working on my. Ullstein, my publisher, sent a stenographer from Berlin to help me. She stayed at the Hotel Crown in the city centre, where I spent the mornings with her, dictating my reminiscences, and then came home. In the afternoons, she would type her notes and then bring them to the house for my mother, Ilse and me to read in the evenings. We gave her our comments, and she returned to the hotel to prepare a final text. She was a very hard worker.'

'All done out in the open, using taxis, I suppose?'

'Of course. We had nothing to hide. But, in no time at all, these comings and goings drew the attention of neighbours and there was a lot of talk about the attractive young woman's daily visits. Once, when I walked with her to the garden gate, a couple of older ladies passed by. It was clear that they could barely restrain their curiosity. They stopped to say hello to me, but their eyes were fastened on the nice young woman with me. Then I got a wonderful, mischievous idea. With a low bow and a sweep of my hand I introduced her: "My fiancée." '

'And what did the stenographer do?'

'I believe she had to bite her lip to keep from bursting out laughing. My discipline failed me this time and I had to laugh. The ladies did not appreciate the joke and simply walked away.'

'No more questions?'

'Not a one. That settled the situation.'

On that note, Salzmann interrupts the conversation and signals the waiter to begin serving. While we were talking, Salzmann had chosen some excellent wine and food. A few hours late, upon our return to the Continental, the receptionist brought out a tray full of telegrams for the alleged bridegroom. Good news – even if untrue – travels fast. Richthofen has the whole batch delivered to his room. Before we part, I ask him about arrangements to go to Schweidnitz, whether we need to book train reservations and so forth. He says with a smile:

'A government car will pick us up at about eleven o'clock and take us to Johannisthal. We will fly from there . . .'

'Fly? Both of us together?'

'Yes, unless you have wings and can fly under your own power. While I am on leave I am allowed to use a two-seater "officially" to maintain my flying proficiency. There is not much room in the plane, so pack only a small bag. And dress warmly. It is quite cold at three thousand metres.'

I nod in agreement and head off to my room. Quickly, I call Hauptmann von Salzmann, who I know has flown with Richthofen, and ask him what I should wear. He laughs and assures me that Richthofen is joking about the need for very warm clothes, as the staff at the airfield will provide me with a flight suit, helmet and goggles.

9

FLYING IN THE RAIN

I marked the first anniversary of my initial meeting with Manfred von Richthofen at my desk in Berlin, no longer enjoying carte blanche to follow him anywhere. Even though his sixty-second and sixty-third aerial victories were national news stories last November, there has been little in the press about the man himself, as the War Ministry has more strategically important tasks for him and those assignments are best kept out of the public eye.

Suddenly, at the end of February, I am packed off to Cambrai to see him again and report on what he has done since our hectic short visit to Schweidnitz almost five months earlier. On the train heading west, I recall that, despite Hauptmann von Salzmann's promise that the flight from Berlin to Schweidnitz would be a 'marvellous experience', I was apprehensive about being in an aeroplane so high in the sky. Even having Germany's most famous fighter pilot at the controls was of little comfort. It took all my courage to peep over the fuselage side to look at the ground. We were at his home barely a day when he and Lothar were summoned back to the Western Front. Before making my way back to Berlin, I fibbed and told Richthofen's mother that I had heard rumours about a romantic interest. She replied only: 'I think that Manfred loves this one girl. It is an honourable man's love of the woman he wants to be the mother of his children. And I am certain that she loves him.' That was her final word on that subject.

* * *

Wednesday, 27 February 1918: The Cambrai area is now familiar to me. North-east of Richthofen's operational area last year is his new airfield at Avesnes-le-Sec. The car ride from Valenciennes is short and I am unescorted this time. What a blessing!

Geschwader-Adjutant Karl Bodenschatz welcomes me to the new field and apologises for its currently rough state. The Kommandeur has requested new wooden hangars, which are due here shortly, as part of the build-up for the Spring Offensive. I learn that Richthofen has just returned from a flight and is in the Officers' Mess warming up with a cup of tea. As we enter, he looks so cheerful – and so much healthier since I last saw him – that I ask: 'Have you just shot down another plane, Herr Rittmeister?'

'No, but we did something almost as interesting. I have long wondered what it would be like in a "gasbag" and so a comrade and I flew to a balloon unit near Cambrai and asked to go up for a short time.'

'Surely, they would not refuse you a request.'

'I doubt that they recognised us. We bundle up in heavy clothing to stay warm in our planes these days. It was a slow day and the balloon crews simply accepted us as fellow German officers and gladly took us aloft. They explained the potential dangers to us, but we said that as fighter pilots, we take risks every day. So, off we went into the wicker basket with one of the balloonists.'

'How high did you go?'

'In general, the gasbags do not go especially high. That is not due to some fear of nasty enemies; rather, it is because they cannot do any better. Fifteen hundred to sixteen hundred metres' altitude is about normal for them. In calm weather the ascent takes place rather simply. It is interesting, but there is little thrill to it.

'No doubt, in a heavy wind it is very easy for one to become seasick, but today, it was absolutely calm. On command, the balloon is released by many men and goes up into the air rather fast. Standing in a small basket beneath the balloon, you can see the whole area. I thought there was much more to be seen from inside the "eyes of the army", as these airships are often called. I saw frightfully little. It is about the same as in a plane when I climb to a thousand metres. I cannot see very much at that height, either.

'I did see the British advanced lines, their artillery positions and quite far behind the lines. But the picture is fairly distorted. As a pilot and earlier as an observer, I was accustomed to a better view. But the balloonists were absolutely satisfied with what they saw and believe it would be impossible to see more.

'The most interesting aspect of all about a balloon, of course, is when the thing is attacked and the crewman must jump out: the famous leap into the unknown. The decision is made relatively easily … as the gasbag above him slowly begins to burn and, if he decides not to jump, he is surely doomed. Then the "unknown" is preferred to certain death. The situation is not at all so uncertain, however, as there is rarely an accident connected to it.

'The young man who took me up could not resist the temptation and had to jump. He did not do it out of fear for his life; rather, purely out of passion. He said they are among life's most beautiful, romantic moments and a young man should not let them slip away. So, he climbed up into the rigging, surveyed the region for awhile, and then he acrobatically swung away from the edge of the balloon basket … in order to make the most of that romantic moment, he swung by his legs for awhile outside the basket … then a quick decision and he jumped. But the jump did not last long, for after a few metres a static line deployed his parachute. He told me there was only a short time in which he was falling freely, which of course was not very pleasant. Suddenly there was a jerk and he hung, held by belts secured under his arms, in the lines of the parachute. He said it was an absolutely secure feeling.

'By then we were quite satisfied with this "other" view of the sky and were quite happy to get into our planes and fly home.'

'So you are not likely to trade your Fokker Triplane for a balloon,' I say, expecting a humorous response. His sudden frown tells me I have touched a raw nerve. He looks from side to side to be sure no one else is nearby and then says:

'The new triplane has not proved to be the great blessing we envisaged. Towards the end of October one of our men was shot down in one … apparently by a German pilot who mistook it for a Sopwith Triplane. Our pilot, Vizefeldwebel Lautenschlager, was killed.

'Then, on the last day of October, it was raining and there were heavy clouds that hide many things. Consequently, Lothar and I went up with a flight of Staffel 11 planes, looking for Englishmen. I noticed that one of our planes was acting strangely. I could not tell whether it was breaking off or even breaking up. It began to go down quickly and then it hit me. It was Lothar! Something was wrong and I rushed down after him. It was clear he had to make an emergency landing so I thought it best to follow him. He found an open space and landed perfectly. I came in behind him and must have snagged something with the undercarriage because my plane was smashed to pieces.'

'What happened to your brother's plane?'

'His engine had packed up and he had to land quickly. We were able to salvage his machine, but mine was a total loss. The same day, we received word that Leutnant Gontermann of Staffel 15 was killed when his triplane crashed. And the following day Staffel 11 lost another triplane when Leutnant Pastor's machine broke up in the air over one of our airfields. Cause unknown. He was killed. Two days later, the Inspectorate of Military Aviation ordered all Fokker Triplanes to be withdrawn from front-line service.'

'What did you use in its place?'

'Our old Albatroses – what else? In my case, we still had the machine in which I was shot down in July.'

'You were not worried about flying a machine in which you were nearly killed?'

'Of course not. The machine had nothing to do with that. Indeed, it was a very good machine to get me through such a harrowing experience. I should send it home to be placed in a special barn and carefully tended like a good old horse.'

'Did you fly it when you shot down Number Sixty-Two on 23 November?'

'Yes. And it worked very well. First, I forced an Englishman to land west of Bourlon Wood. Then I attacked a D.H.5 north of Fontaine-Notre-Dame at about a hundred metres' altitude. After the first shots, the Englishman began to glide downward, but then fell into a corner of Bourlon Wood. I could not see the plane hitting the ground.'

'Did you receive credit for both of them?'

'No, only one. We had absolute proof on that one, because one of my men brought back a swatch of the D.H.5's fabric with the serial number on it.'

Now comes one of the hardest parts of this assignment. I find that I cannot look Richthofen in the eye when I initiate a very sad subject with: 'I was sorry to learn that your old friend Erwin Böhme fell . . .' I steal a look at him and, for the first time, I see his eyes begin to well up. He is near tears. He waits a moment and then clears his throat before responding:

'I have become firm and hard in war, but Böhme's death hit me right in the heart. We were very close friends. On the afternoon before his last flight, he visited me here. He was full of joy about the progress of our dear old Jagdstaffel Boelcke … due to him alone, it is back to its old heights. Now, he and Boelcke are united in Valhalla: this splendid comrade and his great master, to whom, of all of us, he was closest.'

'Excuse me, Herr Rittmeister, but I must ask this question: Do you know what happened during Leutnant Böhme's last flight?'

'I was told that he had just shot down his twenty-fourth opponent, on the other side of the lines, over Zillebeke Lake. Right after that, he was surrounded by an enemy flight and had no chance to escape. Surely, he did not suffer. And we were informed that the English gave him a proper burial with military honours. Meanwhile, waiting for him was a special delivery package from Berlin: the Pour le Mérite he had just been awarded.'

'And the following day, 30 November, you shot down Number Sixty-three. Was it perhaps the same type of plane that shot down Böhme?'

'No, Böhme had the misfortune of falling in among a group of new English two-seaters. They cut him off and he didn't have a chance. I wish I could have avenged him, but my next victory was a single-seater. Lothar, Leutnant Siegfried Gussmann and I were west of Bourlon, just over the front-lines … when we went after a flight of ten enemy single-seaters. After I fired at several of them, I closed in behind one and put a hundred rounds into him. He crashed in flames in a small wooded quarry.'

'Were you able to . . .?' Having heard the question before – perhaps too often – Richthofen cuts me off and says:

'No, we did not learn the pilot's identity. For all I know, he is still out there in no-man's-land. You don't understand – because you don't see it every day, as I do – that war consumes people the way fire consumes paper. We try not to dwell on it.

'The last time I was home on leave, one evening I was sorting through envelopes of photographs from various fronts. One picture showed me with some of my comrades from Feldflieger-Abteilung 69 in Russia. My mother looked over my shoulder, pointed to one happy-looking young airman and asked me: "What has become of him?" "Fallen in combat," I said. When she pointed to another man, I replied: "Also dead." Before she could ask again, I told her: "Please do not ask any more – they are all dead."

'Immediately, I was sorry for speaking out and I tried to reassure her: "You don't need to worry. I have nothing to fear in the air. We are ready for them, even when there are many of them. The worst that could happen to me would be to have to land on the other side." She did not say anything for some minutes and then only: "I firmly believe that the British would treat you decently." I told her that I believe that also and we ended our talk on that subject.'

Now, I am silent. I mention my fatigue from the long journey from Berlin and excuse myself so I may get settled in the very modest quarters provided here on the Cambrai sector. There are no châteaux in this area. Only ruined buildings left from fierce fighting two years earlier. We agree to meet again after dinner.

* * *

Richthofen is absent from the dinner table and Bodenschatz explains that he still suffers headaches from his head wound and often turns in early. Perhaps I will see him tomorrow. Meanwhile, the ever-helpful Adjutant suggests that I might want to talk to a promising newcomer. Perhaps he will be the next Allmenröder or Wolff or Böhme. Bodenschatz points out Leutnant Friedrich-Wilhelm Lübbert, whom Richthofen requested from Flieger-Abteilung 18 in December. I remark that the name is familiar and Bodenschatz tells me that this officer is the brother of Leutnant "Edi" Lübbert, an original Jasta 11 pilot who I now recall died in action almost a year earlier. But sentiment did not bring him to Richthofen's attention. In addition to learning his fighting skills at the Kommandeur's favourite two-seater unit, this nineteen-year-old air warrior had already shot down an enemy plane and had been cited for valour in the Army Weekly Report. And, Bodenschatz notes, 'Lübbert survived being shot down by a gang of S.E.5s on the 17th of this month, but he is a tough character and, after his convalescence, he is looking forward to returning to his Staffel.'

Bodenschatz invites Lübbert to dine with us and I ask him how he likes being a member of this famous unit. Full of enthusiasm, he reacts with almost boyish glee, despite having already been tested severely in battle:

'I am very proud that Rittmeister von Richthofen requested me for Jagdstaffel 11. Until the order arrived, I had met him only once, at my brother's funeral and, even at that sad time, I admired him. Since arriving here, I admire and like him even more. You might think that a man so preoccupied with one of the most strenuous activities there is and who enjoys the great popularity he does, would have no room for friendship and comradeship. Quite the opposite. Richthofen is just as good a superior officer as a comrade for the officers of his Geschwader. He associates with us off duty as any other comrade would. When we cannot fly, he plays hockey with us and in the evenings often joins in our card games. You can go to him with any question and any trouble, and find sympathy and help when they are needed.'

'What have you learned by flying with him?'

'Richthofen is unequalled as an instructor. I have been to different flight training facilities, as well as to the Fighter Pilot School at Valenciennes, and I never met an instructor who could make the theory of air fighting technique so clear to me as Richthofen does. He especially likes it when his pilots are inquisitive. He does not become impatient when our questions seem to be elementary or silly. Every young pilot who comes here has to fly a few times to the Front alone with Richthofen. After the flight, he and the beginner discuss every aspect thoroughly.'

'Is he a demanding man?'

'He asks no more from the pilots than he is willing to give himself. But Richthofen is very firm on one point: he keeps only pilots who really accomplish something. He watches each beginner for a time … then if he feels that the person is not up to the requirements that Richthofen places on a fighter pilot – either in his moral character or technical ability – that man is transferred out.'

Bodenschatz slips away from the table for a few moments and I use this unguarded moment to ask Lübbert: 'How does he treat the lower-ranking men?'

'I can tell you honestly that, as a superior, Richthofen is loved by all. You can talk to any of the enlisted men, especially the mechanics, with whom the pilots are very close … and they will tell you that they love and respect him above all others. So it is only natural that such a superior gets on so well with his officers, too. It is truly remarkable how calmly he deals with all his subordinates even at times when, inwardly, we know that he must be very upset. Richthofen is an ideal leader.'

* * *

Thursday, 28 February 1918: The rest of last night's conversation was idle chatter. I wonder, for example, whether Lübbert thinks I can influence Richthofen and help him be recalled to active flying? Surely, it is every German fighter pilot's ambition to fly with Jagdgeschwader I. In any event, at breakfast today Richthofen seems to be refreshed and eager to talk. With so much of his story already told in his book, I am looking for new insights and, even though I have been cautioned about discussing new aircraft developments, I cannot resist asking: 'Have the improvements to the Fokker Triplane been to your satisfaction?' He winces and replies:

'For the most part. Changes have been made and it is no secret that more triplanes have been ordered. Indeed, it seems that every company wants to produce triplanes these days. In December, I went with some other pilots to the Pfalz Works at Speyer to test fly their triplane design.'

'How was the Pfalz?'

'I was not impressed. Like so many Pfalz designs, it is a very nice-looking plane, but it does not handle as well as the Fokker Triplane. Pfalz is supposed to have a more powerful engine for their triplane, but it did not feel any better to me. I told Falkenhayn and the others in Berlin that, of the two, I prefer the Fokker. Until the newer Fokkers arrived, we continued to use the Albatros D.Vs and Pfalz D.IIIs that we had on hand.'

'And, as I saw when I arrived, the Fokker Triplanes are back . . .'

'Yes, but there is an even better Fokker coming. It is a biplane, which I tested at Adlershof last month. Until the new plane arrives, we have to use triplanes. The problem is not just the plane itself. A few days ago I sent a report to Berlin about the synthetic lubricant that the Rizinus factory produces from coal tar for use in our rotary engines. That lousy oil is probably what caused Lothar's engine to seize up and have to make the emergency landing ... when

I followed him and ruined my machine. I wrote that, because we have only this poor-quality oil, rotary engines are no longer suitable for this war. Therefore, I want no more rotary engines for my Geschwader, even if they produce two-hundred horsepower. When the new Fokker biplane is ready, it will have a stationary engine and I want the BMW engine or the supercharged Mercedes. Of course, if the new Fokkers are issued with unsupercharged engines, I would not refuse them.'

'Well, thank goodness, it has been relatively quiet at the Front since our success at Cambrai. What have you been doing during this quiet period?'

'Three days before Christmas we flew what we call a protective patrol over Solesmes, south-east of here. The Kaiser likes to visit the troops during the holidays and, when he was in our area, we made sure that no enemy planes could come over.

'It rained on Christmas Eve, which was perfect for us. My father came here from his post and, once again, my brother and I spent Christmas with him. The pilots and the men all call him father of the airmen and they like it when he visits. In typical Silesian fashion, he is a bit stand-offish with strangers, but he takes an especially active interest in aviation and our flying comrades. He often sits for hours on end among our comrades in the Officers' Mess and listens intently as they talk about their air fights. He enjoys every daring morsel about flying and, as he has been an eyewitness to many fights from the ground, he has a great appreciation for what we do. He understands our talk and shares our joys and sorrows.'

'Were you able to fly during the bad weather at the New Year?'

'No, a few days later Lothar and I were invited to the peace conference at Brest-Litovsk by Prinz Leopold of Bavaria, Commander-in-Chief of German Forces in the East. As the war with Russia is over, I suppose we were among the celebrities brought in to impress the Russian delegation. We rode for three and a half days in an unheated railway coach, only to arrive at Brest-Litovsk just as the Russians were returning home for consultations with their government.'

'So what did you do in Russia – in the winter, of all times?'

'Fortunately, Lothar and I were invited to go to hunting in Bialowicz Forest. It was wonderful! We lived in the Tsar's hunting-lodge and did as we liked.

'Once there were great herds of bison there, but, unfortunately, our hearty troop columns and others have very energetically diminished a stock some seven-hundred head strong and many a bison has ended up in a rifleman's stew-pot. Now the herd is estimated at about a hundred and fifty head. It is a very great pity that this animal has been almost completely exterminated by the war.'

'Did you shoot a bison?'

'No, a stag. But after we returned to Brest-Litovsk, we wished we had remained at Bialowicz. The peace conference was boring. It is impossible to deal with those Bolsheviks. One Russian woman delegate in particular was a real witch.'

'Who was she and why do you call her a witch?'

'She is called Madame Anastasia Bitsenko, although all of the Bolshie leaders seem to have false names. Everyone there knew she had murdered a Russian general during the 1905 revolt, and had been sent to a labour camp in Siberia. Now she is a member of the Presidium of the Moscow Soviet. I almost got Madame Bitsenko as a dinner table companion. It would have been a grand, amusing conversation. I would have enjoyed it, as she has also hunted down some of her enemies. Although they were ministers and grand dukes and the like, whom she had banned to the penal colonies in Siberia. Nevertheless, the experience of hunting would have been a common point of conversation for us.'

Richthofen pauses, perhaps thinking about Madame Bitsenko and her ruthless treatment of Russians of his own class. Obviously, she was one woman he failed to charm. Having little interest in politics and anxious to learn more about the new Fokker fighter, I ask: 'And after that you went to Adlershof to see the new fighters?'

'Yes, and other duties as well.'

'What other duties?'

'Surely, you are aware of the social and labour problems back home. I was asked to visit munitions factories where workers were on strike to protest about working conditions, food shortages and other problems. It was a very humbling experience. When I arrived at the factories, the workers all rushed up to me and pleaded for me to speak to them. What could I say? They did not want to hear stories about the war. I could only tell them how important their work is and how the soldiers and airmen at the Front need their support. For the most part, they went back to their work, but who knows what will happen next?'

I always find Manfred von Richthofen to be a very well disciplined and self-aware person. So it is not surprising that he catches himself slipping deeper into a gloomy subject and quickly turns around his mood:

'Oh, I must tell you about one visit to Adlershof – and ask you to accept my apologies for not calling you while I was in Berlin last month. One rainy day we were driving back from the airfield by car. Due to the rain, not much had been accomplished at the aircraft tests. Along the way, I got out at Schulte's Art Gallery to look at some new pictures.

'As it was raining, I wore an overcoat with a big collar, typical of officers' coats worn before the war. With the collar pulled up, it acts like a disguise. I went into the gallery and came to a painting that showed me in my plane, captioned "Rittmeister Freiherr von Richthofen."

'An elderly gentleman came up and stood beside me. I said to him: "I beg your pardon, but I am told I have some likeness to the person in this painting." The gentleman put on his spectacles, looked at the picture, looked at me, and finally said: "I think you can forget that notion."

'Ten minutes later, I was back at the hotel, laughing my head off every time I told the story. So much for well-known war heroes!'

'What was the purpose of your visits to the Adlershof airfield?'

'That is where the Aircraft Test Establishment is and, of course, it attracts the aeroplane manufacturers who compete for production contracts. Last year, after I had proved myself and people in the War Ministry had begun to ask for my opinion, I proposed that our aviation branch establish aircraft type tests to select front-line planes. I do not believe that some home-front pilot, especially someone working for one of the manufacturers, should determine the aircraft to be flown at the Front. Now, pilots from many front-line units come to these tests. We fly the individual types and then agree among ourselves on which types we feel are best suited at the moment.'

'The idea is sound, but it seems very dangerous to fly unproven aircraft.'

'As we have seen with the Albatroses and the Fokker Triplanes, even aircraft that have been well proven at the factory can be dangerous at the Front. You never know from one day to the next.

'When I was home on leave the last time, my sister saw me off at the train and said to me: "Please be a bit careful. We do want to see you again." I simply told her: "Can you imagine, Ilse, that I could ever die in some common way, in some wretched bed of straw?"'

That seemed to me to be an odd comment for a brother to tell his sister, who is concerned about his well-being. It is my turn to change the mood of the conversation. I ask: 'Now that you are away from 4th Army's sector, does 2nd Army's Air Operations Officer allow you to undertake Geschwader-strength flights?' He gives me a look of total disgust as he responds:

'Here, we have mostly bad weather and extremely scant enemy flying activity in our Army sector. So we have been redeployed and it seems like I have become the leader of four ground support units and am no longer a Jagdgeschwader-Kommandeur. The change is not overly interesting.'

'Then why does your Geschwader remain in this sector?'

'I have no idea. The British are much more active over 17th Army and 6th Army than they are in this sector.'

'Could it be that the High Command is holding your units in reserve for the Spring Offensive? Surely, that can be only weeks away.'

'You should ask your contacts in Berlin. If they have some secret plan, they have not shared it with me.'

I know that 2nd Army's Air Operations Officer, Hauptmann Wilhelm Haehnelt, is highly regarded in Berlin and so I cannot imagine that he is taking some unilat-

eral action in his use of the first Jagdgeschwader. In anticipation of the expected Spring Offensive, my editor encourages me to travel to other locations to find stories. Now I believe it would be a good time to visit 2nd Army Headquarters.

* * *

Friday, 15 March 1918: Unlike other Prussian bureaucrats, Hauptmann Haehnelt was quite approachable and, when I asked why Jagdgeschwader I was not employed as originally planned, he assured me: 'We are waiting for the right time.' As proof of the value of the four-Jagdstaffel groupings, Haehnelt noted that JG II and JG III were formed in early February and are preparing to go into action.

While I have been off chasing other stories, Richthofen has shot down his sixty-fourth and sixty-fifth opponents. I sense that change is coming and is, as Haehnelt said, a matter of 'the right time'. During my absence, the new wooden hangars have been erected and Avesnes-le-Sec is now a fully operational airfield. It has rained steadily this morning and the small lorry provided for my transport has leaked the whole time. Consequently, I am soaking wet when I arrive at the field and I am very glad when Bodenschatz escorts me to the small (but warm and dry!) room that is to be my quarters. I must give these airmen credit: they live well.

My hopes of spending a nice afternoon by a stove, catching up with Richthofen, are dashed when he suggests we go for a ride to Le Cateau after lunch. In the rain.

The car is a nice little Opel with a new roof and side curtains that keep out the rain. To make sure I am warm, Richthofen lends me his fur coat and leather helmet, while he wears only a leather jacket and peaked cap. He is much younger than I and more accustomed to this raw weather, so I am not at all embarrassed at being over-dressed. Once we are under way, I ask him: 'Did you fly a new Fokker Triplane when you shot down your sixty-fourth enemy three days ago?'

'Yes. Lothar, Leutnant Steinhäuser and I were in triplanes north of Nauroy when we saw a flight of Bristol Fighters. They were flying north between Caudry and Le Cateau at an altitude of fifty-five-hundred metres, far behind our lines. We went after them and the plane I attacked immediately dived to a thousand metres and tried to escape. The observer had only fired when we were up high and then disappeared in his seat. He began shooting again shortly before the machine landed.

'During the fight, we drifted off to Le Catelet. There I forced my adversary to land and, after doing this, both crewmen left the plane.'

'What happened to them?'

'Our troops in the area captured them. I believe one of them was wounded and sent to a field hospital.'

'And the following day, you shot down Number Sixty-Five. I understand that fight involved far more aeroplanes – on both sides – and so I wonder whether, at last, you go into battle in Geschwader strength?' When he answered, I tried to not act surprised that he echoed Hauptmann Haehnelt's philosophy:

'Oh, yes, now is the time for us to confront the enemy with sheer force of numbers. I took off with my brother and other comrades from Staffel 11 and later on joined up with two Staffeln of my Geschwader against twenty to thirty Englishmen in D.H.4s, S.E.5s and Sopwith Camels. I forced down a D.H.4 from four thousand to two thousand metres. My opponent glided down towards Caudry with his engine running very slowly. The fight took place quite a distance behind our lines. The Englishman landed south of La Terrière.

'He was being harassed by the Albatroses of other Staffeln, so I let my doomed adversary off, and climbed up to thirty-two-hundred metres, where I engaged with several Sopwith Camels. At this moment, I saw an Englishman attacking one of my Staffel's planes. I followed him, closed in on him and at twenty metres put holes through his fuel tank. Apparently I had hit the pilot, as the machine dived and dashed to the ground. The Englishman tried to land near Gonnelieu, but smashed his machine just behind our lines.

'So, yes, the good news was that I had achieved my sixty-fifth, but, as we later learned, my brother was shot down . . .'

'I have heard about that,' I say, remaining calm so that I can observe his reaction. 'I was told at Headquarters that you would have more information about this unfortunate event – on the thirteenth of the month, which surely did nothing to dispel his superstitious nature. Just what happened?'

'I was among the last to land. Only my brother was missing and, when I asked about him, I was told: "Someone saw the top wing of his triplane fall off at fifty-five-hundred metres and then go down in a glide."

'I went with the pilots to the operations hut. They had no news yet. Suddenly, a report by telephone came in: "Leutnant von Richthofen has crashed near Cambrai and is dead." I was stunned, but fought to keep my composure. Soon there was a second report: "Leutnant von Richthofen has made an emergency landing and has badly injured an eye." No one knew which report to believe.

' "We must wait," I said, and to keep up the men's spirits, I began my usual evaluation of the day's flight and remarked casually: "By the way, I shot down two today."

'After waiting some time, I got into my crate and flew to the crash site. I wanted to find out for myself what had happened to my brother, whose injuries turned out to be relatively light, fortunately, despite the bad crash.'

'Did he tell you what happened?'

'Yes. He said that, when the fight developed, he went after one Englishman and followed him into a dive. Then there was a loud crash within his machine. It had been hit and, suddenly, his triplane became a biplane. There he was, at four thousand metres, minus a wing. What a horrible feeling that must have been. Of course, he broke away from his opponent, who, fortunately, did not follow him. He would have been an easy target. His luck held and the machine did not go into a dive. Both remaining wings enabled him to bring it into a normal glide, but he could fly only straight ahead; he had no rudder control.'

'How is your brother? Have you been to see him?'

'Yes, I check on him daily. Overall, he is in good condition. His nasal bone was broken but will heal and his jawbone was cracked, but all of his teeth have been saved. Over the right eye he has a big gash, but the eye itself has not been damaged. On the right knee some blood vessels have burst, and on the left leg from the calf down, there is some haemorraghing.

'He has coughed up some blood, but it did not come from any internal injuries; rather, he swallowed it in the crash. He is in hospital in Cambrai … he regrets very much not being with us now, preparing for the Spring Offensive.'

Despite his seemingly detached manner, with odd little pauses, I sense that Richthofen does not wish to speak further about his brother. I mention what

Haehnelt has told me about the creation of two additional Jagdgeschwader and how these fighting forces will surely give rise to 'a whole crop of new Richthofens'. My attempt at flattery falls flat. With a cynical look, he replies:

'For many people ambition has an important role. Everyone must have a certain amount of ambition. But it should not become an unhealthy ambition. Aerial combat is always singular combat. I have flown with my Staffel against entire enemy formations and annihilated them. This can be achieved only with very well-trained comrades, where each individual is an ace and knows the other like his brother. With a poorly prepared Geschwader one cannot get the better of any Englishman at all. In that case, you sit mostly alone below a swarm of enemy planes and are lucky to come out of it with your hide intact.'

With that, Richthofen becomes silent. I cannot seem to coax a word out of him and simply look at the dreary bombed buildings and other destruction along the main road from Cambrai to Le Cateau. Eventually, just outside the city we see aeroplane hangar tents being erected and Richthofen pulls off the road. As we get out of the car, I ask: 'What unit is this and what are you looking for?' He points to an officer who is clearly in charge of the activity and says:

'I am looking for that man. He is Leutnant Udet and he is in charge of Jagdstaffel 37, which has just come to our sector. I have watched his progress for some time and now I want him to lead Jasta 4.'

So this is how Richthofen gathers promising pilots and prospective Staffel leaders. He approaches the other man, taps him on the shoulder and, when he turns around, gives him a tip of the hat salute and begins this conversation:

'Hello, Udet. Wonderful weather for ducks, isn't it?'

The other man recognises him immediately and salutes very smartly and replies 'Yes, sir, Herr Rittmeister!' Both laugh and Richthofen asks:

'How many planes have you shot down, Udet?'

'Nineteen confirmed and waiting to hear about one more,' Udet replies.

'For all practical purposes, twenty. Now you are truly ready for us. Are you so inclined?'

Udet is bewildered by the offer and is overly candid in his response: 'There are many good Jagdstaffeln in this sector, Herr Rittmeister, and Jasta 37 is not the worst. But there is only one Jagdgeschwader Richthofen.'

'And now it is your time to join it, don't you think?'

'Jawohl, Herr Rittmeister!' Udet blurts out. They shake hands on it and, before returning to the car, Richthofen says:

'The paperwork will be ready in a day or so. I look forward to seeing you at Avesnes.'

Without a word between us, we get back into the car. Richthofen says nothing on the way back. He smiles and hums a little song which I do not recognise. He has had a very good day.

10

THE SPRING OFFENSIVE

*S*aturday, 30 March 1918: At the railway station in Valenciennes this
morning I met three rumpled-looking members of parliament on their way
back to Berlin. These parliamentary leaders came to the Front to experience the thrill of victory that prevails among German forces since the thundering
offensive – Operation Michael – began on the 21st. Unfortunately for these poor
fellows, they visited Jagdgeschwader Richthofen when 'a huge swarm of those
damned English devils', to use their words, 'carried out a fierce night-time aerial
bombardment'. They say they feel lucky to have emerged with their skins intact
and have only the highest praise for the front-line troops who 'bravely endure
such punishment every day'.
The Geschwader is moving ever forward and, indeed has changed airfields twice
since my last visit. When I arrive at Jasta 11's newest field, at Léchelle, south-east
of Cambrai, and inquire about the air raid, Adjutant Bodenschatz smiles and
suggests I ask the Kommandeur. What is this? Who smiles about an air raid? As
we approach the small, half-round metal-covered building that is Richthofen's
quarters, an officer emerges still chuckling after what seems to have been a light-
hearted exchange with his superior. Richthofen invites me in and I am hardly
seated when I ask: 'What happened during the last British air raid here? I talked
to some politicians in Valenciennes who told me it was horrible.' Composing
himself, he replies:

'For them I am sure it <u>was</u> horrible. But for us it was quite amusing. We are
still enjoying it. Let me explain. With the success of the offensive, some political figures want to be seen among Germany's front-line troops. We do not
have time for inexperienced visitors – and that is no reflection on you,
because you understand our situation. Those three arrived late yesterday
afternoon in a limousine with a driver and expected to have a fine time here.
They strutted around as if they were at a party in Berlin. One fellow even
wore a cutaway coat. He bowed and gestured so much that his coat-tails
swayed like the tail of a bird – which we thought was very funny.

'Not so amusing, however, were the long-winded speeches at dinner. They
brought their own wine with them and consumed it liberally … adding fuel to

their pronouncements. One of them said to me: "When you motor on against the enemy in your flying machine, Herr Baron …" as if we go off on some sort of Sunday excursion. "Motor on," indeed! The damned fool! I endured him in silence.'

'I believe I understand. But how did you get rid of them so quickly?' With a big, broad smile, he says:

'Ah, that is a tale well worth telling – although you must promise not to repeat it or associate the Geschwader with it in any way.

'When the evening finally ended – thank God! – the "guests" were put up for the night in one of these small "Nissen huts" put up by the Englishmen we evicted in recent days. Of course, that meant that some of my men had to double up in their own sleeping quarters. All so that the politicians would be able to return home and say they had endured front-line hardships. One pilot who had been dispossessed by these unwanted characters had a brilliant thought: "They should be allowed to experience more of the war before they return home." Another pilot piped up: "Air raid!"

'Our training enables us to coordinate our actions in aerial battle … we were of the same mind to make the evening interesting. One fellow had already fetched a flare pistol and some blank ammunition. Then the fun began.

'There was a clatter inside the barracks, then the crackle of gunfire and the dull thud of bombs being detonated. Other men hooted and hollered loudly. The moon was full and we hid in the dark shadows of the other barracks. Suddenly, across the way, the guest-hut door flew open and out charged three forms in flapping white nightshirts. I laughed so hard that tears ran down my cheeks.

"Air raid! Back into the barracks!" Bodenschatz shouted. Frantically, the three white forms disappeared back behind the door. I am certain they hid under their beds and did not sleep a wink all night.

'They left in a hurry early the next morning – without even joining us for breakfast. We are having a good laugh about our brave home-front warriors. There are few joys out here; so, whenever there is a chance for some fun, we enjoy it for a long time.'

'In a way, I suppose, everyone benefited from last night's exercise,' I say and Richthofen nods in agreement. 'But I am surprised they would travel this far.

In any case, you are making great gains these days. Your move from Avesnes-le-Sec to Awoingt was less than fifteen kilometres and it was more than another twenty-five to Léchelle . . .'

'My next move will be at least as long. At this rate, I may celebrate my next birthday in Paris!'

'And your victory list continues to grow, I understand that you achieved Number Sixty-Six on 18 March. Were you part of a Staffel flight?' For a moment it was as if the extra years that the events since July had seemed to pile on his face have simply disappeared. Once again, he has that boyish quality I found when I first met him. Now, almost smugly, he replies:

'No, that was a Geschwader flight. About thirty of our planes going after the English! As we approached the Front, I saw several groups of English planes flying over our lines in the direction of Le Cateau. The first one I encountered was at about fifty-five-hundred metres' altitude. Leutnant Gussmann of Jasta 11 and I fired at the last of the opponents, a Bristol Fighter. He lost his wings and Gussmann brought him down at Jonecourt.

'After that, I gathered my planes, climbed to fifty-three hundred metres ... we followed two groups that had broken through, heading toward Le Cateau. When they attempted to turn away and head back toward the Front ... I attacked the enemy closest to me, apparently a Bréguet or a Bristol Fighter. Leutnant Lowenhardt of Jasta 10 and I fired at him and shot his fuel tank to pieces. Loewenhardt sent him crashing down.

'Then I attacked a plane with streamers out of an English single-seater group, and forced the pilot to land near Molain.'

'And after that you moved to Awoingt?'

'Yes, but it was still not close enough to our main hunting area. A few days later, while leading twenty-five machines, I shot down Number Sixty-Seven near Combles ... just a few kilometres from where we are now.'

'And, as I see from the records, Number Sixty-Eight was shot down even farther west, over Contalmaison. Another Geschwader triumph?'

'No, I was with five planes of Jagdstaffel 11 when we attacked some low-flying

171

English single-seaters north-east of Albert. I came up to within fifty metres of one Englishman, fired a few shots and set him on fire. The burning plane crashed between Contalmaison and Albert and continued to burn on the ground. Apparently, he was carrying bombs, because they exploded some minutes later.'

'And the following day you shot down two . . .'

'Yes, both in the afternoon. Do you remember Leutnant Udet, whom you met at Le Cateau? He was up for his first flight with me. We were at low altitude, when he and I encountered a Sopwith single-seater. At the beginning, the Englishman attempted to escape by skilful flying. I fired from a plane's length away and set him on fire. During the fall the plane broke into pieces ... and the fuselage fell into some small woods.

'A quarter of an hour later, I encountered an R.E. two-seater at the same location at about seven hundred metres. I went into a dive behind it and fired about a hundred rounds at close range and set it on fire. At first the observer defended himself with his machine-gun. The plane burned until it hit the ground. Half an hour later it was still burning on the ground.

'And when we landed, it was here at this new field.'

'The records show that the next day, 27 March, was even more successful. You shot down <u>three</u> enemy aeroplanes!' I exclaim enthusiastically. Richthofen begins to blush as I pull out a copy of a congratulatory notice from the Commanding General of the Air Force, and read:
' "To the father of Rittmeister Freiherr von Richthofen I have expressed my and the Air Force's best wishes on the occasion of the one-hundredth victory of both brothers. To Leutnants Udet and Loewenhardt, who, in quick succession und exemplary fashion, have raised the number of their victories continuously, I express my most sincere appreciation. The 27th of March was again a proud day for Jagdgeschwader I."

'You once said that Boelcke referred to this area as "the El Dorado for fighter pilots". Do you think, at the rate you are going, that you will repeat your success of last April, when you shot down twenty planes?' His face is still bright-red, as he replies:

'Of course Boelcke said the right thing for that time. But the sky does not have favoured hunting spots the way I find them in the woods. That day, many low-flying Englishmen were attacking our troops as they advanced north of Albert and we were determined to stop them.

'Vizefeldwebel Hemer and Leutnant Loewenhardt had each shot down an Englishman that morning … then I led five machines from Jasta 11 after a Sopwith single-seater at low altitude. I approached very close to him and fired about a hundred and fifty bullets into him. He fell into a flooded part of the Ancre River.

'Early that evening, I was with six machines of Jasta 11 when we spotted low-flying English two-seaters attacking our troops. I managed to get close to one of them without being noticed. At some fifty metres' distance I fired about a hundred rounds into it. The machine fell burning and crashed into the ground near our positions.

'About five minutes after I shot down my seventy-second opponent, I saw a two-seater attack one of my gentlemen from Jasta 11. I got behind the Englishman and, from fifty metres, shot him down in flames. I noticed that the observer's compartment was closed and I presume filled with bombs. I shot the pilot dead and the plane seemed to hang on its propeller in a stall. I fired a few more shots and it caught fire and broke up in the air. The fuselage fell into some woods and continued to burn.'

'And the next day, 28 March, you shot down an Armstrong Whitworth two-seater, which was, possibly, the same type that shot down Erwin Böhme. Do you feel that you have avenged him with Victory Number Seventy-Four?' Richthofen ponders the question, creating an awkward silence that makes me wonder whether I have opened an old emotional wound. He replies curtly:

'Yes, it was an Armstrong Whitworth. No, I did not connect it to Böhme. There is simply no time to do that. My thoughts are fully occupied with stopping any enemy plane from attacking our troops or reconnoitring our lines. On this occasion, I was flying at a very low altitude when I saw shell explosions. Coming closer, I recognised an English plane at five hundred metres' altitude, flying home. I cut him off and went after him. After a hundred shots it caught fire and then went crashing down and hit the ground near the small wood at Méricourt, where it continued to burn.'

Manfred von Richthofen has suddenly become morose. As his mother told me when I visited Schweidnitz: 'He has seen death too often.' I note that, even though he becomes quite animated when he is describing his triumphs, at some point he always seems to drift into an emotional void. Further discussion is impossible, as, at such a point, he only mumbles a few words and seems very distracted, very far away.

I thank him for his time and ask to be excused so that I may see more of his new airfield. With a brushing wave of his hand, confirming that the conversation is over, he returns to his paperwork.

* * *

Tuesday, 2 April 1918: I am visiting other airfields in the area when word comes that today Richthofen has shot down Number Seventy-Five. Quickly, I return to Léchelle to hear the story first-hand.

I am lucky to be there by dinner-time. Bodenschatz hustles me over to the Officers' Mess, where victors from the late afternoon patrol are being congratulated. He tells me that, this afternoon, before Richthofen went out by car to find a new advance airfield closer to the Front, he asked who would lead the next flight. 'Most of the men looked to Leutnant Hans Weiss, the oldest pilot there. Richthofen nodded in agreement and made a little joke by saying: "I will watch to see whether all of you are brave." Weiss proved himself worthy of the honour by shooting down his fourteenth enemy plane,' Bodenschatz says. Now, Weiss is being roundly congratulated and I am able to sit next to Richthofen and ask him about the milestone in his career. Very matter-of-factly, he says:

'It was a normal event. At about 12:30 p.m. I attacked an English R.E. two-seater over the woods at Moreuil, and just below the clouds. As he did not see me until late, I managed to get very close to him and opened fire. I was about five metres away when the flames shot out. I could see the pilot and observer twisting out of their seats to escape the flames. The machine was burning on the way down. It fell out of control to the ground, where it exploded and was reduced to ashes.'

'Were there any survivors?'

'No. And it is a strange feeling. There, once again a couple of men shot dead. They are somewhere out there all burned up and I myself sit here every day at the table and the food tastes as good as ever. I once mentioned something similar to His Majesty when I was invited to visit him. He only replied: "My soldiers do not shoot men dead; my soldiers annihilate the opposition!"'

Before I can ask a question, the Mess door opens and we hear Bodenschatz's stentorian voice reading a telegram announcing that the Kaiser has awarded Richthofen the Order of the Red Eagle Third Class with Crown and Swords. That is a regimental commander's award and highly unusual for a Rittmeister to receive it! Everyone congratulates Richthofen and, as usual, he becomes all red-faced and flustered for some moments. Then he stands and addresses his comrades:

'I know that on my seventieth victory, General Ludendorff himself forwarded a nomination for me to be awarded the Oak Leaves to the Pour le Mérite. But the Cabinet Council members proved quite clearly that I could not receive this distinction because it is awarded only for winning a battle. General Ludendorff, of course, said: "Richthofen has won more than a battle."'

There is a great clamour among the men, all insisting that Richthofen has won many battles in the air. He calls for silence and says:

'No, there was never a strategic victory. Every air battle, no matter how big it is, always ends up in individual combats.'

There is another uproar. Finally, Richthofen takes his thick walking stick – made from the remnants of an English propeller – and thumps the floor several times to restore order. It has the desired effect and he tells the men to finish their dinner and get a good night's sleep so that they will be ready for tomorrow's missions. Then he sits down and turns to me and says with a weary smile:

'They don't realise that, now more than ever, we need new and better planes. Once again, I wrote to my friend Falkenhayn in Berlin and asked about receiving Fokker biplanes with the supercharged engines. Despite our recent gains, the superiority of English single-seater and reconnaissance aircraft makes it even more unpleasant here. The single-seaters come over at high altitudes and stay up there. We cannot even shoot at them. The two-seaters drop their bombs without our being able to reach them. Speed is the most important point. We could shoot down five to ten times as many enemy planes if ours were faster.'

'What about the newer models of the Fokker Triplane?' I ask. He shakes his head:

'During the offensive we liked the low cloud ceiling, about a hundred metres, because at low altitude the triplane has its advantages. But with better weather coming, I need to know when we can count on receiving new, faster machines.

'The need has become very great now, as every emergency landing in the old bombarded area of the Somme wasteland results in a total wreck. After a fight, frequently my men must land urgently and, due to the soft soil, there are many wrecks.'

To change the direction of the conversation, I pull out a copy of Richthofen's book, in which I have underlined some points to discuss with him. Before I can ask, he laughs out loud as his frame of mind becomes more positive. He points to the small yellow-covered paperback volume and exclaims:

'Ach, the book! Now even <u>you</u> have it! Ever since it came out I have received many letters and cards from people who write how much they like it. That really makes me very happy. I read them all, but I doubt if I can reply to half of them. I try to write to as many people as possible.

'It is very amusing to see the various impressions the book makes on different readers. For instance, a comrade who is probably a great glutton and who is obviously profiting from the war writes: "Very honoured comrade, please write to me immediately where you managed to obtain oysters. I would also like to eat oysters." '

'Referring to that time, over a year ago, when you were royally "entertained" by the engineering officer at Hénin-Liétard?'

'Yes! I couldn't stop laughing when I received this letter! I vaguely remember mentioning oysters, but this fellow thinks the oyster affair is the quintessence of the book.

'A schoolboy sent me a hand mirror and noted that he had concluded from the book that I was lacking such an instrument in my red plane.

'A young woman from a well-known family wrote to tell me that, even though she is a novice and will become a nun, she kept a postcard photo of me in her cell. One day the abbess saw the picture and scolded her for keeping a picture of a man, even if he is a fighter pilot in the nation's service. She was ordered to remove the picture. But what do you suppose this clever girl did? She obtained a similar-sized photo from a friend who is a nun and cut out her friend's face and placed the rest over my photo – so my "sweet" face peers out from under a nun's habit!

'And I receive an extraordinary amount of mail from the Cadet Corps. The cadets write to me that they share my opinions of teachers. Theirs also give them trouble, and they learn only what is most necessary in order to be promoted.

'My youngest brother, Bolko, wrote a long letter of complaint to the family. He is a cadet at Wahlstatt and complains that I portrayed the teachers in the Cadet Corps badly in my book. He is having so much unpleasantness in the Corps that he can no longer bear it. He asks the family to see to it that I first submit the manuscript of my next book for his approval. I think he demands quite a bit of me, good Bolko, besides accusing me of lies. I wrote that I once clambered up the church tower in Wahlstatt and tied a handkerchief there. Bolko has established beyond a doubt that the handkerchief no longer hangs there, and that because of that I could scarcely have told the truth. I think it is too much to ask of a handkerchief to adorn a church tower for fifteen years.'

'Why would you tie a handkerchief on a church tower?' I ask, even though I recognise instantly that Richthofen's adventurous nature must be boundless. Grinning broadly, he replies:

"I like to take risks. One fine day my best friend, Frankenberg, and I climbed the well-known steeple of Wahlstatt by shinnying up the lightning rod. I tied my handkerchief to the top of the steeple. I remember vividly how difficult it had been to negotiate the gutters along the way. When I visited Bolko at Wahlstatt ten years later, I saw my handkerchief still tied high in the air.'

'Who is this Frankenberg? He sounds as though he would make an ideal pilot.'

'My friend – Helmut von Frankenberg und Ludwigsdorf, to be entirely correct – fell very early in the war. In August 1914. He was a fellow Silesian and, even though he was a year younger than I, we became the closest of friends. When I shot down my forty-seventh enemy plane, on 23 April 1917, I remembered that day would have been Frankenberg's twenty-fourth birthday. In my mind, I can still see him, following me up the steeple as seriously as if we were on a military mission of the greatest importance. He became a Grenadier officer. What a fine fellow he was . . . '

* * *

177

Wednesday, 3 April 1918: It is becoming very painful to me when I inadvertently touch on an emotional subject, as I did last night with my question about Richthofen's Cadet Corps friend. His face takes on such a haunted look. I make a note to myself to be sure I am not with him twenty days from now, which will be the anniversary of Frankenberg's birthday.

Leutnant Ernst Udet, the impishly smug Bavarian who is Richthofen's current protégé, has a terrible ear infection and must go to a hospital in Valenciennes. I ask to accompany him to learn more about the Kommandeur – although my real need is to be away from Léchelle. Through some bit of administrative magic, Richthofen arranges for a big Benz landau, a very elegant and comfortable car, to take us up north to Valenciennes.

Although his injury is obviously uncomfortable, Udet is very talkative. Indeed, he begins the conversation by saying he has discovered the secret of Richthofen's success:

'Other Staffeln take over castles, villas or small villages twenty or thirty kilometres behind the front-lines. The Richthofen-Geschwader resides in corrugated metal sheds that can be taken down and reassembled in a few hours. They seldom stay more than twenty kilometres behind the Front. Other Staffeln take off two to three times a day; Richthofen and his people go up five times. Others cancel flight operations in bad weather; we fly continually.

'Most surprising to me are the advance landing fields. They were Boelcke's idea and Richthofen, his most gifted pupil, continues to use them. Only a few kilometres behind the Front, often within reach of enemy shells, we all lie suited up in deck-chairs in the middle of open fields, with our aircraft ready to take off nearby. As soon as we spot an opponent on the horizon, we take off. Sometimes just one or two or three of us; other times the entire Staffel.

'Immediately after a fight we land, stretch out in our chairs again, search the skies with binoculars and wait for the next opponent. There are no defensive patrols, as Richthofen sees no use for them. "Such outposts in the sky weaken a fighter pilot's eagerness for battle," he says. These days he likes to patrol over the enemy rear areas. So we go up only to fight.'

'When you came to Jasta 11, you were already a proven fighter pilot and a Staffel leader. Did the Kommandeur simply let you go after the enemy in the ways you have learned?'

'Oh no. He is very careful. I arrived at the Geschwader at about ten in the morning and at noon that day I took off on my first flight with Jagdstaffel 11, led by Richthofen himself. He places a great value on personally testing every newcomer, no matter how experienced the man may be.

'It was the first time I had flown a Fokker Triplane, so I followed the Rittmeister. In fact, Vizefeldwebel Scholtz and I were fourth and fifth at the end of the formation. We swept over the shell holes, heading west at about five hundred metres.

'There was an English R.E. observation plane over the riddled ruins of Albert, below the low-hanging cloud cover. No doubt he was working with his artillery batteries. We were lower than he probably didn't notice us, because he calmly continued to circle the area. I exchanged a quick glance with Scholtz. He nodded in agreement and I left the flight to rush towards the Englishman. I came up under his nose like a shark and fired from a short distance. His engine seized up. He rolled over and the burning wreckage fell near Albert.'

'Where was the Rittmeister while all of this as going on?'

'Watching. He seems to have eyes everywhere. When I rejoined the Staffel, he looked over at me and waved in greeting to let me know that he had seen my handiwork, and immediately led us towards the old Roman Road out of Albert. Through the latticework of barren trees he had spotted a column of retreating Englishmen, marching westwards. Nearby, there was a flight of Sopwith Camels to protect them. My mind had hardly grasped the entire picture when Richthofen went zooming after them in his red Fokker. We were right behind him. The Sopwiths scattered like chicks when a hawk swoops down.'

'I gather that this was when he shot down his seventy-first?'

'I don't know what number it was, but he closed in on the Englishman so fast that I thought he was going to crash into him. He couldn't have been more than ten metres away when he opened fire and sent the Sopwith down with a plume of fuel and smoke trailing behind.'

'I know he was credited with two more victories that day, but not until early evening. What did you do after scoring these morning victories – his and yours?'

179

'We followed Richthofen, who, like the Staffel's steely wedge, continued down towards the Roman Road. At about ten metres' altitude, he flew level with the ground and fired both machine-guns continuously at the column of men on the road below. We were right behind him and also fired our guns. A dreadful fright seemed to paralyse the troops. As our shots kicked up the dirt only a few leaped into the roadside trenches and the rest fell where they stood.

'At the end of this stretch of road, the Rittmeister made a tight turn-around and flew back the same way, just over the treetops. Now we could see what we had done. But this time the infantrymen were ready and fired back. One man in a trench even had a machine-gun. But, even though the Rittmeister's wings were being hit by bullets, he flew right along, firing all the way. We did the same. The Staffel moved as if it were a solid mass held together by his willpower. When he pulled out and climbed to five hundred metres, we were right with him and stayed with him all the way back to the airfield.'

'Did he say anything to you after the flight?'

'While my mechanics looked at the damage to my machine, he walked over to me and, with that thin-lipped smile of his, asked: "Do you always fire from so far back?" I said: "I have had some success doing it that way." He just laughed and turned to go, saying over his shoulder: "Well, you can take over Staffel 11 in the morning." I knew I would lead a Staffel, but the method of informing me surprised me a bit.'

'Do you socialise with him at all? Can you tell me anything about him from a personal standpoint?'

'To be sure, he eats, drinks and sleeps like everyone else. But he eats, sleeps and drinks to fight. When our food supplies begin to dwindle, he sends Bodenschatz, the very model of an adjutant, to the rear with an old box to request provisions for us, and Bodenschatz always takes a pile of photos with Richthofen's handwritten inscription "dedicated to my dear comrade in arms" on each. These photos are highly prized among rear area supply officers, who send back a veritable feast.'

As Udet has a bit of an ego himself, he begins to tell me about his aerial adventures, which he is writing down with a view to producing a book. He has quali-

fied for the Pour le Mérite and, he lets slip, he is hopeful that his home state of Bavaria will honour him with its highest award, the Military Order of Max-Joseph, which carries with it a lifetime elevation to the nobility. That would be a nice boost for a man from modest circumstances. Everything around us seems so dreary, but Udet seems to smell the scent of victory and is beginning to think about his career after the war.

* * *

Friday, 12 April 1918: Five days ago Richthofen shot down Number Seventy-Eight. No doubt he will soon double Boelcke's victory score of forty and then go on to even greater triumphs. Now his airfield is at Cappy, more than twenty kilometres south-west of Léchelle, and so he is moving as fast as he said he would.

The Kommandeur is occupied at the moment and Bodenschatz introduces me to another Richthofen assigned to Jasta 11. This is Wolfram, a twenty-two-year-old cousin and former hussar, who has fought on the Eastern and Western Fronts. He says little so I can only wonder how he will turn out. At length the Kommandeur returns, greets me warmly and takes me to his office. I congratulate him on his latest victories, to which he only shrugs. 'Oh, come on, now,' I chide in a fatherly sort of way. 'Tell me all about them, beginning with Number Seventy-Six on 6 April.' He feigns a protest and then tells me the details:

'But you have heard and read so many of these stories before. Well, I got only one that day. As usual, I led five planes of Staffel 11 against enemy single-seaters flying at low altitude near Villers- Bretonneux. The Englishman I attacked began to burn after only a few shots from my gun. Then it crashed to the ground in the small woods outside Villers-Bretonneux and continued to burn.'

'The following day, as you know, I got two. Late in the morning, I went with four machines of Staffel 11 and we attacked several S.E.5s near Hangard, south of Villers-Bretonneux. I shot at an enemy plane some two hundred metres away and, after I had fired a hundred rounds, it broke apart. The remnants came down near Hangard.'

'A little over half an hour later, I observed three Germans pursuing an Englishman and attacking him from the rear. I dashed to their aid and attacked an English plane until it fell. The plane smashed into the ground and was reduced to splinters.'

'With seventy-eight enemy planes to your credit, you are among the most famous men in the world,' I practically shout at him. Richthofen swings back in his chair with his hands over his ears, as if to deny his status. His smile fades as he locks his eyes on to mine and he says:

'Famous? What is so wonderful about being famous?'

Trying a light-hearted approach, I remind him: 'Well, Bodenschatz says that he can take a pack of postcards signed by you and come back from the supply depot with enough food to feed the Geschwader for some time. People want a remembrance of you because you are famous.'

'I wonder how many of those postcards will be kept as mementoes and how many will be converted to cash? I say that because, after the first postcard appeared, a woman stopped me on the street in Berlin and asked me to sign fifty of them for her. They cost her twenty Pfennigs apiece and so I was flattered that she would spend so much money for souvenirs. Later I saw her selling them on the street for one Reichsmark apiece. So she turned her ten-Mark "investment" into a quick profit of forty Marks. After that, when I went home to Schweidnitz and a woman asked me to autograph a hundred cards, I became furious with her, which made my mother angry with me because of my outburst. So much for fame. I simply want to do my job.'

Once again, the dark side of Richthofen's personality surfaces. By now I know that such spells last longer and longer. Even though I have only recently arrived at Cappy, it might be good for me to move out.

11

THE LAST FLIGHT

*S*aturday, 20 April 1918: As I make my way towards the Front by lorry and *car, there are reports that today Manfred von Richthofen shot down two more enemy airplanes – his seventy-ninth and eightieth victories – a stunning achievement. His score is exactly twice that of his mentor, the great Oswald Boelcke. Only bad weather during the past four days has kept him from achieving this goal sooner, but today's clear skies brought victory.*

Upon arrival at Cappy airfield in the early evening, I find a festive mood like that of a front-line Oktoberfest. The whole place is a hive of activity. Men running in and out of various huts, apparently sampling various beverages while repeating the good news and loving the sound of it, unable to contain their enthusiasm. They say that the Kommandeur's latest triumphs are wonderfully symbolic of the German Army's spring offensive. The men are convinced that their field grey troops will smash the Tommy soldiers just as their great air hero has knocked down Tommy's best fighter planes.

It is impossible to speak with Richthofen during dinner, amid the celebrations. Afterwards, he offers his usual shy smile and, with a quick motion of the hand that has guided his planes with deadly efficiency, signals me to join him. We leave the Officer' Mess and head for his quarters, where he customarily retreats during even the most deserved of festivities. His small workroom is as sparse as a monk's cell, but it offers the solitude he seems to crave. Then, as we settle in our chairs, he beams in a way that indicates that he already knows what I am going to say, but the thought is so incredible that, like his overjoyed comrades, I must give voice to it: 'Now you have shot down eighty enemy aeroplanes!'

'Yes. Eighty. A respectable number, don't you think? It has been a good day, even though this morning's fine weather turned cloudy. At first, it looked as though we would have nothing to report. But then we saw a large flight of English planes crossing the lines. Perhaps they were emboldened because there were only six of us. We dived down … they came up at us eagerly, like brown-coloured spear-points. Then, just before we smashed into each other, everyone scattered and went off, looking for targets.

'Manoeuvring for position amid the swirl of planes, I saw one of my triplanes being fired at from below by a Sopwith Camel. Immediately, I flew round and got above and behind the Camel and dived at him. I came so close that it took only a few shots to send him down in flames. He crashed and burned on the ground.

'I pulled up and, a few minutes later, I went after another Camel. I followed him into a dive and, when he pulled up, I did the same and lost some distance. He did that again and again, no doubt thinking that he could shake me off. But I waited until I had come close to him and then fired about fifty rounds at him. His fuselage caught fire and he crashed.

'Do you know what happened to the two pilots you shot down?'

'No. There were still many English planes above me and I had to watch out for them and see whether any of my men needed help. These men crashed behind our lines and, if they survived, were taken prisoner by our ground troops. On the way back to Cappy, I flew low over our troops and waved to them. They know my red bird by now and help to confirm my victories.'

'The spring offensive has gone on for more than a month and, with this latest pair, you have shot down fifteen during that time. Will you go on leave soon and get some rest?'

'Yes, I will get away for a short time. Next week, in fact, one of my best young pilots, Hans Joachim Wolff, and I are scheduled to take a short leave to go hunting in the Black Forest. It is not that far from the Front and the rest will do us good.

'Now, I am tired and in wretched spirits after every fight. But that is surely one of the consequences of my head wound. Lately, when I put my foot on the ground again, I come directly to this place. I do not want to see anyone or hear anything.'

He points to the blanket separating this space from another and continues:

'On the ceiling of my bedroom, there is a lamp that I had made from the rotary engine of a plane that I shot down. I had light bulbs mounted in the cylinders and at night, when I lie awake and let the light burn, Lord knows, this chandelier on the ceiling looks fantastic and weird enough. When I lie there like that I have much to think about.

'I now feel that the image of the "red air fighter" has exposed people to quite another Richthofen than I truly am deep inside of myself. Things are very different now, from when I wrote my book last year. I no longer feel so impudent. Not because I can imagine how it would be one day when death is breathing down my neck; surely not for that reason, although I have thought often enough that it can happen. People "higher up" – and even my father – have told me that I should give up flying, because one day it will catch up with me. I would be miserable with myself if now, weighed down with glory and decorations, I were to hide behind my own dignity in order to save my precious life for the nation ... while those poor fellows in the trenches continue to endure their duties.

'I am considering doing a continuation of *The Red Air Fighter* and, indeed, for quite a good reason. The battle now taking place on all fronts has become dreadfully serious; there is nothing left of the "lively, merry war", as we thought of it at the beginning. Now we must arm ourselves against despair and prevent the enemy from violating our homeland.

'I believe that the war is not as the people at home imagine it, with a hurrah and a roar; it is very serious, very grim.'

He seems to be trying to smile, to put up a brave front. But his acting skills – or whatever special inner forces he has – fail him. He looks so sad. By now, he and I have a little game we play at this point in our conversation. I know he does not want to talk further, but does not want to be rude, so – as usual – I make the excuse that I am tired and need to rest. I can only hope that he will be able to find some escape in sleep.

* * *

Sunday, 21 April 1918: It begins as a bright day, with sunshine and a strong wind out of the east, blowing away the mist. At a late breakfast, Rittmeister von Richthofen is in wonderful spirits, enjoying the glorious weather. He lets loose a big belly-laugh when I say that his gaudily painted aeroplanes look like medieval war horses, ready for the joust. Still chuckling, he says:

'You may have a point there. Air battles in this war are all that remain of knights in individual combat. A hundred years ago, the leader of an army stood on his field commander's promontory, directing the battle from there and, when things went awry, rode off to lead the battle himself. These days, the army leader seems to be on the telephone forever, has a map under his nose and storms the English positions with little paper flags. It is not at all like that in the air, where there is no General Staff officer to lead the attack against an enemy formation. The chart-makers are truly sorry that they cannot devise theoretical air battles. There is no turning a flank or attack from the rear.'

Ah, this is the Richthofen I want to hear! Animated and alive with ideas! His keen mind is ready to solve any problem. I ask: 'Do you have some special way to use your guns on this new battlefield of the air? Some way that perhaps will be charted for the benefit of future military airmen?' He blurts out excitedly:

'No, no, it is not just a matter of weaponry! When I attack an enemy, I say that I do it "with the plane" and not "with the machine-gun" and I do that on purpose. Aerial combat is not the usual shooting with a firearm – not at all! It involves manoeuvring and aiming with the entire plane. Now, as we enter the final battles of the war, you can expect to see hundreds of such planes within quite a small space during major battles. The machine is an extension of the man. It goes where he wills it to go.'

'Have I missed something since we last talked or have you refined some of your thinking on aerial combat?'

'Perhaps I have. It is on my mind constantly. You must remember that when I first flew, in a two-seater, I had to act defensively so as not to be shot down. And then I went to a Fokker Eindecker, in which I could not fly defensively, but only offensively. I have learned that a cautious fighter pilot can never be effective.'

Still concerned about the haggard-looking Richthofen whom I saw last evening, I probe a bit: 'Do you mean that a combat pilot must continually seek danger to prove his worth?' He pauses before replying:

'Normally, a fighter pilot passes through the following phases: He arrives as a young pilot, intending to fight, shoot down the enemy and be successful. He goes at it with great fervour, but catches on very quickly when an experienced Englishman fills his crate full of holes. This situation repeats itself a few times until – if he survives – his recklessness is singed and he becomes fully aware of the danger of what he is doing. Then comes a critical moment: he realises that this business is mortally dangerous and not as simple as he thought. Now he must fight his fear and attack the enemy with the same recklessness he had at the beginning – and that combination of fear and courage will lead to success. He must not lose his nerve. Boelcke once said: "When you show your nerve, anything can be forgiven."

'In addition to raw courage and unbending will, a pilot needs above all to have a good eye in order to defeat his opponent. He can of course wear pince-nez or a monocle. For example, despite the fact that Kurt Wintgens, one of the first fighter pilots, was near-sighted, he shot down twenty Englishmen.

I hesitate to remind Richthofen that Wintgens himself was shot down. There is no need to, as he continues to reinforce the value of courage by mentioning another comrade who has since gone to Valhalla:

'And the Bavarian pilot Oberleutnant Kirmaier, Boelcke's successor, maintained that he could fly only in a straight line. The list goes on and on. All good men who pursued their objectives relentlessly!'

Richthofen's high spirits are so infectious that they inspire me to ask an imperti-
nent question: "Rumour has it that, when mail was distributed before breakfast
today, you received a perfumed envelope, addressed by a delicate hand – and not
from your mother or your sister – which makes me wonder again: Is there "a
special person" in your life?' He turns his face away from me to hide what I sense
is a smile. Then he shakes his head in mock disbelief and turns back to me and
bellows:

'You journalists! Must you know <u>everything</u>?'

At first I am shocked by the tone of his voice, but I soon sense that it is not
real anger. Exasperation, perhaps. I look him in the eye and reply: 'I must tell you,
Herr Rittmeister, that there is great interest in this side of your life. People in
Berlin ask me about it all the time. One story I have heard, for example, is about
an Austrian lady you met last year in Freiburg and then again in Vienna.' The
smile fades and he replies:

'I know who you mean and she is hardly more than a girl.'

'Right now. But in a few years. After the war . . .' Richthofen interrupts:

'After the war? First I must survive the war! And, as for my time in Vienna, Menzke was with me the whole time and he can vouch for my whereabouts for every minute.'

'Ha!' Now it is my turn to laugh. 'Menzke! Your faithful servant! He would endure horrible torture before he would betray you. As would every other person in your Geschwader.' Now, with *an exaggerated frown, Richthofen answers:*

'Is that so? Then who told you this ridiculous story about a perfumed envelope?'

'No one in particular. I heard some men talking about it and, when I tried to learn more, they simply walked away from me. They are incredibly loyal to you. But my instincts tell me there is a good story here and I am trying to gather more information. Or, as with other matters we have discussed, at least to have material for a story which I can write after the war.' Just then, Oberleutnant Bodenschatz pokes his head into the room and announces there is an urgent telephone call for the Kommandeur. English planes have been spotted heading this way. Richthofen looks at me with an indulgent half-smile and says:

'Sorry, but I must go. We can discuss this subject when I return.'

'Wonderful!' I exclaim, savouring the thought of obtaining such a story first-hand. 'Good luck, Herr Rittmeister! I hope you bring down Number Eighty One and Eighty Two today!' I run to a window and watch as masses of fighters take off and climb, then circle the airfield while waiting for the last two planes: the Kommandeur in his dark red Fokker triplane and Leutnant Weiss in a white-winged triplane.

* * *

It is now late afternoon and the flights have returned. All the planes, that is, except the red triplane. The skies have been scanned hundreds of times and there is no trace of the Kommandeur. Calls to various outposts, inquiring whether he had been seen landing, all receive negative answers. The festive mood is turning black. The last comrade to see him, Leutnant Hans Joachim Wolff, is distraught and near tears as he recounts what he saw during the morning flight:

'Scarcely had we arrived at the Front, when from this side, below us, in the area around Hamel, we saw about seven Sopwith Camels. In addition to the five of us, aircraft of another Jagdstaffel were still in the area, but much farther away, near Sailly-le-Sec. Above us were seven more Sopwith Camels, some attacked the other Staffel, some remained above.

'One or two came at us. We began to fight. In the course of the fight, Herr Rittmeister was often near me, but he had not yet fired at anything. Of our flight, only Oberleutnant Karjus was next to me. While Karjus and I fought against two or three Camels, suddenly I saw the red machine near me, as he fired at a Camel that first went into a spin, and then slipped away in a steep dive towards the west, on the other side, over the heights of Hamelet.

'Now the air was clear around me and I drew closer to a Camel and shot it down. As it went down, I looked over at Herr Rittmeister and saw that he was at an extremely low altitude over the Somme near Corbie, right behind an Englishman. I shook my head instinctively and wondered why he was following an opponent so far across the other side.

'Suddenly, while I was looking to see where my opponent had fallen, I heard a machine-gun behind me. I was being attacked by another Camel, which had already put about twenty holes in my machine. Luckily, I got free of that one, but, when I looked around for Herr Rittmeister, I saw no one except Karjus, who was close to me. Then I became a bit uneasy, as I certainly should have seen Herr Rittmeister by now. We circled the area for a time, and were again attacked by an Englishman who followed us up to about nine hundred metres over Corbie – but there was no trace of Herr Rittmeister.

'I came home with a sense of foreboding. Reports had already come in, saying that a red triplane had landed smoothly north-west of Corbie. That another Englishman could have shot him down from behind was out of the question – I would vouch for that.

'That would also have been the most terrible thing for me, as I considered myself to be Herr Rittmeister's personal shield. Indeed, if he had shot down the Englishman, then he would have pulled up, but he suddenly went into a steep dive and landed smoothly. Now there were two possibilities. The machine was overstressed, a valve let go, and the engine quit. The other possibility was that

shots fired from the ground hit the engine. We did not know what had happened.'

* * *

Tuesday, 23 April 1918: Today would have been the twenty-fifth birthday of the Kommandeur's best friend at Wahlstatt, Leutnant Helmut von Frankenberg und Ludwigsdorf. No one is here to mark the occasion, as Rittmeister Manfred Frei-herr von Richthofen is dead at the age of twenty five, according to a widely accepted news article. I know my assignment is over when I read it:

'As a British war correspondent reported, Rittmeister Freiherr von Richthofen was shot down as he flew behind the Australian Front at a very low altitude on April 21. To all appearances, he fell victim to fire from an Australian battery that had directed a Lewis machine-gun at him. The body of Rittmeister Freiherr von Richthofen showed only one wound: a bullet had hit him in the heart. He was buried with military honours appropriate to his rank.'

VICTORY LIST
OF MANFRED VON RICHTHOFEN

No	Date	Time	Location	Aircraft	Crew and Disposition
n/c	26.10.15		Champagne Sector	Farman Two-seater	
n/c	26.4.16		Fleury, south of Fort Douaumont	Nieuport	
1	17.9.16	1100	Villers Plouich	F.E.2b 7018	2/Lt Lionel B.F. Morris (DoW), Capt Tom Rees (DoW), No 11 Squadron, RFC
2	23.9.16	1100	Beugny	Martinsyde G.100 7481	Sgt Herbert Bellerby(KiA), No 27 Squadron, RFC
3	30.9.16	1150	Frémicourt	F.E.2b 6973	Lt Ernest C. Lansdale (KiA), Sgt Albert Clarkson (KiA), No 11 Squadron, RFC
4	7.10.16	0910	Equanacourt	B.E.12	2/Lt William C. Fenwick (KiA), No 21 Squadron, RFC
n/c	10.10.16	1800	Rouex	F.E.2b 4292	(disputed; credit awarded to *Vzfw* Fritz Kosmahl, *Fl.-Abt 22*)
5	16.10.16	1710	north of Ytres	B.E.12 6580	2/Lt John Thompson (KiA), No 19 Squadron, RFC
6	25.10.16	0935	north of Bapaume	B.E.12 6629	2/Lt Arthur J. Fisher (KiA), No 21 Squadron, RFC
7	3.11.16	1410	Loupart Wood	F.E.2b 7010	Sgt Cuthbert G. Baldwin (KiA), 2/Lt George A. Bentham (KiA), No 18 Squadron, RFC
8	9.11.16	1030	Beugny	B.E.2c 2506	2/Lt Ian G. Cameron (DoW), No 12 Squadron, RFC
9	20.11.16	0940	south of Grandcourt	B.E.2c 2767	2/Lt James C. Lees (PoW), Lt Thomas H. Clarke (PoW), No 15 Squadron, RFC
10	20.11.16	1615	Guedecourt	F.E.2b 4848	2/Lt Gilbert S. Hall (DoW), 2/Lt George Doughty (KiA), No 18 Squadron, RFC

No	Date	Time	Location	Aircraft	Crew and Disposition
11	23.11.16	1500	Bapaume	D.H.2 5964	Maj Lanoe G. Hawker, VC, DSO (KiA), No 24 Squadron, RFC
12	11.12.16	1155	Mercatel	D.H.2 5986	Lt Benedict P.G. Hunt (PoW), No 32 Squadron, RFC
13	20.12.16	1130	Monchy le Preux	D.H.2 7927	Lt Arthur G. Knight, DSO, MC (KiA), No 29 Squadron, RFC
14	20.12.16	1345	Noreuil	F.E.2b A.5446	Lt Lionel G. D'Arcy (KiA), Sub/Lt Reginald C. Whiteside (KiA), No 18 Squadron, RFC
15	27.12.16	1625	Ficheux / Arras	F.E.2	No matching RFC casualty
16	3.1.17	1615	Metz en Couture	Sopwith Pup N.5193	F/S/Lt Alan S. Todd (KiA), No 8 Squadron, RNAS
17	23.1.17	1610	southwest of Lens Lens	F.E.8 6388	2/Lt John Hay (KiA), No 40 Squadron, RFC
18	24.1.17	1215	west of Vimy 6997	F.E.2b	Capt Oscar Greig (WiA/PoW), 2/Lt John E. MacLenan (WiA/PoW), No 25 Sqdn, RFC
19	1.2.17	1600	southwest of Thelus	B.E.2d 6742	Lt Percival W. Murray (DoW), Lt Duncan J. McRae (DoW), No 16 Squadron, RFC
20	14.2.17	1200	Lens – Hulluch road, east of Loos	B.E.2d 6231	2/Lt Cyril D. Bennett (WiA/PoW), 2/Lt Herbert A. Croft (KiA), No 2 Squadron, RFC
21	14.2.17	1645	Loos (over British lines)	B.E.2c 2543	Capt George C. Bailey, DSO (WiA), 2/Lt George W.B. Hampton, No 2 Squadron, RFC
22	4.3.17	1250	north of Loos	B.E.2d 5785	Lt James B.E. Crosbee, Fl/Sgt John E. Prance (WiA), No 2 Squadron, RFC
23	4.3.17	1620	Acheville, south of Vimy	Sopwith 1½ Strutter A.1108	2/Lt Herbert J. Green (KiA), 2/Lt Alexander W. Reid (KiA), No 43 Squadron, RFC
24	6.3.17	1700	Souchez	B.E.2e A.2785	2/Lt Gerald M. Gosset-Bibby (KiA), Lt Geoffrey J.O. Brichta (KiA), No 16 Squadron, RFC

No	Date	Time	Location	Aircraft	Crew and Disposition
25	9.3.17	1200	Roclincourt – Bailleul	D.H.2 A.2571	2/Lt Arthur J. Pearson, MC (KiA), No 29 Squadron, RFC
26	11.3.17	1200	Vimy	B.E.2d 6232	2/Lt James Smyth (KiA), 2/Lt Edward Byrne (KiA), No 2 Squadron, RFC
27	17.3.17	1145	Bailleul / Oppy	F.E.2b A.5439	Lt Arthur E. Boultbee (KiA), 2/AM Frederick King (KiA), No 25 Squadron, RFC
28	17.3.17	1700	Souchez	B.E.2c 2814	2/Lt George M. Watt (KiA), Sgt Ernest A. Howlett (KiA), No 16 Squadron, RFC
29	21.3.17	1725	north of La Neuville	B.E.2f A.3154	Fl/Sgt Sidney H. Quicke (KiA), 2/Lt William J. Lidsey (KiA), No 16 Squadron, RFC
30	24.3.17	1155	Vimy	SPAD S.7 A.6706	2/Lt Richard P. Baker (WiA/ PoW), No 19 Squadron, RFC

(25 March 1917: German time synchronized with Allied time)

No	Date	Time	Location	Aircraft	Crew and Disposition
31	25.3.17	0820	Tilloy	Nieuport 17 A.6689	2/Lt Christopher G. Gilbert (PoW), No 29 Squadron, RFC
32	2.4.17	0835	Farbus, northeast of Arras	B.E.2d 5841	Lt Patrick J.G. Powell (KiA), 1/AM Percy Bonner (KiA), No 13 Squadron, RFC
33	2.4.17	1120	Givenchy	Sopwith 1? Strutter A.2401	2/Lt Algernon P. Warren (PoW), Sgt Reuel Dunn (KiA), No 43 Squadron, RFC
34	3.4.17	1615	Lens	F.E.2d A.6382	2/Lt Donald P. McDonald (WiA/Pow), 2/Lt John I. M. O'Beirne (KiA), No 25 Squadron, RFC
35	5.4.17	1100	Quincy	F.2A A.3343	Lt Alfred T. Adams (PoW), Lt Donald J. Stewart (WiA/ PoW), No 48 Squadron, RFC
36	5.4.17	1100	Lewaarde, southeast of Douai	F.2A A.3340	2/Lt Arthur N. Lechler (WiA/ PoW), Lt Herbert D.K. George (DoW), No 48 Squadron, RFC
37	7.4.17	1745	Mercatel	Nieuport 17 A.6645	2/Lt George O. Smart (KiA), No 60 Squadron, RFC

No	Date	Time	Location	Aircraft	Crew and Disposition
38	8.4.17	1145	Farbus	Sopwith 1? Strutter A.2406	2/Lt John S. Heagerty (WiA/PoW), Lt Leonard H. Cantle (KiA), No 43 Squadron, RFC
39	8.4.17	1640	Vimy	B.E.2e A.2815	2/Lt Keith I. MacKenzie (KiA), 2/Lt Guy Everingham (KiA), No 16 Squadron, RFC
40	11.4.17	0925	Willerval	B.E.2c 2501	Lt Edward C.E. Derwin (WiA), Gnr H. Pierson (WiA), No 13 Squadron, RFC
41	13.4.17	0856	Vitry	R.E.8 A.3190	Capt James M. Stuart (KiA), Lt Maurice H. Wood (KiA), No 59 Squadron, RFC
42	13.4.17	1245	west of Monchy, near Feuchy	F.E.2b A.831	Sgt James A. Cunniffe (WiA), 2/AM W.J. Batten (WiA), No 11 Squadron, RFC
43	13.4.17	1930	Hénin-Liétard	F.E.2b 4997	2/Lt Allan H. Bates (KiA), Sgt William A. Barnes (KiA), No 25 Squadron, RFC
44	14.4.17	0915	Fresnoy	Nieuport 17 A.6796	Lt William O. Russell (PoW), No 60 Squadron, RFC
45	16.4.17	1730	Gavrelle	B.E.2c 3156	2/Lt Alphonso Pascoe (WiA), 2/Lt Frederick S. Andrews (WiA), No 13 Squadron, RFC

(17 April 1917: German time one hour ahead of Allied time)

No	Date	Time	Location	Aircraft	Crew and Disposition
46	22.4.17	1710	Lagnicourt	F.E.2b 7020	Lt Waldemar Franklin (WiA), Lt William F. Fletcher (WiA), No 11 Squadron, RFC
47	23.4.17	1213	Avion / Méricourt east of Vimy	B.E.2f A.3168	2/Lt William E.A. Welch (KiA), Sgt Amos G. Tollervey (KiA), No 16 Squadron, RFC
48	28.4.17	0930	east of Pelves	B.E.2e 7221	Lt Reginald W. Follit (DoW), 2/Lt Frederick J. Kirkham (WiA/PoW), No 13 Squadron, RFC
49	29.4.17	1215	Lecluse	SPAD S.7 A.1573	Lt Richard Applin (KiA), No 19 Squadron, RFC
50	29.4.17	1644	southwest of Inchy	F.E.2b 4898	Sgt George Stead (KiA), 1/AM (A/Cpl) Alfred Beebee (KiA), No 18 Squadron, RFC

No	Date	Time	Location	Aircraft	Crew and Disposition
51	29.4.17	1925	Roeux	B.E.2e 2738	2/Lt David E. Davis (KiA), Lt George H. Rathbone (KiA), No 12 Squadron, RFC
52	29.4.17	1945	Lens / Billy - Montigny / Sallaumines	Sopwith Triplane N.5463	F/S/Lt Albert E. Cuzner (KiA), No 8 Squadron, RNAS
53	18.6.17	1315	north of Ypres	R.E.8 A.4290	Lt Ralph W.E. Ellis (KiA), Lt Harold C. Barlow (KiA), No 9 Squadron, RFC
54	23.6.17	2115	north of Ypres (Dickebusch)	SPAD B.1530	2/Lt Robert W. Farquhar No 23 Squadron, RFC
55	24.6.17	0930	Becelaere	D.H.4 A.7473	Capt Norman G. McNaughton (KiA), Lt Angus H. Mearns (KiA), No 57 Squadron, RFC
56	25.6.17	1735	Le Bizet	R.E.8 A.3847	Lt Leslie S. Bowman (KiA), 2/Lt James E. Power-Clutterbuck (KiA), No 53 Squadron, RFC
57	2.7.17	1020	Deulemont	R.E.8 A.3538	Sgt Hubert A. Whatley (KiA), 2/Lt Frank G.B. Pascoe (KiA), No 53 Squadron, RFC
58	16.8.17	0755	southwest of Houthulst Forest	Nieuport 23 A.6611	2/Lt William H.T. Williams (KiA), No 29 Squadron, RFC
59	26.8.17	0730	Poelcappelle	SPAD S.7 B.3492	2/Lt Coningsby P. Williams (KiA), No 19 Squadron, RFC
60	1.9.17	0750	Zonnebeke	R.E.8 B.782	2/Lt John B.C. Madge (PoW), 2/Lt Walter Kember (KiA), No 6 Squadron, RFC
61	3.9.17	0735	south of Bousbecque	Sopwith Pup B.1795	Lt Algernon F. Bird (PoW), No 46 Squadron, RFC
62	23.11.17	1400	Bourlon Wood	D.H.5 A.9299	Lt James A.V. Boddy (WiA), No 64 Squadron, RFC
63	30.11.17	1430	Moeuvres	S.E.5a B.644	Lt Donald A.D.I. MacGregor (KiA), No 41 Squadron, RFC

(10 March 1918: German time synchronized with Allied time)

No	Date	Time	Location	Aircraft	Crew and Disposition
64	12.3.18	1110	Nauroy	F.2B B.1251	2/Lt Leonard C. F. Clutterbuck (PoW), 2/Lt Henry J. Sparks (PoW), No 62 Squadron, RFC
65	13.3.18	1035	Gonnelieu / Banteaux	Sopwith F.1 Camel B.5590	Lt Elmer E. Heath (WiA/PoW), No 73 Squadron, RFC
66	18.3.18	1115	Andigny	Sopwith F.1 Camel B.5243	Lt William V. Ivamy (PoW), No 54 Squadron, RFC
67	24.3.18	1445	Combles	S.E.5a C.1054	Lt John P. McCone (KiA), No 41 Squadron, RFC
68	25.3.18	1555	Contalmaison	Sopwith F.1 Camel C.1562	2/Lt Donald Cameron (KiA), No 3 Squadron, RFC
69	26.3.18	1645	south of Contalmaison	S.E.5a B.511	2/Lt Allan M. Denovan (KiA), No 1 Squadron, RFC
70	26.3.18	1700	northeast of Albert	R.E.8 B.742	2/Lt Vernon J. Reading (KiA), 2/Lt Matthew Leggatt (KiA), No 15 Squadron, RFC
71	27.3.18	0900	Aochny	Sopwith F.1 Camel C.6733	Capt Thomas S. Sharpe (WiA/ PoW), No 73 Squadron, RFC
72	27.3.18	1630	Foucaucourt	Armstrong Whitworth F.K.8 B.288	2/Lt Edward T. Smart (KiA) Lt Kenneth F. Barford (KiA) No 2 Squadron, RFC
73	27.3.18	1635	northeast of Chuignolles	Sopwith 5F.1 Dolphin C.4016	2/Lt George H. Harding (KiA), No 79 Squadron, RFC
74	28.3.18	1230	east of Mancourt F.K.8	Armstrong Whitworth No 82 C.8444	2/Lt Joseph B. Taylor (KiA), 2/Lt Eric Betley (KiA), Squadron, RFC
75	2.4.18	1235	east of Moreuil	R.E.8 A.3868	2/Lt Ernest D. Jones (KiA), 2/Lt Robert F. Newton (KiA), No 52 Squadron, RAF
76	6.4.18	1545	Villers- Brettoneux	Sopwith F.1 Camel D.6491	Capt Sidney P. Smith (KiA), No 46 Squadron, RAF

No	Date	Time	Location	Aircraft	Crew and Disposition
77	7.4.18	1130	Hangard	S.E.5a	No matching RAF casualty
78	7.4.18	1205	east of Hill 104, north of Villers-Brettoneux	Sopwith F.1 Camel D.6550	2/Lt Albert V. Gallie No 73 Squadron, RAF

(16 April 1918: German time one hour ahead of Allied time)

No	Date	Time	Location	Aircraft	Crew and Disposition
79	20.4.18	1840	south of Bois de Hamel	Sopwith F.1 Camel D.6439	Maj Richard Raymond- Barker, MC (KiA), No 3 Squadron, RAF
80	20.4.18	1843	Villers- Brettoneux	Sopwith F.1 Camel B.7393	2/Lt David G. Lewis (WiA/ PoW), No 3 Squadron, RAF

SOURCES

BOOKS

Bodenschatz, K., *Jagd in Flanderns Himmel – Aus den sechzehn Kampf-monaten des Jagdgeschwaders Freiherr von Richthofen*, Munich, 1935

Böhme, E. (ed J. Werner), *Briefe eines deutschen Kampffliegers an ein junges Mädchen*, Leipzig, 1930

Boelcke, O., *Hauptmann Boelckes Feldberichte*, Gotha, 1916

Bruce, J., *British Aeroplanes 1914–1918*, London, 1969

Dickhuth-Harrach, G. (ed.), *Im Felde unbesiegt*, vol I, Munich, 1921

Eberhardt, W. von (ed.), *Unsere Luftstreitkrafte 1914–1918*, Berlin, 1930

Ferko, A., *Richthofen*, Berkhamsted, 1995

Fipts, A., and Faillie, M. and R., *Marke Wereledoorlog I*, Marke, 1984

Foerster, W. and Greiner, H. (eds), *Wir Kämpfer im Weltkrieg – Selbstzeugnisse deutscher Frontsoldaten*, Berlin, (n.d.)

Franks, N., Giblin, B., and McCrery, N., *Under the Guns of the Red Baron*, London, 1995

Gibbons, F., *The Red Knight of Germany*, New York, 1927

Goote, T. (W. Von Langsdorff), *... rangehn ist Alles!* Berlin, 1938.

Henshaw, T., *The Sky Their Battlefield*, London, 1995

Hobson, C., *Airmen Died in the Great War 1914–1918*, Suffolk, 1995

Hoeppner, E. von, *Deutschlands Krieg in der Luft*, Leipzig, 1921

Hoffmann, R. (ed.), *Der deutsche Soldat – Briefe aus dem Weltkrieg*, Munich, 1937.

Italiaander, R., *Manfred Freiherr von Richthofen – Der beste Jagdflieger des grossen Krieges*, Berlin, 1938

Kilduff, P., *Germany's First Air Force 1914–1918*, London, 1991

— *Richthofen – Beyond the Legend of the Red Baron*, London, 1993

— *The Red Baron Combat Wing – Jagdgeschwader Richthofen in Battle*, London, 1997

— *The Illustrated Red Baron – The Life and Times of Manfred von Richthofen*, London, 1999

Langsdorff, W. von, *Flieger am Feind*, Gütersloh, 1934.

Neumann, G. (ed.), *Die deutschen Luftstreitkräfte im Weltkriege*, Berlin, 1920

— *In der Luft unbesiegt*, Munich, 1923

Nowarra, H. and Brown, K., *von Richthofen and the Flying Circus*, Letchworth, 1964

O'Connor, N., *Aviation Awards of Imperial Germany in World War I and the Men Who Earned Them, vol II – The Aviation Awards of the Kingdom of Prussia*, Princeton, 1990

Richthofen, K. von, *Mein Kriegstagebuch*, Berlin, 1937

Richthofen, M. von, *Ein Heldenleben*, Berlin, 1920

— *Der rote Kampfflieger*, Berlin, 1917

— *Der rote Kampfflieger*, Berlin, 1933

— (transl. P. Kilduff), *The Red Baron*, New York, 1969

Schäfer, K., *Vom Jäger zum Flieger*, Berlin, 1918

Schilling, F., *Flieger an allen Fronten*, Berlin, 1936.

Schnitzler, E., *Carl Allmenröder der Bergische Kampfflieger*, Wald, 1927

Schröder, H., *Erlebter Krieg*, Bern, (n.d.)

Schweckendiek, O., *Der Kampfflieger Lothar von Richthofen*, Hamburg, 1938.

Shores, C., Franks, N. and Guest, R., *Above the Trenches*, London, 1990

Udet, E., *Mein Fliegerleben*, Berlin, 1935

'Vigilant' (C. Sykes), *Richthofen – The Red Knight of the Air*, London, (n.d.)

Wenzl, R., *Richthofen-Flieger*, Freiburg im Breisgau, (c. 1930)

Zuerl, W., *Pour le Mérite-Flieger*, Munich, 1938

DOCUMENTS

Jagdstaffel 11 Berichte, published in the field, 1917, 1918

Kommander der Flieger der 4. Armee Wochenberichte, 1917

Kommander der Flieger der 6. Armee Wochenberichte, 1917

Kommandeur der Flieger der 7. Armee Fliegertagesmeldungen, 1918

KoGenLuft, *Nachrichtenblatt der Luftstreitkräfte vol I*, Berlin, 1917

— *Nachrichtenblatt der Luftstreitkräfte vol II*, Berlin, 1918

Richthofen Combat Reports (Translations), Public Record Office, London, (n d) (PRO File No Air 1/686/21/13/2250 XC15183)

ARTICLES, MONOGRAPHS AND PERIODICALS

Bodenschatz, K., 'Das Jagdgeschwader Frhr v.Richthofen Nr 1 im Verbande der 2. Armee', *In der Luft unbesiegt*, Munich, 1923

Evans, W., 'Manfred Freiherr von Richthofen List', *Over the Front*, 1992

Ferko, A., *Fliegertruppe 1914–1918*, Salem, Ohio, 1980

— 'The Origin of the First Jagdstaffeln', in *Cross & Cockade Journal*, 1965

Ferko A. and Grosz, P., 'The Circus Master Falls: Comments on a Newly Discovered Photograph', in *Cross & Cockade Journal*, 1968

Grosz, P. and Ferko A., 'The Fokker Dr. I – A Reappraisal', in *Air Enthusiast*, 1978

Kriegs-Echo, Berlin, 1916, 1917, 1918

Lampel, P., '*Als Gast beim Rittmeister Frhr. v.Richthofen*', *In der Luft unbesiegt*, Munich, 1923

von der Osten, G. (ed. L. Zacharias), 'Memoirs of World War I With Jagdstaffeln 11 and 4', in *Cross & Cockade Journal*, 1974

von Richthofen, L., '*Das letzte Mal an der Front, Juli-August 1918*', *Im Felde unbesiegt*, vol I, Munich, 1921

INDEX

I. MILITARY FORMATIONS

II. PERSONNEL

FURTHER INFORMATION

Readers interested in obtaining additional information
about military aviation of the First World War may wish to contact
research-oriented, non-profit organizations, including:

Cross & Cockade International
URL: http://www.crossandcockade.com

League of World War I Aviation Historians
URL: http://www.overthefront.com

World War One Aeroplanes
URL: http://www.avation-history.com/ww1aero.htm